AutoCAD 2
Training guide

by
Linkan Sagar
Nisha Gupta

FIRST EDITION 2019

Copyright © BPB Publications, INDIA

ISBN: 978-93-88511-25-4

All Rights Reserved. No part of this publication can be stored in a retrieval system or reproduced in any form or by any means without the prior written permission of the publishers.

LIMITS OF LIABILITY AND DISCLAIMER OF WARRANTY

The Author and Publisher of this book have tried their best to ensure that the programmes, procedures and functions described in the book are correct. However, the author and the publishers make no warranty of any kind, expressed or implied, with regard to these programmes or the documentation contained in the book. The author and publisher shall not be liable in any event of any damages, incidental or consequential, in connection with, or arising out of the furnishing, performance or use of these programmes, procedures and functions. Product name mentioned are used for identification purposes only and may be trademarks of their respective companies.

All trademarks referred to in the book are acknowledged as properties of their respective owners. This book is written solely for the benefit and guidance of the students.

Distributors:

BPB PUBLICATIONS
20, Ansari Road, Darya Ganj
New Delhi-110002
Ph: 23254990/23254991

BPB BOOK CENTRE
376 Old Lajpat Rai Market,
Delhi-110006
Ph: 23861747

MICRO MEDIA
Shop No. 5, Mahendra Chambers
150 DN Rd. Next to Capital Cinema,
V.T. (C.S.T.) Station,
MUMBAI-400 001
Ph: 22078296/22078297

DECCAN AGENCIES
4-3-329, Bank Street,
Hyderabad-500195
Ph: 24756967/24756400

Published by Manish Jain for BPB Publications, 20, Ansari Road, Darya Ganj, New Delhi-110002 and Printed by Repro India Ltd., Mumbai

Contents

Chapter 1: Introduction 1
What is AutoCAD? 1
History of AutoCAD? 1
Usage of AutoCAD? 2
What is New in AutoCAD 2019? 2
What is Workspace? 3

Chapter 2: Overview 5
Welcome Screen 5
Mouse use 6
Difference between Command Work & Visual Work 7
Coordinate System with Line Command 7
Zoom and Extents 10
Regen 14

Chapter 3: Draw tools 15
Line 15
Pline 16
Xline 19
Spline 22
Circle 24
Arc 26
Rectangle 31
Polygon 34
Ellipse 36
Hatch 37
Gradient 39
Boundary 40
Ray 41
Point 42
Divide 43
Measure 45
Region 46
Wipeout 47
3D Polyline 48
Helix 49
Revision Cloud 49

Solid 50
Fill 51

Chapter 4: Modify Tools 53

Move 53
Copy 54
Stretch 54
Rotate 56
Mirror 57
Scale 58
Trim 60
Extend 61
Fillet 62
Chamfer 63
Blend Curves 64
Array 65
Explode 68
Offset 69
Lengthen 70
Align 71
Break 72
Join 73
Delete Duplicate Object 73
Draw Order 75
Blocks 77

Chapter 5: Annotation 79

Text 79
Multiline Text 80
Text Style 81
Dimensioning 82
Linear 83
Aligned 84
Angular 85
Arc Length 86
Radius 87
Diameter 88
Jogged Radius Dimension 89
Ordinate 90
Quick Dimension 91
Continue 93
Baseline 93

Centre Mark	94
Centre Line	95
Inspection Dimension	95
Dimension Break	96
Dimension Space	97
Dim Style	98
Qleader	98
Leader	99
Table	100
Smart Dimension	103

Chapter 6: Inquiry 105

List	105
Angle	105
Dist	106
Volume	107
Area	107

Chapter 7: Parametric 109

Geometric Constraints	110
Dimensional Constraints	113
Manage Constraints	113

Chapter 8: Setting & Option 115

Infer Constraint	115
Grid & Snap	116
Osnap	117
Polar	123
Ortho	123
Otrack	124
Lwt	124
Dyn	124
Qp (Quick Properties)	125
Colour	125
Ui Colour Changes	127
Pan	129
Steering Wheels	129
Grips Editing	130
Regen	131
Multline Style	131
Pointstyle	132
Tablestyle	132

Background Mask ... 133
Units ... 134
Layers ... 135
Purge ... 137

Chapter 9: 3D Modeling & View ... 139

Box ... 139
Cylinder ... 140
Helix ... 141
Cone ... 142
Torus ... 144
Pyramid ... 145
Wedge ... 147
Polysolid ... 148
Sphere ... 149
Extrude ... 151
Presspull ... 152
Loft ... 153
Revolve ... 156
Sweep ... 158

Chapter 10: 3D Modify Tools ... 159

3D Move ... 159
3D Rotate ... 160
3D Scale ... 161
3D Mirror ... 162
3D Array ... 163
Subtract ... 165
Union ... 166
Intersect ... 167
Slice ... 168
Fillet Edge ... 169
Chamfer Edge ... 170

Chapter 11: 3D Surface & Mesh ... 171

Network ... 171
Planar ... 172
Surface Blend ... 172
Patch ... 173
Surface Offset ... 174
Surface Extend ... 176
Surface Trim ... 177

Surface Fillet 178

Chapter 12: What Are the New Features Introduced In 181
AutoCAD 2019?

DWG compare 181
Revision Cloud 183
Smart Dimension 184
Geometric Center (Osnap) 185
Center Marks and Center Lines 185
Pdf File Import 186

CHAPTER-1

Introduction

WHAT IS AutoCAD?

Autodesk Company who develop a software named AutoCAD, stands for Autodesk's Computer aided design. It's a drafting and designing software. There are several software for drafting and designing available in market, Out of them The AutoCAD is best, because it Works on co-ordinate system that help's in survey drawing and drafting.

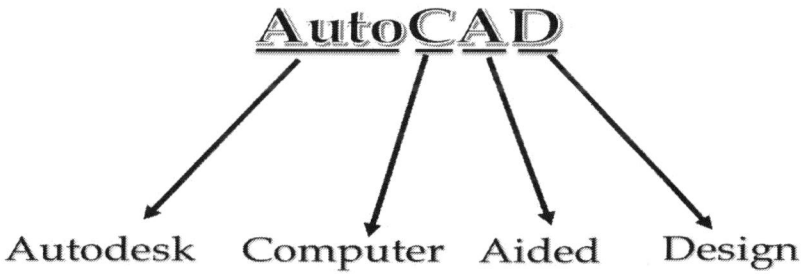

Figure 1: full form of AutoCAD

HISTORY OF AutoCAD?

AutoCAD was Came in concept during 1977, and it's first commercial release was in 1979 with the name Interact CAD. Later on Autodesk Company develop it and Release in 1982 for Microcomputer. Gradually the lighter version for small PC and Notebook were release. In 2010 AutoCAD 360 app was released for mobile.

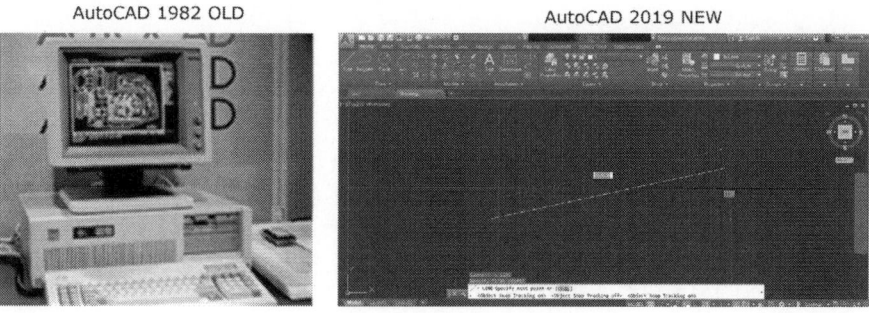

Figure 2: AutoCAD version

USAGE OF AutoCAD

AutoCAD is used for 2D and 3D design, mostly for Civil, Mechanical, Electrical, Interior & Architecture domain. You can design & draw layout, building plan, mechanical part etc. This software is very popular among small to large scale Companies.

AutoCAD stands for Automatic Computer Aided Design.

1. As an Architectural planning tool.

Figure 3: Architectural

2. As an Engineering drafting tool.

Figure 4: Drafting

3. As a Graphic design tool.

Figure 5: Graphic Design

4. In the fashion industry.

Figure 6: Fashion Industry

5. As an industrial design tool.

Figure 7: Industrial Design

WHAT IS NEW IN AutoCAD 2019?

Every year AutoCAD new version is released with some new tools and feature as well as carrying previous feature.

AutoCAD 2019 is also released with some new and enhanced feature.

For ex.

Introduction

- PDF import
- External file references
- Object selection
- Text to Mtext
- User interface
- Share design views
- High-resolution monitor support
- AutoCAD mobile app

WHAT IS WORKSPACE?

Workspace provides us a platform for carrying out our work with definite sets of Menus, toolbars, palettes, which are displayed according to the work space selected. A workspace may also display the ribbon toolbar; it is a distinct palette with task specific Control panels. One can easily switch between workspaces. We are aided with thefollowing task based Workspaces in AutoCAD 2019:

- 2D Drafting & Annotation
- 3D Modeling
- 3D Basic

Say for example, if we have to create 3D models, we can use the 3D modeling Workspace, which provides us only 3D-related toolbars, menus, and palettes. And Hides the other interface items that we do not need for 3D modeling, thus maximizing the screen area available for our work. Depending upon our drawing requirement, we can modify a selected workspace with our choices of tools and pallets and save it as a new workspace with a different name for easy access in future.

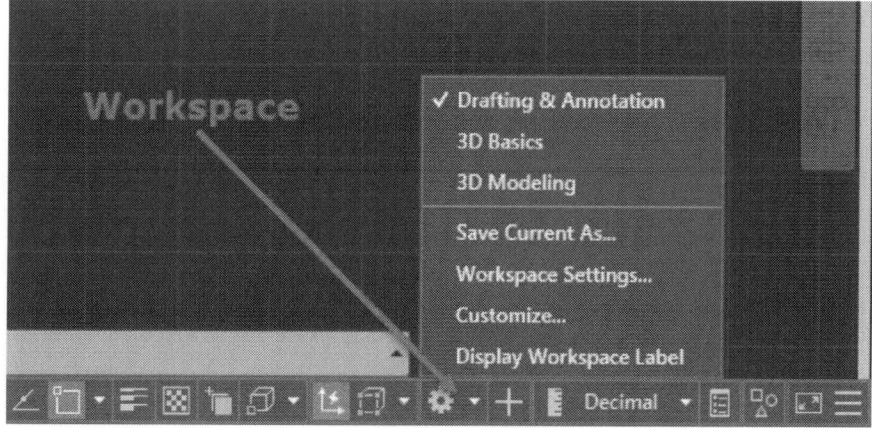

Figure 8: Workspace

2D Drafting & Annotation

Figure 9: 2D Drafting & Annotation

3D Modeling

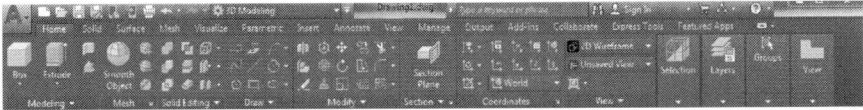

Figure 10: 3D Modeling

3D Basic

Figure 11: 3D Basic

CHAPTER-2

Overview

WELCOME SCREEN

It is the first time that Autodesk AutoCAD has introduced a welcome screen in its version of 2019. In this version when we open the AutoCAD we get to see a welcome screen. The welcome screen provides easy learning, starting, and exploring AutoCAD. In this screen, we will get to see two different types of tab at the bottom namely LEARN and CREATE. In this version, we can add the number of new tab according to our requirement. When we choose to add a new tab, we get Create page by default.

- **What is NEW TAB CREATE?**

In this tab, we will have three columns providing us options to proceed as per our Requirement. Three columns namely Get Started, Recent Documents and Get connected. The name of columns gives us a notion of its use. Let's begin with "GET STARTED" it is for starting a fresh new drawing page, or we can work upon our previously drawn file by browsing the folder. Next is "RECENT DOCUMENT" this column provides instant access to the file that we lastly worked upon in AutoCAD. And finally "GET CONNECTED" provides us web access to Autodesk 360 and also shows us notifications (if any) regarding AutoCAD.

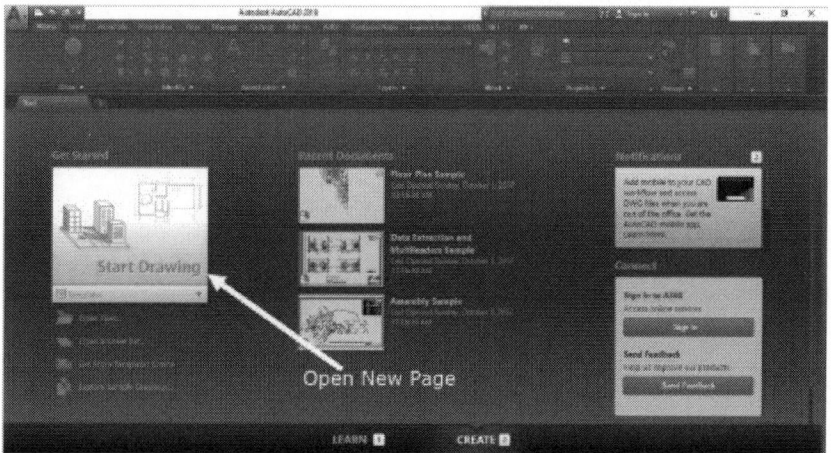

Figure 12: Create tab

▪ What is NEW TAB LEARN?

Day by day increasing use of AutoCAD is attracting new users, Keeping this in mind AutoCAD 2019 comes with a learn tab providing its new users easy learning via its three columns namely:

What's new, Getting Started Videos and TIP/Online Resources.

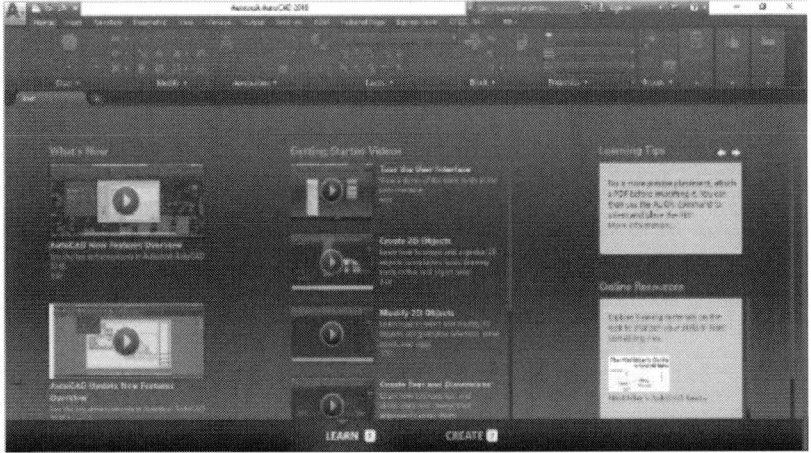

Figure 13: Learn tab

GUI (Graphical User Interface) Overview

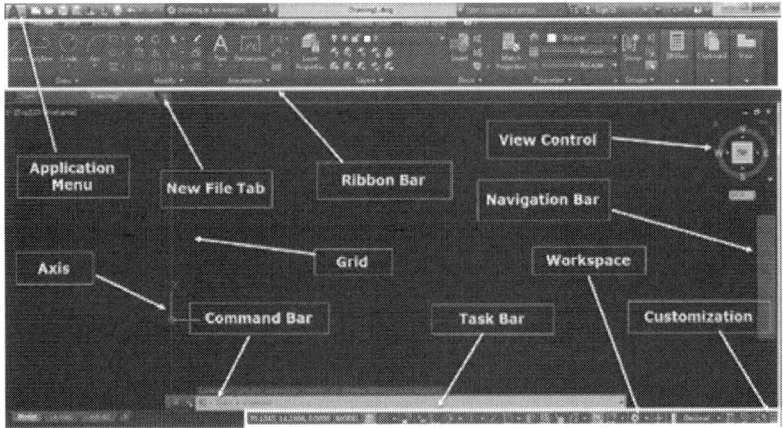

Figure 14: GUI

MOUSE USE

Left button of mouse is used to CLICK and Right button is used for ENTER. To move the AutoCAD page press the scroll button and move the mouse. If you have to do zoom in and zoom out the page just revolve the scroll button.

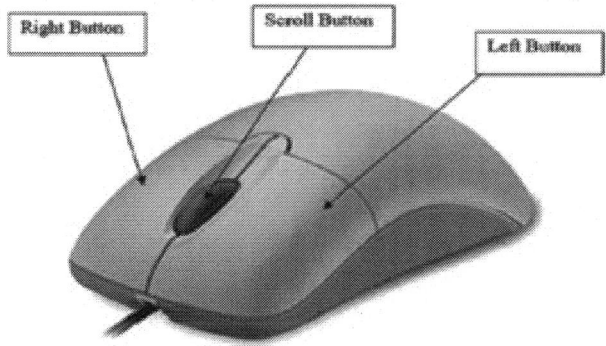

Figure 15: Mouse setting

DIFFERENCE BETWEEN COMMAND WORK & VISUAL WORK

AutoCAD provide two mode of operation, first is Command based work and another is visual work.

When you work using GUI (Graphical User Interface), consider an example of using tools icon this is visual work and when you do same thing using command that is visual work. For Example if you have to draw line using command write L in command bar and press ENTER, And if you want to draw using visual click on line Icon.

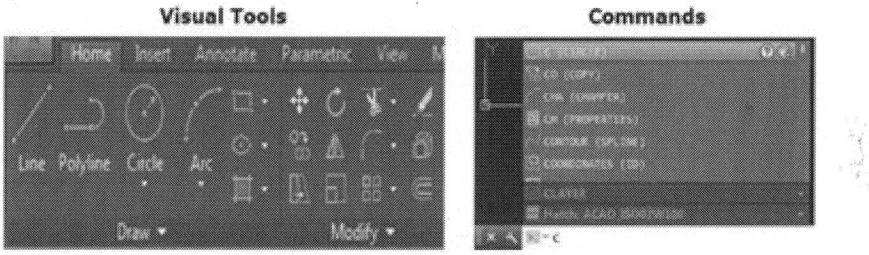

Figure 16: Visual/Command

COORDINATE SYSTEM WITH LINE COMMAND

Our AutoCAD page is based on graphical coordinate system that constitutes three axis viz. x, y, z. As we know these three axis starts from a point origin (0, 0, 0) one in the vertical direction, next horizontal and the last parallel to the page. Moving forward in any of the axes increases the value of the coordinate in that axis.

We can draw using any of the three coordinates system given below:

- **Absolute Coordinate System (X, Y)**

We use absolute coordinate system when we know the precise distance of x coordinate and y coordinate from the origin.

Step 1: Command: L
Step 2: Specify first point: 0, 0
Step 3: Specify next point or [Undo]: 10, 0
Step 4: Specify next point or [Undo]: 10, 2
Step 5: Specify next point or [Close/Undo]: 8, 2
Step 6: Specify next point or [Close/Undo]: 8, 5
Step 7: Specify next point or [Close/Undo]: 6, 5
Step 8: Specify next point or [Close/Undo]: 6, 7
Step 9: Specify next point or [Close/Undo]: 4, 7
Step 10: Specify next point or [Close/Undo]: 4, 5
Step 11: Specify next point or [Close/Undo]: 2, 5
Step 12: Specify next point or [Close/Undo]: 2, 2
Step 13: Specify next point or [Close/Undo]: 0, 2
Step 14: Specify next point or [Close/Undo]: C
(**Note:** Enter command and then follow instructions.)

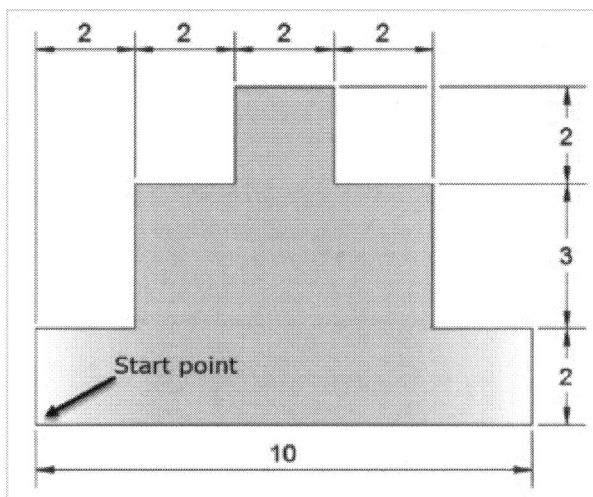

Figure 17: Absolute coordinate system

- **Relative Rectangular Coordinate System (@X, Y)**

We use this coordinate system when we have a relative distance, i.e., distance of the next point with respect to previous drawn point.

Step 1: Command: L
Step 2: Specify first point: Pick any point
Step 3: Specify next point or [Undo]: @2, 0
Step 4: Specify next point or [Undo]: @0, -2

Overview

Step 5: Specify next point or [Close/Undo]: @3, 0
Step 6: Specify next point or [Close/Undo]: @0, 3
Step 7: Specify next point or [Close/Undo]: @5, 0
Step 8: Specify next point or [Close/Undo]: @0, 3
Step 9: Specify next point or [Close/Undo]: @-3, 0
Step 10: Specify next point or [Close/Undo]: @0, 3
Step 11: Specify next point or [Close/Undo]: @-3, 0
Step 12: Specify next point or [Close/Undo]: @0, -1
Step 13: Specify next point or [Close/Undo]: @-2, 0
Step 14: Specify next point or [Close/Undo]: C
(**Note:** Use always @ Symbols for relative rectangle.)

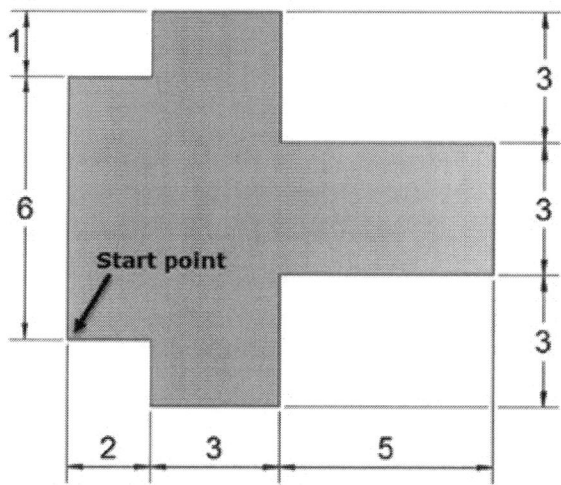

Figure 18: Relative Rectangular Coordinate System

- **Relative Polar Coordinate System (@ distance < angle)**

We use relative polar coordinate system when we have a relative distance and angle of a point to draw with respect to the previous point. The use of angle is compulsory in this coordinate system which is measured in Anti clock direction, taking towards the right.

Step 1: Command: L
Step 2: Specify first point: Pick any point
Step 3: Specify next point or [Undo]: @30<0
Step 4: Specify next point or [Undo]: @30<-60
Step 5: Specify next point or [Undo]: @30<60
Step 6: Specify next point or [Close/Undo]: @30<0

Step 7: Specify next point or [Close/Undo]: @30<120
Step 8: Specify next point or [Close/Undo]: @30<60
Step 9: Specify next point or [Close/Undo]: @30<180
Step 10: Specify next point or [Close/Undo]: @30<120
Step 11: Specify next point or [Close/Undo]: @30<240
Step 12: Specify next point or [Close/Undo]: @30<180
Step 13: Specify next point or [Close/Undo]: @30<-60
Step 14: Specify next point or [Close/Undo]: C
(**Note:** Use always @ Symbols for relative and < for angle)

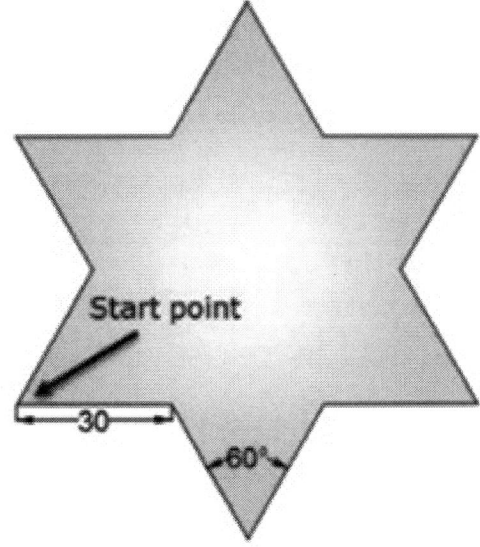

Figure 19: Relative Polar Coordinate System

ZOOM AND EXTENTS

Use the mouse scroll bar to ZOOM IN ZOOM OUT the drawing created on AutoCAD page, in case scroll does not support then type z in command bar and press enter to zoom.

If created drawing have unexpected size then zoom it and extend after.

Step 1: Command: Z
Step 2: Zoom [All Center Dynamic Extents Previous Scale Window Object]: E

 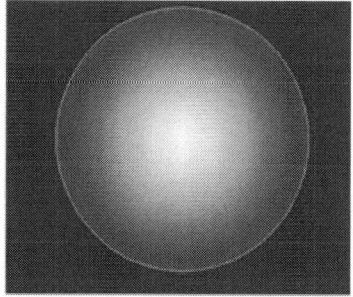

Figure 20: Zoom

If you want to select an option like-

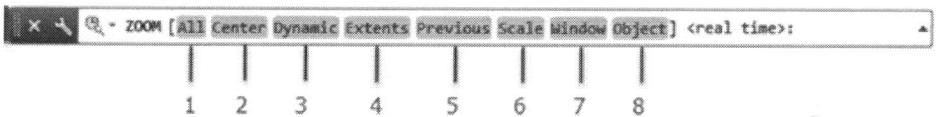

Figure 21: Zoom option

1. All

It is used to only for gird limits.
Step 1: Z ⏎ Then A ⏎

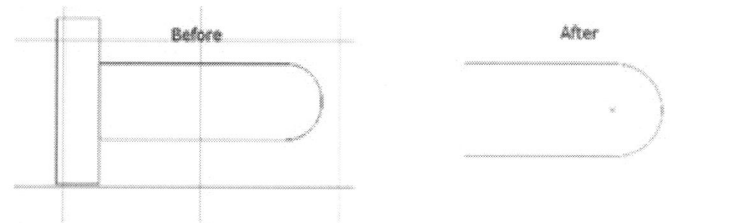

Figure 22: Zoom all

2. Center

It is used as s center point and a magnification value or a height.
Step 1: Z ⏎ Then C ⏎
Step 2: Pick center point
Step 3: Specify height

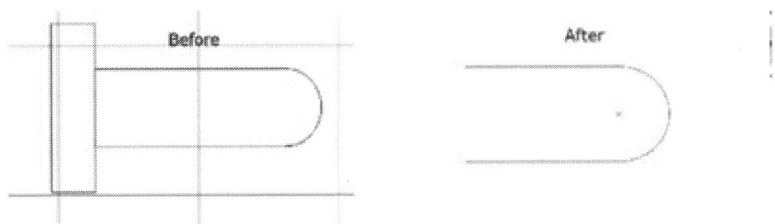

Figure 23: Zoom center

3. Dynamic

Pans and zooms using a rectangular view box. The view box represents your view, which you can shrink or enlarge and move around the drawing. Positioning and sizing the view box pans or zooms to fill the viewport with the view inside the view box. Not available in perspective projection.

Step 1: Z ⏎ Then D ⏎

Step 2: Specify the area again ⏎

Figure 24: Zoom dynamic

4. Extents

It is used to zoom all objects.

Step 1: Z ⏎ Then E ⏎

Figure 25: Zoom extents

5. Previous

Zooms to display the previous view. You can restore up to 10 previous views.

Step 1: Z ⏎ Then P ⏎

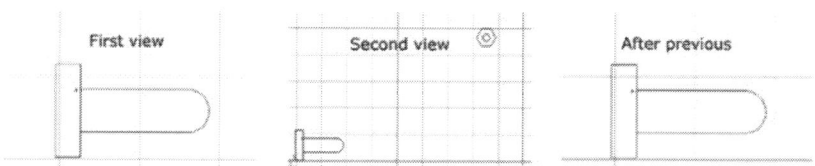

Figure 26: Zoom previous

6. Scale

It is used to zoom scale like 2 times, 3 times.
Step 1: Z ⏎ Then S ⏎
Step 2: 3x (for 3 times zoom) ⏎

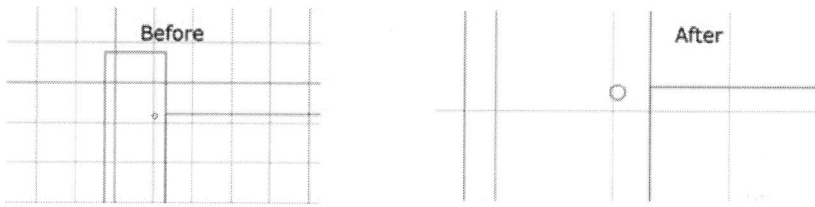

Figure 27: Zoom Scale

7. Window

Zooms to display an area by rectangle window.
Step 1: Z ⏎ Then W ⏎
Step 2: Select window area corner to corner.

Figure 28: Zoom window

8. Object

It is used to zoom select object.
Step 1: Z ⏎ Then O ⏎
Step 2: Select object

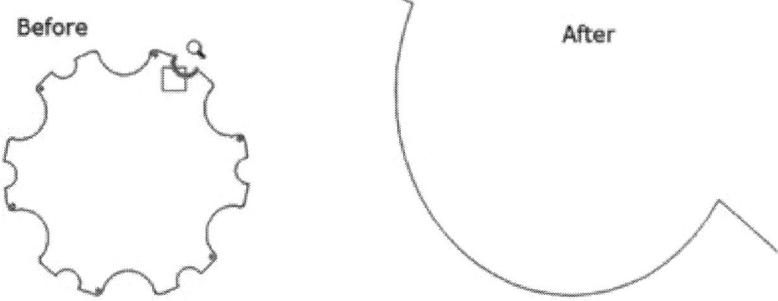

Figure 29: Zoom object

REGEN

Usually and mostly during zoom in and zoom out of AutoCAD pages, it's not working properly, Or when you move the page it refrain to move, Or when you create circle and want to view by zoom in it appear like polygon. So, to resolve these problem use the REGAN command to overcome such type of problem.

Step 1: Re

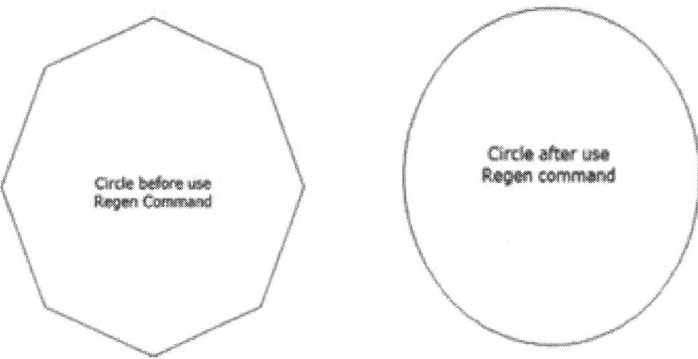

Figure 30: Regen command

CHAPTER-3

Draw Tools

What do you mean by LINE?

Line command is straight continuous joining points without any curve and infinite if we do not mention its start point and end point.

Step 1: Ribbon: Home tab ➤ Draw panel ➤ Line

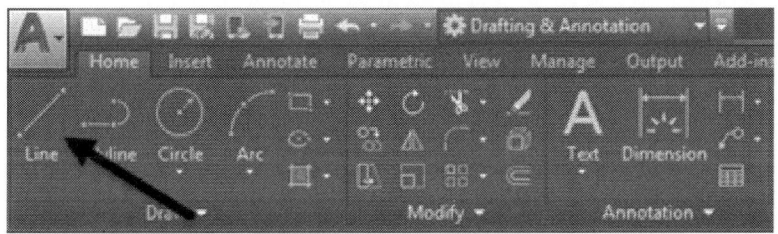

Figure 31: Line tool icon

OR

Command: L ⏎

Step 2: Specify first point: Pick any point
Step 3: Specify next point: 4 ⏎
(Give Direction then specify distance)
Step 4: Specify next point or [Undo]: 1.5 ⏎
Step 5: Specify next point or [Close/Undo]: 4 ⏎
Step 6: Specify next point or [Close/Undo]: 3 ⏎
Step 7: Specify next point or [Close/Undo]: 1 ⏎
Step 8: Specify next point or [Close/Undo]: 2 ⏎
Step 9: Specify next point or [Close/Undo]: 3 ⏎
Step 10: Specify next point or [Close/Undo]: 3 ⏎
Step 11: Specify next point or [Close/Undo]: 4 ⏎
Step 12: Specify next point or [Close/Undo]: 3 ⏎
Step 13: Specify next point or [Close/Undo]: 2.5 ⏎
Step 14: Specify next point or [Close/Undo]: 1.5 ⏎
Step 15: Specify next point or [Close/Undo]: 2.5 ⏎
Step 16: Specify next point or [Close/Undo]: 1 ⏎
(**Note:** Use again Enter or Esc for finish line command)

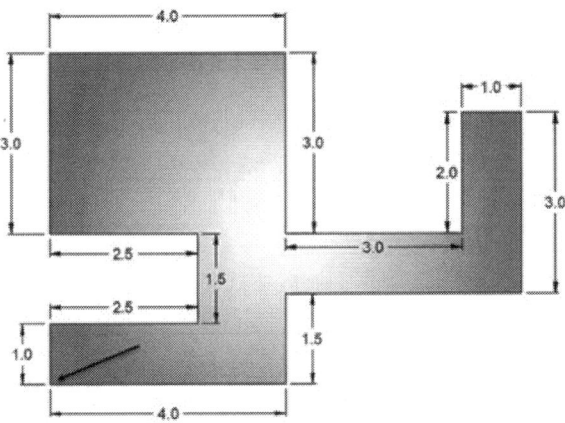

Figure 32: Line drawing

What do you mean by PLINE?

Command Pline stands for polyline and is same as line and created in the same way as line is created but it requires 1st and 2nd endpoints. It is an object but may have different segments. In polyline, each segment can be given required width and can be also given different width to the start and end of the polyline.

Step 1: Ribbon: Home tab ➢ Draw panel ➢ Pline (polyline)

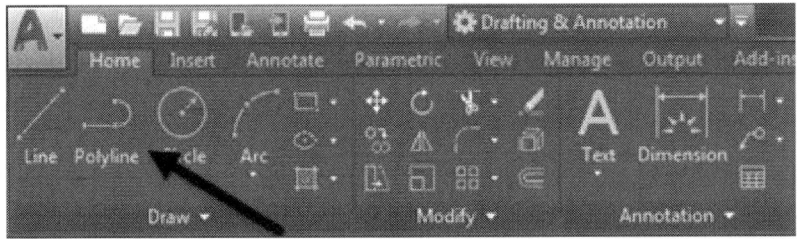

Figure 33: Pline tool icon

OR

Command: PL

Step 2: Specify first point: 1, 1

Step 3: PLINE Specify next point or [Arc Halfwidth Length Undo Width]:2, 2

Step 4: PLINE Specify next point or [Arc Halfwidth Length Undo Width]:3 (give right side direction then enter value)

Step 5: PLINE Specify next point or [Arc Close Halfwidth Length Undo Width]: 1 (give down side direction then enter value)

Draw Tools 17

Step 6: PLINE Specify next point or [Arc Close Halfwidth Length Undo Width]: 2 (give right side direction then enter value)

Step 7: PLINE Specify next point or [Arc Close Halfwidth Length Undo Width]: @2<45

Step 8: PLINE Specify next point or [Arc Close Halfwidth Length Undo Width]: 3 (give up side direction then enter value)

Step 9: PLINE Specify next point or [Arc Close Halfwidth Length Undo Width]: 1 (give left side direction then enter value)

Step 10: PLINE Specify next point or [Arc Close Halfwidth Length Undo Width]: 1 (give up side direction then enter value)

Step 11: PLINE Specify next point or [Arc Close Halfwidth Length Undo Width]: 3 (give left side direction then enter value)

Step 12: PLINE Specify next point or [Arc Close Halfwidth Length Undo Width]: 1.4 (give down side direction then enter value)

Step 13: PLINE Specify next point or [Arc Close Halfwidth Length Undo Width]: 2.6 (give left side direction then enter value)

Step 14: PLINE Specify next point or [Arc Close Halfwidth Length Undo Width]: C (C for close line)

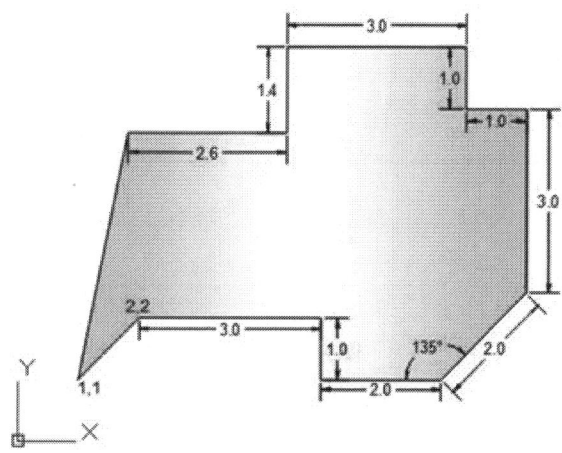

Figure 34: Pline drawing

If you want to select an option like-

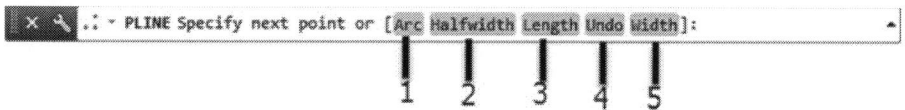

Figure 35: Pline command option

1. Arc

It is used to create Arc. Arc is a part of circle.

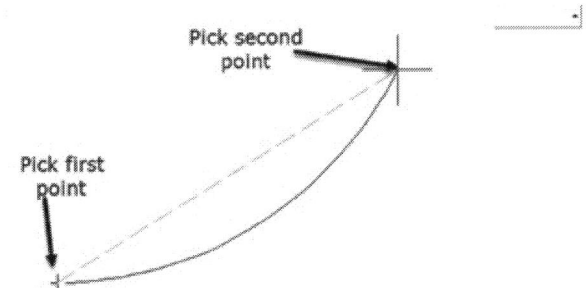

Figure 36: Pline arc option

2. Halfwidth

It is used to change the line width. But it is two directional.

Figure 37: Pline halfwidth option

3. Length

It is used to create a line with same direction.

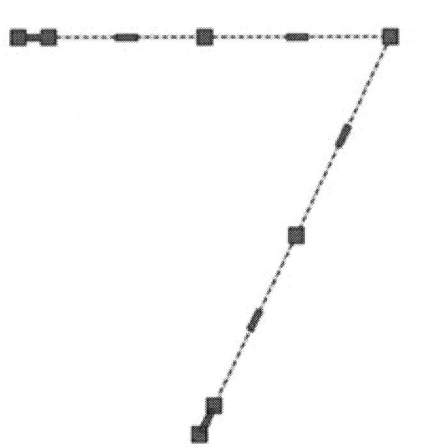

Figure 38: Pline length option

4. Undo

It is used to reverse step.

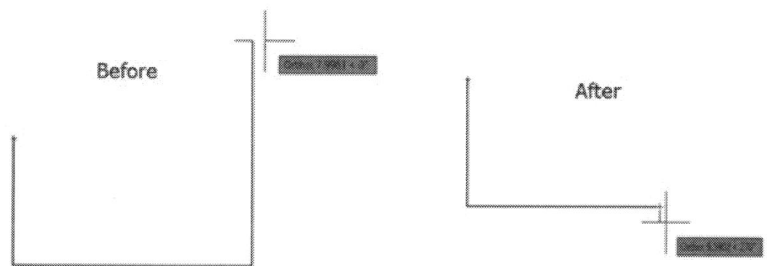

Figure 39: Pline undo option

5. Width

It is used to Change the line width.

Figure 40: Pline width option

What do you mean by XLINE?

It is a command which is infinite and used to create construction line, reference line and for trimming boundaries.

Step 1: Ribbon: Home tab ➢ Draw panel ➢ Xline

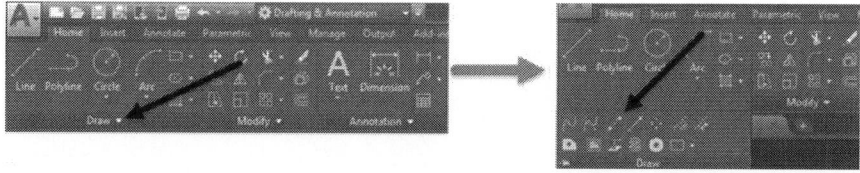

Figure 41: Xline tool icon

OR

Command: XL

Step 2: Specify a point or [Hor Ver Ang Bisect Offset]: **Use one of the points fixing methods or enter an option**

Step 3: Specify through point: **Pick through point**

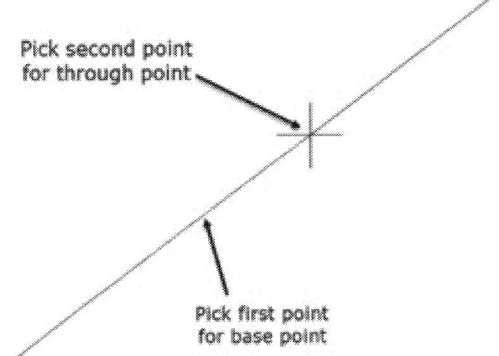

Figure 42: use of xline

If you want to select an option like-

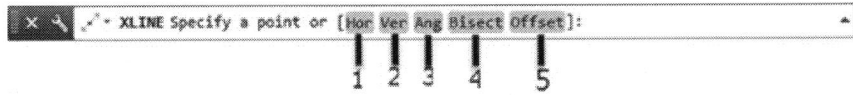

Figure 43: xline option

1. Hor

Creates a horizontal xline passing through a selected point.

Figure 44: Xline hor

2. Ver

Creates a Vertical xline passing through a selected point.

Figure 45: xline ver

Draw Tools 21

3. Ang

Creates a xline at a specified angle.

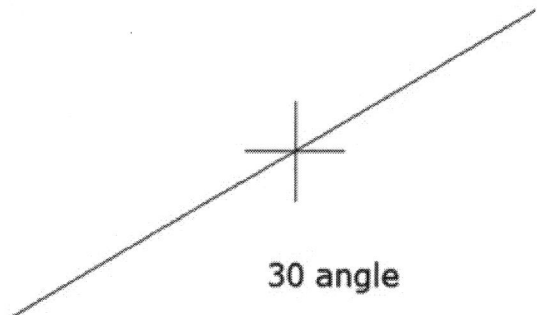

Figure 46: xline angle

4. Bisect

It creates a xline that passes through a selected angle vertex and bisects the angle between first and second line.

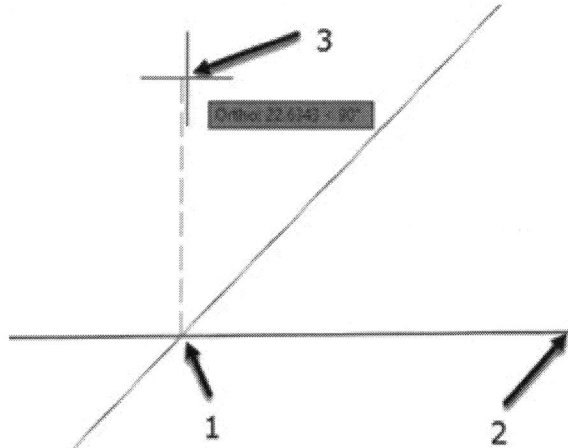

Figure 47: xline bisect

5. Offset Distance

Specifies the distance the xline is offset from the selected object.

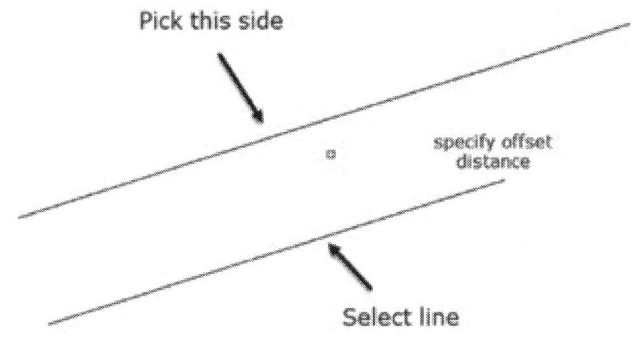

Figure 48: xline offset distance

What do you mean by SPLINE?

It is a command for making smooth curves and can be constructed along specific points.

Step 1: Ribbon: Home tab ➢ Draw panel ➢ Spline

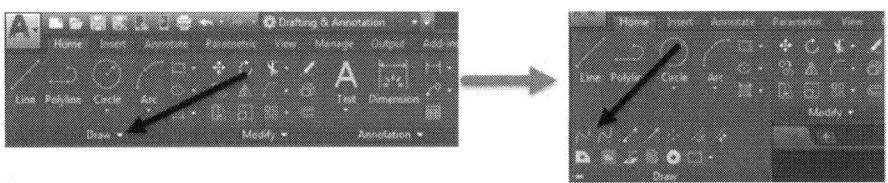

Figure 49: spline tool icon

OR

Command: SPL

Step 2: SPLINE Specify first point or [Method Knots Object]: pick point 1

Step 3: Specify Enter next point or [start Tangency toLerance]: pick point 2

Step 4: Specify Enter next point or [end Tangency toLerance Undo]: pick point 3

Step 5: Specify Enter next point or [end Tangency toLerance Undo Close]: pick point 4

Step 6: Specify Enter next point or [end Tangency toLerance Undo Close]: pick point 5

Step 7: Specify Enter next point or [end Tangency toLerance Undo Close]: pick point 6

Step 8: Specify Enter next point or [end Tangency toLerance Undo Close]: pick point 7

Step 9: Specify Enter next point or [end Tangency toLerance Undo Close]: pick

Draw Tools

point 8

Step 10: Specify Enter next point or [end Tangency toLerance Undo Close]: pick point 9

Step 11: Specify Enter next point or [end Tangency toLerance Undo Close]: pick point 10

Step 12: Specify Enter next point or [end Tangency toLerance Undo Close]: C ⏎

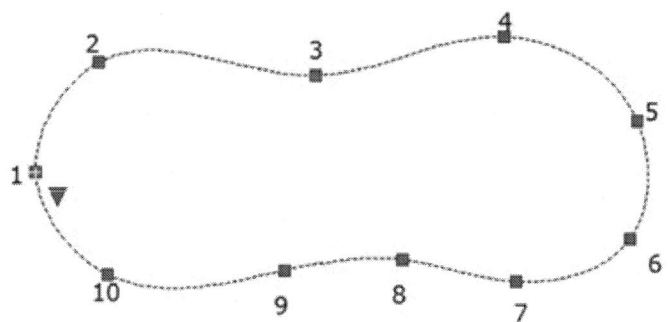

Figure 50: spline drawing

If you want to select an option like-

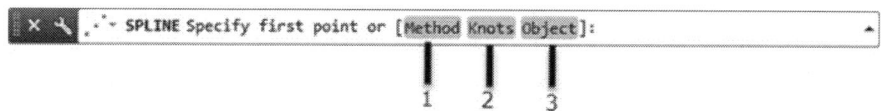

Figure 51: spline option

1. Method

It is used to create Fit and CV spline.

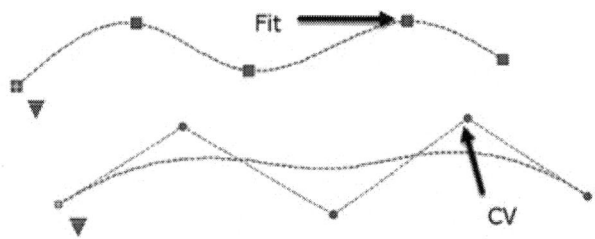

Figure 52: spline method

2. Knots

It is used to create knots.

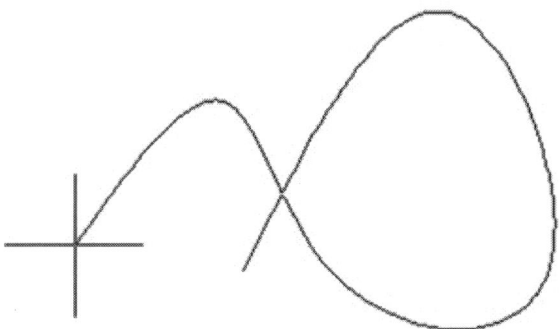

Figure 53: spline knots

3. Method

It is used to create Fit and CV spline.

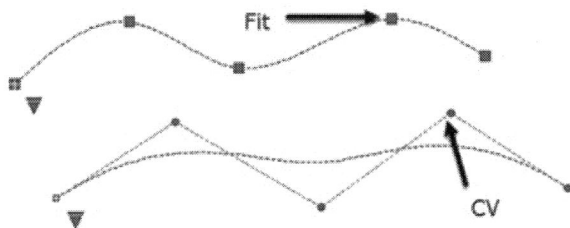

Figure 54: wrong

What do you mean by CIRCLE?

It is a command by which we can make a curved line joined in the end having equal distance from the center point. Circle help us to create two-way normal. But in AutoCAD there are three ways to create Circle. One is by specifying the radius and second by specifying Diameter. Besides this 2point, 3point, and tan tan radius. Here we have five ways to create Circle.

Step 1: Ribbon: Home tab ➤ Draw panel ➤ Circle

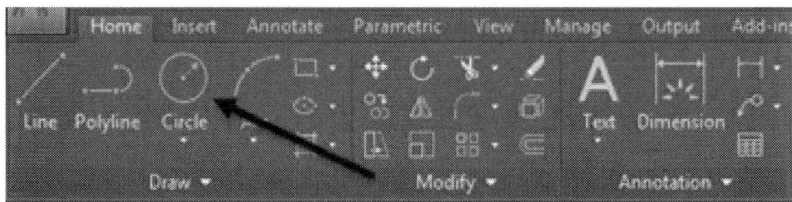

Figure 55: circle tool icon

OR

Command: C

Step 2: Specify center point for circle or [3P/ 2P/ Ttr (tan tan radius)]: **Pick a point**
Step 3: Specify radius of circle or [Diameter]: **10**

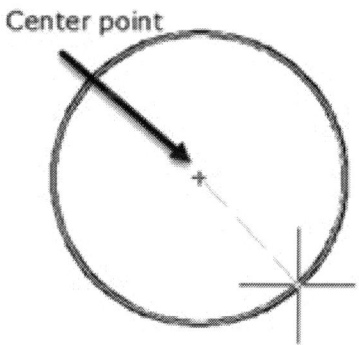

Figure 56: circle radius

Circle diameter

Command: C

Step 1: Specify center point for circle or [3P/ 2P/ Ttr (tan tan radius)]: **Specify a point**
Step 2: Specify radius of circle or [Diameter]: **D**
Step 3: Specify diameter of circle: **20**

3P (Three point)

Draws a circle based on three points on the circumference.

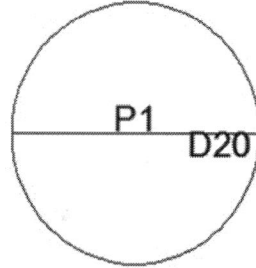

Figure 57: circle diameter

Command: C

Step 1: Specify center point for circle or [3P/ 2P/ Ttr (tan tan radius)]: **3P**
Step 2: Specify first point on circle: **Specify a point (1)**
Step 3: Specify second point on circle: **Specify a point (2)**
Step 4: Specify third point on circle: **Specify a point (3)**

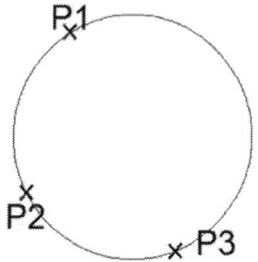

Figure 58: circle 3point

2P (Two point)

Draws a circle based on two endpoints of the diameter.

Command: C

Step 1: Specify center point for circle or [3P/ 2P/ Ttr (tan tan radius)]:**2P**

Step 2: Specify fxirst endpoint of circle's diameter: **Specify a point**

Step 3: Specify second endpoint of circle's diameter: **Specify a point**

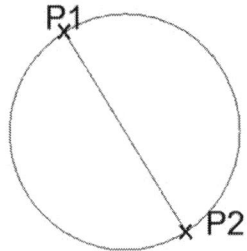

Figure 59: circle 2point

TTR (Tangent, Tangent, Radius)

Draws a circle with a specified radius tangent to two objects.

Command: C

Step 1: Specify center point for circle or [3P/ 2P/ Ttr (tan tan radius)]: **T**

Step 2: Specify point on object for first tangent of circle: **Select a line**

Step 3: Specify point on object for second tangent of circle: **Select a line**

Step 4: Specify radius of circle < *current*>: **Enter radius**

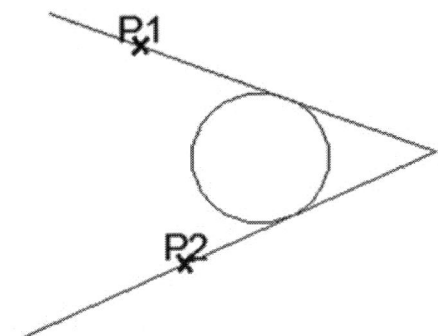

Figure 60: circle ttr

What do you mean by ARC?

It is a command by which we can create a circle segment (part of a circle) or part of the curve. An arc can be a 2-point or 3-point. In case of 3-point Arc, we can specify the angle, endpoint, start point, combination of centers, chord length, direction values and radius.

Step 1: Ribbon: Home tab ➤ Draw panel ➤ Arc

Draw Tools

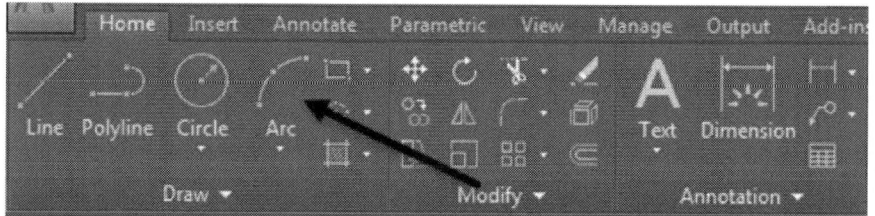

Figure 61: arc tool icon

OR

Command: A

Step 2: Specify start point of arc or [Center]: **Pick 1 point**
Step 3: Specify second point of arc or [Center/End]: **Pick 2 point**
Step 4: Specify end point of arc: **Pick 3 point**

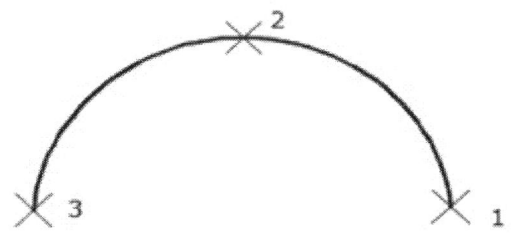

Figure 62: Arc drawing

Eleventh types of Arc-

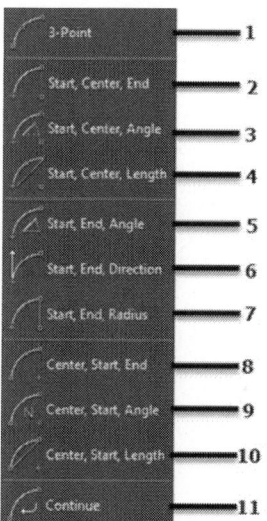

Figure 63: arc types

1. **3-point**

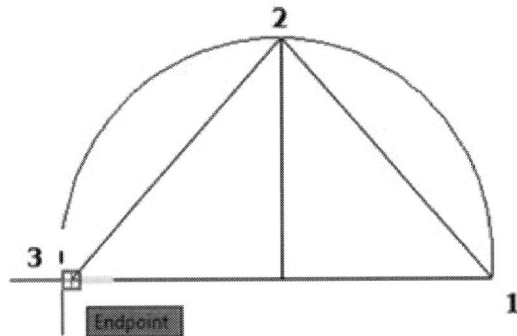

Figure 64: arc 3 point

2. **Start, Center, End**

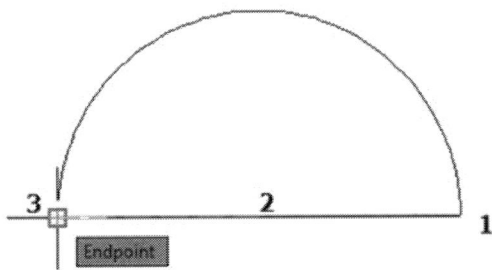

Figure 65: arc Start, Center, End

3. **Start, Center, Angle**

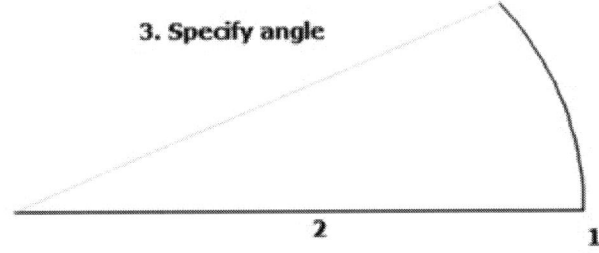

Figure 66: arc Start, Center, Angle

4. Start, Center, Length

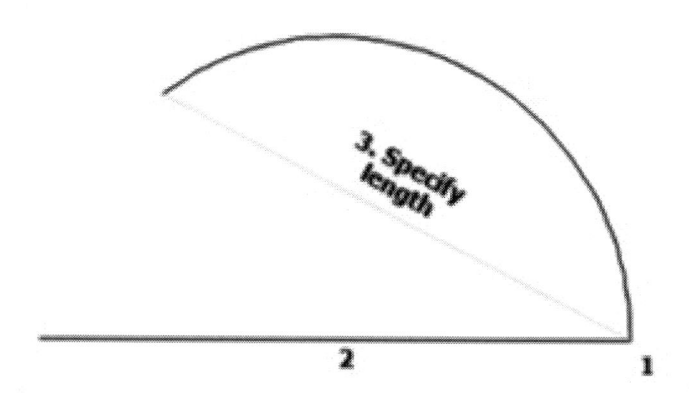

Figure 67: arc Start, Center, Length

5. Start, End, Angle

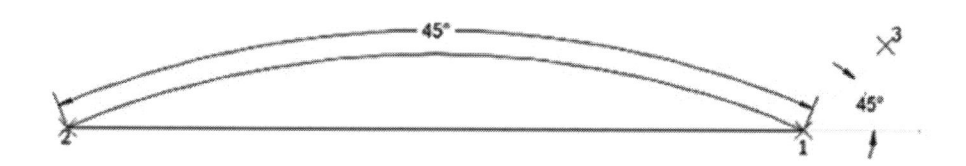

Figure 68: arc Start, End, Angle

6. Start, End, Direction

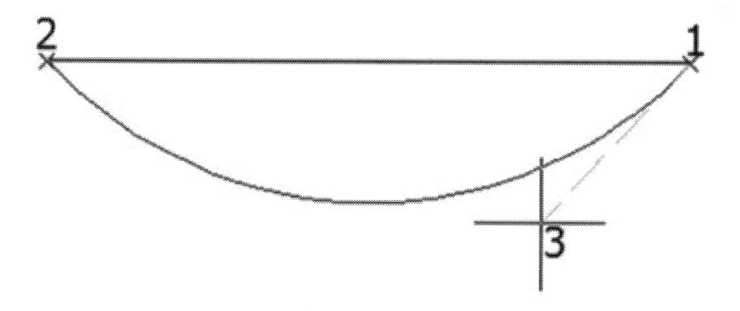

Figure 69: arc Start, End, Direction

7. **Start, End, Radius**

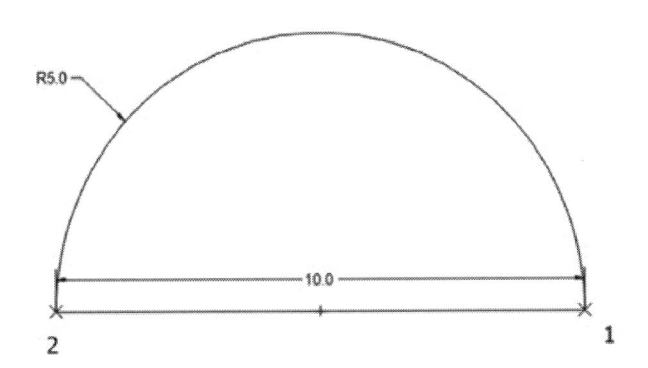

Figure 70: arc Start, End, Radius

8. **Center, Start, End**

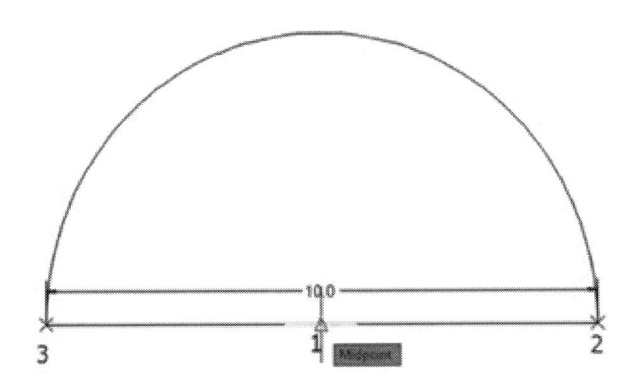

Figure 71: arc Center, Start, End

9. **Center, Start, Angle**

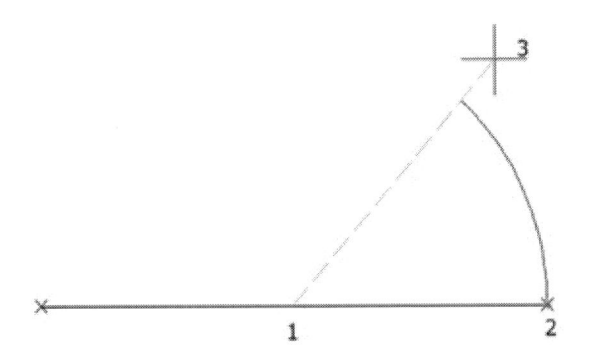

Figure 72: arc Center, Start, Angle

Draw Tools

10. Start, Center, Length

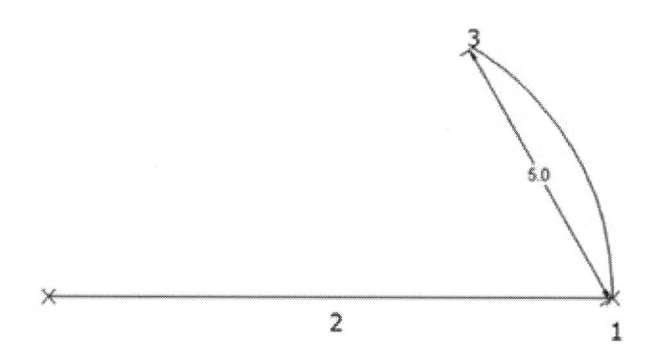

Figure 73: arc Start, Center, Length

11. Continue

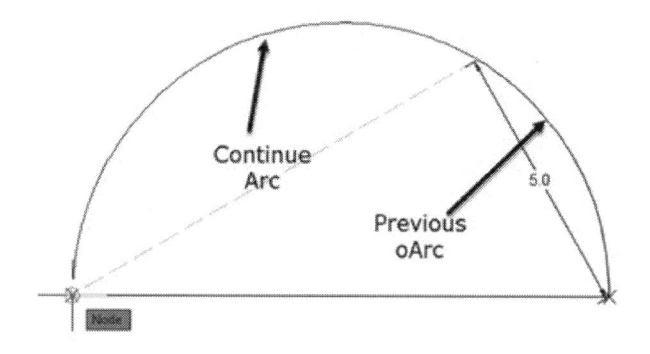

Figure 74: arc Continue

What do you mean by RECTANGLE?

It is a command by which we can make a rectangle having similar right angles and two sides are also similar.

Step 1: Ribbon: Home tab ➢ Draw panel ➢ Rectangle

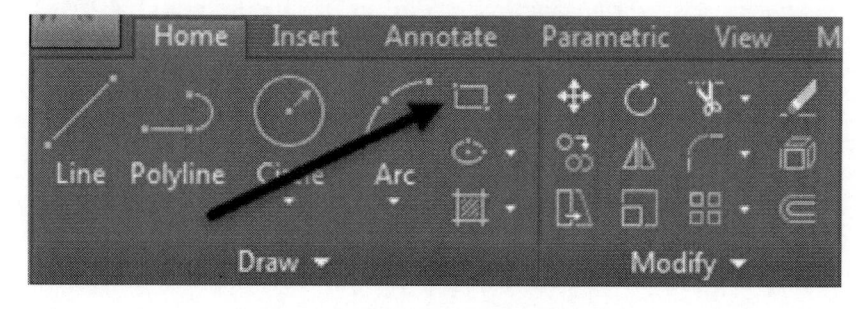

Figure 75: rectangle tool icon

OR

Command: REC

Step 2: Specify first corner point or [Chamfer/ Elevation/ Fillet/ Thickness/ Width]: **Pick 1 point**

Step 3: Specify other corner point or [Area/Dimensions/Rotation]: **Pick 2 point**

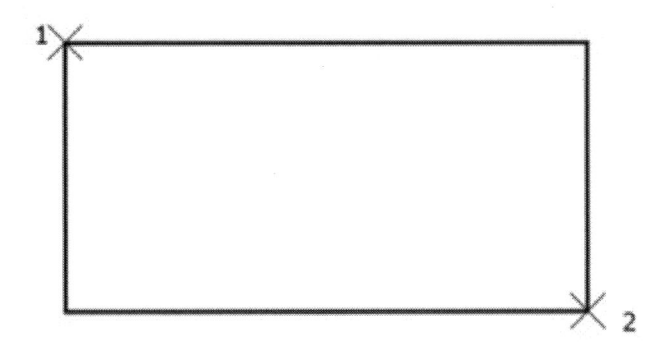

Figure 76: rectangle

If you want to select an option like-

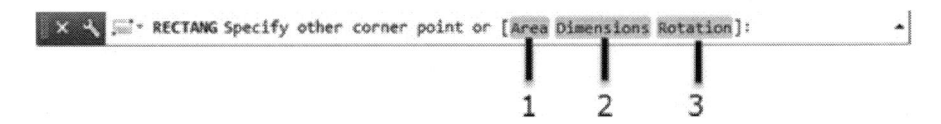

Figure 77: rectangle option

1. Area

It can be explained as the region inside the boundary of any 2D

Step 1: Command: **REC**

Step 2: Specify first corner point or [Chamfer/ Elevation/ Fillet/ Thickness/ Width]: **Pick 1 point**

Step 3: Specify other corner point or [Area/Dimensions/Rotation]: **A**

Step 4: Enter area of rectangle in current units: **500**

Step 5: Calculate rectangle dimensions based on [Length/Width]: **L**

Step 6: Enter rectangle length: **50**

Draw Tools

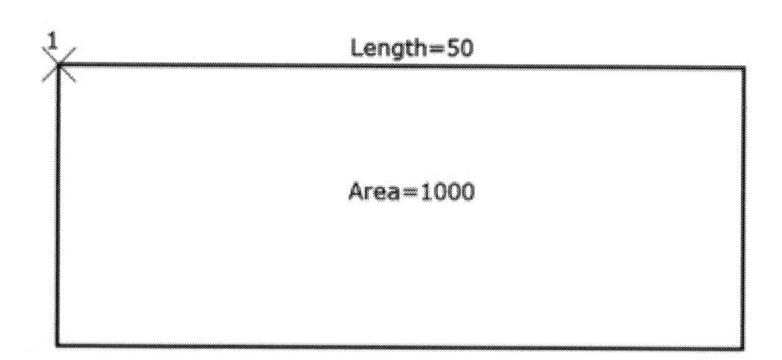

Figure 78: rectangle area

2. Dimensions

Creates a rectangle by using length and width values.

Step 1: Command: **REC**

Step 2: Specify first corner point or [Chamfer/ Elevation/ Fillet/ Thickness/ Width]: **Pick 1 point**

Step 3: Specify other corner point or [Area/Dimensions/Rotation]: **D**

Step 4: Specify length for rectangles: **50**

Step 5: Specify width for rectangles: **10**

Step 6: Specify other corner point or [Area/Dimensions/Rotation]: **Pick 2 point**

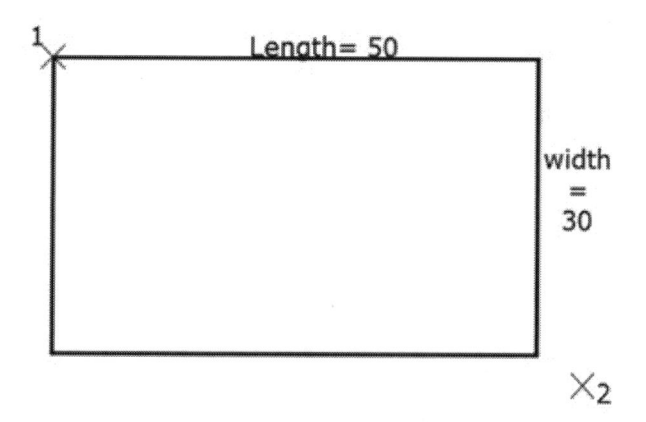

Figure 79: rectangle dimensions

3. Rotation

Creates a rectangle at a specified rotation angle.

Step 1: Command: **REC**

Step 2: Specify other corner point or [Area/Dimensions/Rotation]: **R**

Step 3: Specify rotation angle or [Pick point]: **45**

Step 4: Specify other corner point or [Area/Dimensions/Rotation]: D ↵
Step 5: Specify length for rectangles: 50 ↵
Step 6: Specify width for rectangles: 10 ↵
Step 7: Specify other corner point or [Area/Dimensions/Rotation]: **Pick 2 point**

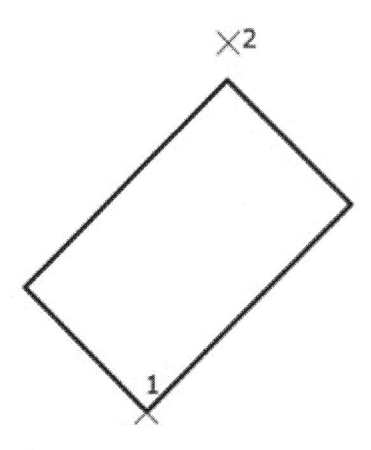

Figure 80: rectangle rotation

What do you mean by POLYGON?

It is a command by which we can create a plane figure having at least three straight sides and angles. Triangle, rectangle and pentagon can be created through this command. In AutoCAD we can construct a polygon object that has a minimum of three closed sides and maximum of 1024 sides. There are two type Polygon. First inscribed in the circle and second circumscribed about circle.

Step 1: Ribbon: Home tab ➤ Draw panel ➤ Polygon

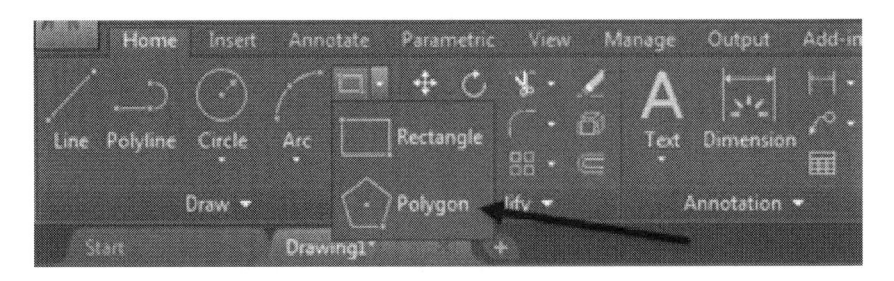

Figure 81: polygon tool icon

Command: POL

Inscribed in the Circle

In this, the polygon lies inside the circle with its vertices on the circumference.

Step 2: Polygon enter number of sides: 8 ↵

Draw Tools 35

Step 3: Specify center of polygon or [Edge]: **Specify a center point**
Step 4: Enter an option [Inscribed in circle/Circumscribed about circle]: **I**
Step 5: Specify radius of circle: **12**

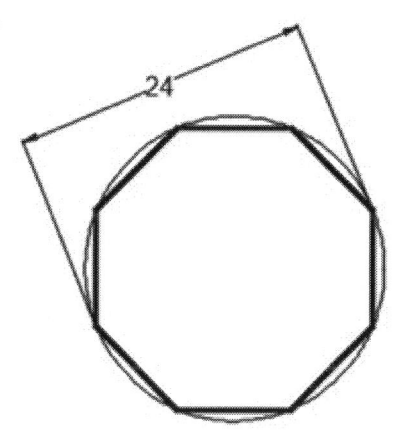

Figure 82: Inscribed in the Circle

Circumscribed about Circle

It is a polygon constructed such that circles lies within it and its circumference crosses through the mid-points of the vertices of polygon.

Step 1: Command: **POL**
Step 2: Polygon enter number of sides: **8**
Step 3: Specify center of polygon or [Edge]: **Specify a center point**
Step 3: Enter an option [Inscribed in circle/Circumscribed about circle]: **C**
Step 4: Specify radius of circle: **10**

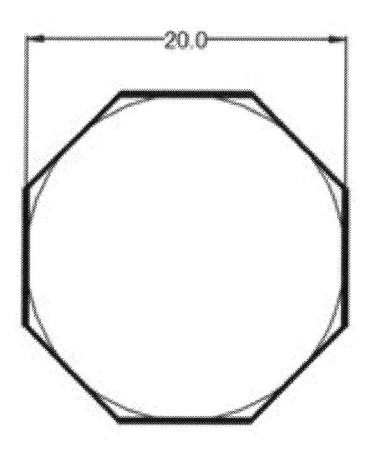

Figure 83: Circumscribed about Circle

What do you mean by ELLIPSE?

It is a command to create an Elliptical type arc. The first two points determine the location and length of the first axis whereas the third point fixes the distance from the center of the ellipse to the end point of the second axis.

Step 1: Ribbon: Home tab ➢ Draw panel ➢ ELLIPSE

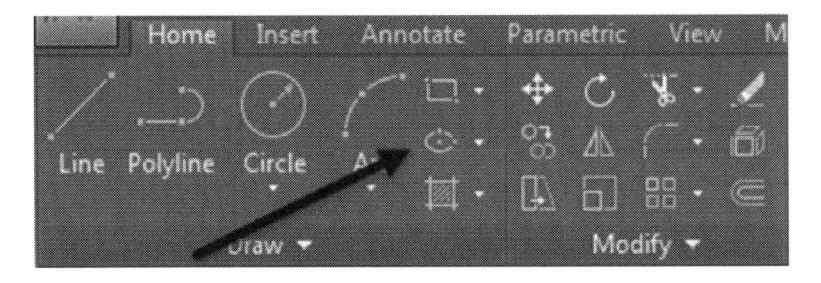

Figure 84: ellipse tool icon

OR

Command: EL

Step 2: Specify axis endpoint of ellipse or [Arc/Center]: **Pick 1 point**

Step 3: Specify another endpoint of the axis: **10** (Give direction then enter value)

Step 4: Specify the distance to other axis or [Rotation]: **10**

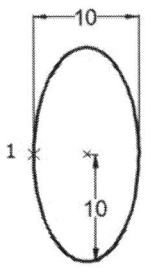

Figure 85: ellipse

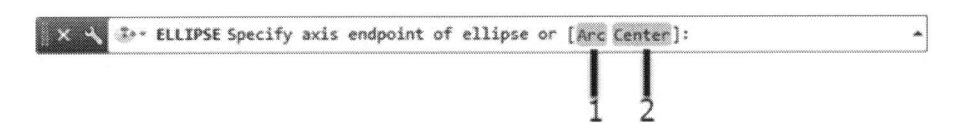

Figure 86 ellipse option

1. Arc

First of all. Specify first axis dimension then specify second axis dimension. Then specify start angle and end angle.

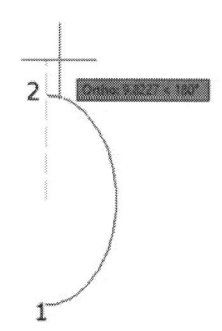

Figure 87: ellipse arc

2. Center

Specify center point of ellipse.

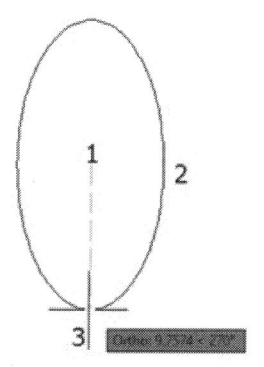

Figure 88: ellipse center

What do you mean by HATCH?

It is a command to create lines for section viewing and filling of an area of an object so that it is distinguished from other objects.

Step 1: Ribbon: Home tab ➤ Draw panel ➤ Hatch

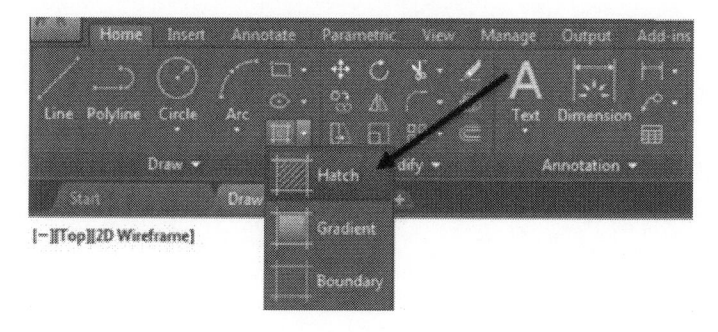

Figure 89: hatch tool icon

OR

Step 2: H

Step 3: Give the command 'H' enter, a ribbon toolbar will appear.

Step 4: Click "Hatch Pattern" and select the type of pattern.

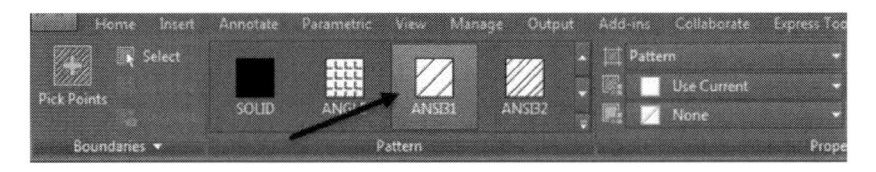

Figure 90: hatching pattern

Step 5: Click on pick points and select an area that is required to be hatched. (Remember only a closed area can be hatched)

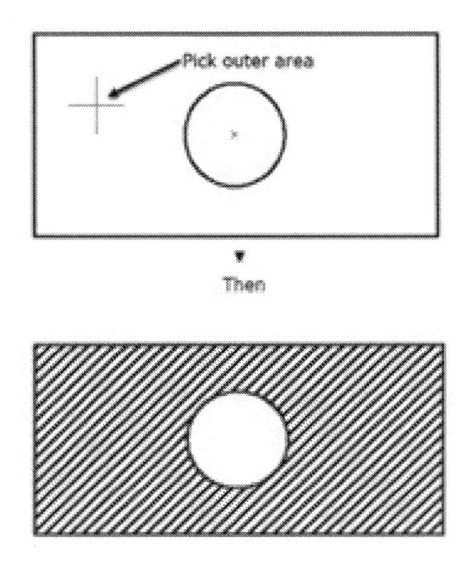

Figure 91: use of hatch

Step 6: In the ribbon toolbar, give the scale of the pattern and properties like color and background color.

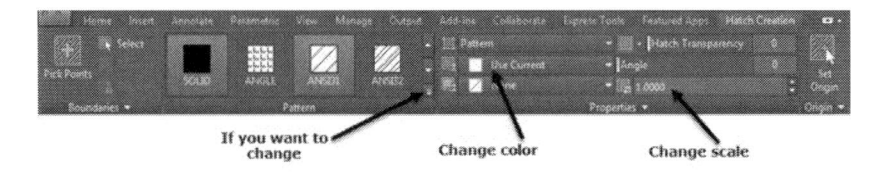

Figure 92: hatching setting

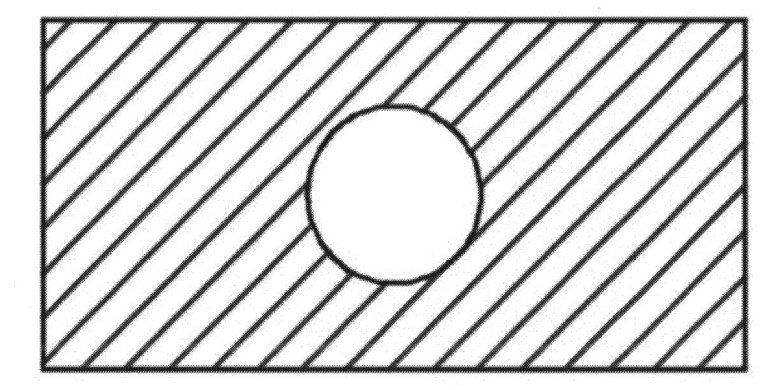

Figure 93: after hatching editing

What do you mean by GRADIENT?

Gradient command is used to create a gradient type of fill which means "two color types of filling." This two color types of filling is "transition filling."

Step 1: Ribbon: Home tab ➢ Draw panel ➢ Gradient

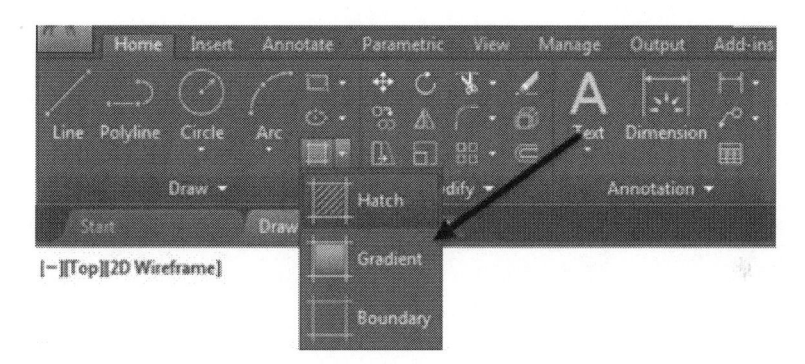

Figure 94 gradient tool icon

OR

Command: GD

Step 2: Give the command 'GD' and press enter. A ribbon toolbar will appear.

Step 3: Select the gradient pattern from 'Hatch Pattern' option.

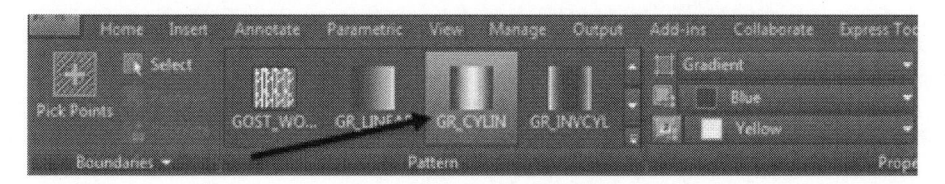

Figure 95: gradient pattern

Step 4: Give the required color, such as a single or a pair of two color.

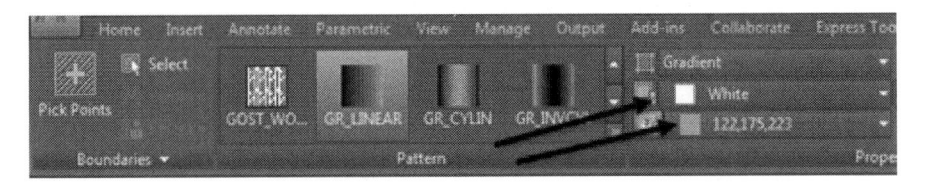

Figure 96: gradient color

Step 5: Click 'Pick Point' to select a point in a closed area.

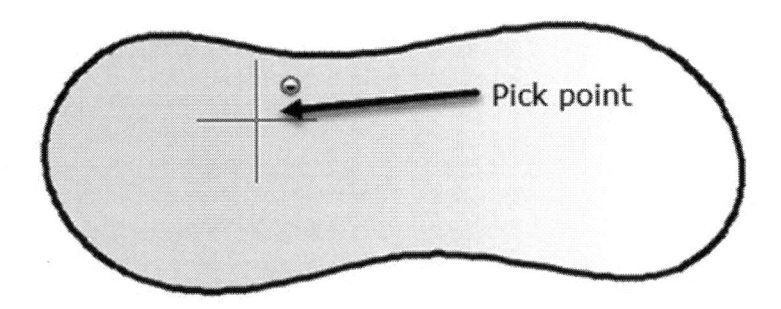

Figure 97: use of gradient

What do you mean by BOUNDARY?

Boundary command is used to create a region in an enclosed area.

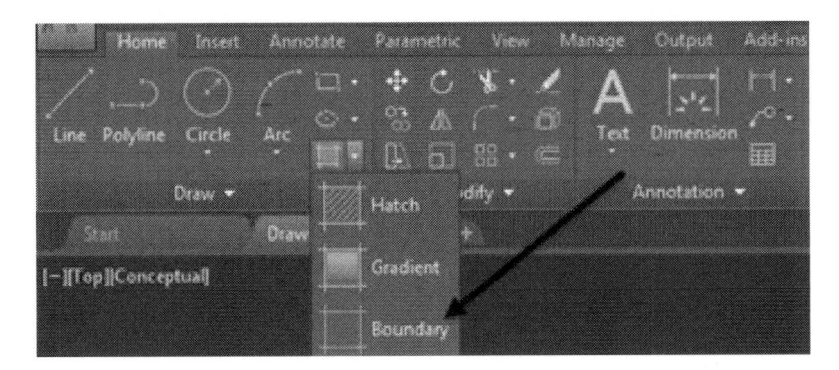

Figure 98: boundary tool icon

OR

Command: BO

Step 2: On giving command 'BO' enter, a boundary creation tab appears.

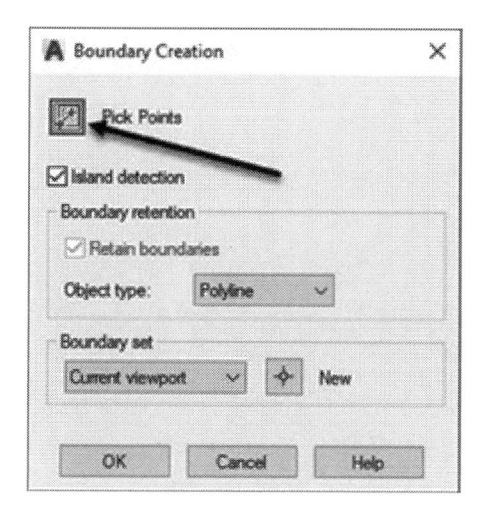

Figure 99: Boundary creation

Step 2: Click the option of 'pick points,' then select an enclosed point in an enclosed area that you need to make a boundary.

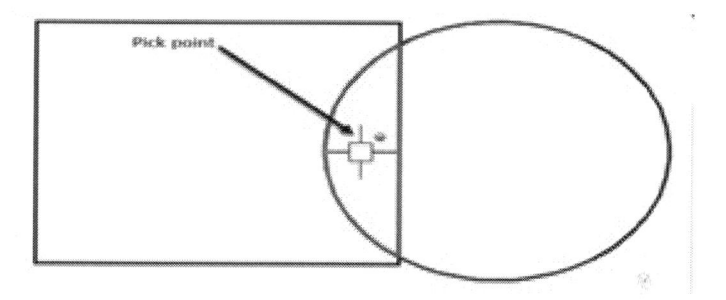

Figure 100: use of boundary tool

Step 3: Then enter.

What do you mean by RAY?

It is a command to create a line starting from a point to infinity in one direction. It can be used as a reference for creating other objects.

Step 1: Ribbon: Home tab ➤ Draw panel ➤ Ray

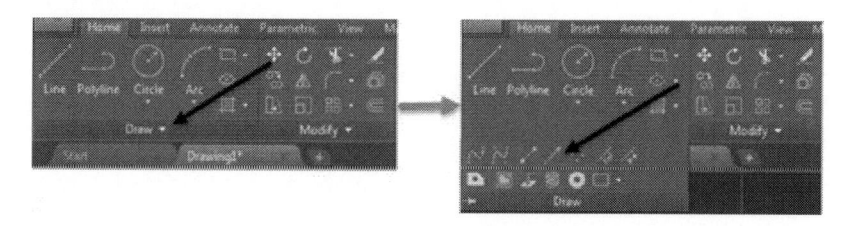

Figure 101: ray tool icon

OR

Command: RAY

Step 2: Pick Start Point.
Step 3: Pick through point.

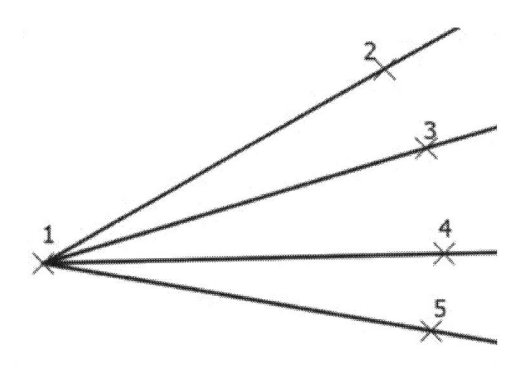

Figure 102: use of ray

What do you mean by POINT?

We used point to create point objects. With the help of this command we specify the 3d location for a point, can snap objects, view current elevation (if we neglect the z axis.)

Step 1: Ribbon: Home tab ➤ Draw panel ➤ Multiple points

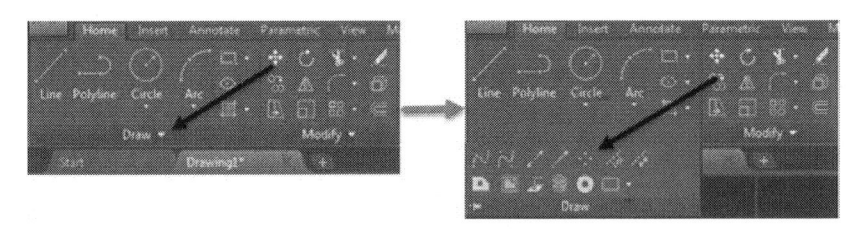

Figure 103: point tool icon

OR

Command: PO

Step 2: Pick point.

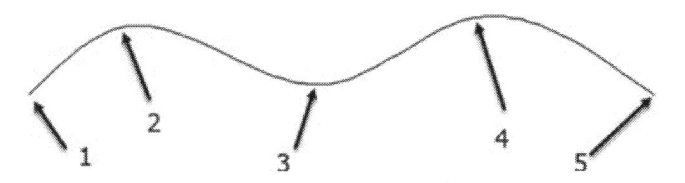

Figure 104: pick point

Draw Tools

Step 3: Command: DDPTYPE (for point style).

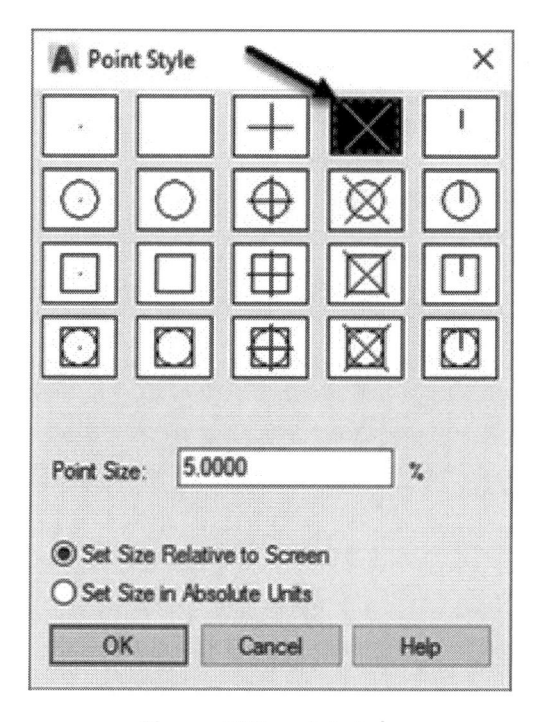

Figure 105: point style

Step 3: Select point style then ok.

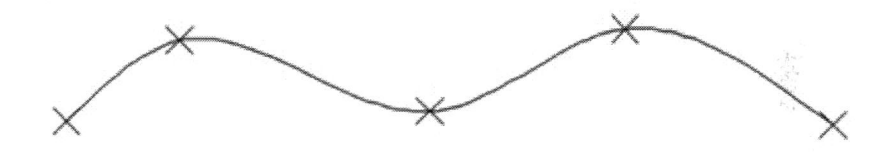

Figure 106: point style result

What do we mean by DIVIDE?

When we use the command divide, it places a point along the line, arc, circle, polyline dividing it into the required number of segments.

Step 1: Ribbon: Home tab ➢ Draw panel ➢ Divide

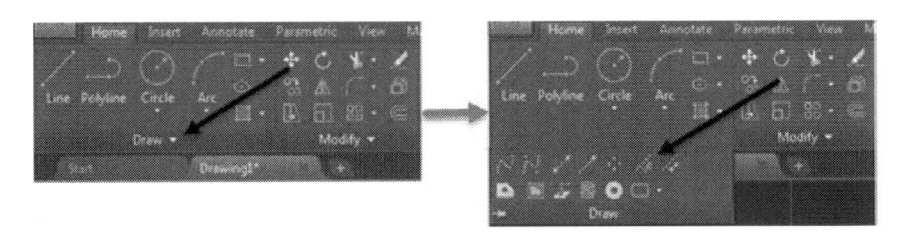

Figure 107: divide tool icon

OR

Command: DIV

Step 2: Select object to divide: **Select object**

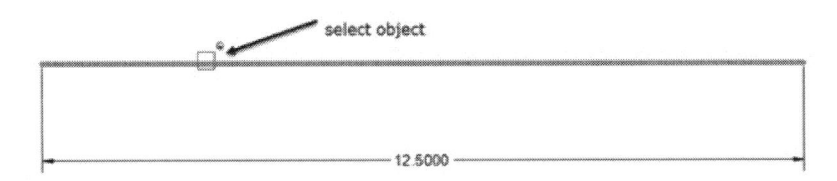

Figure 108: use of divide tool

Step 3: Enter the number of segments or [Blocks]: **5**
Step 4: Command: PTYPE (Select any point style and OK)

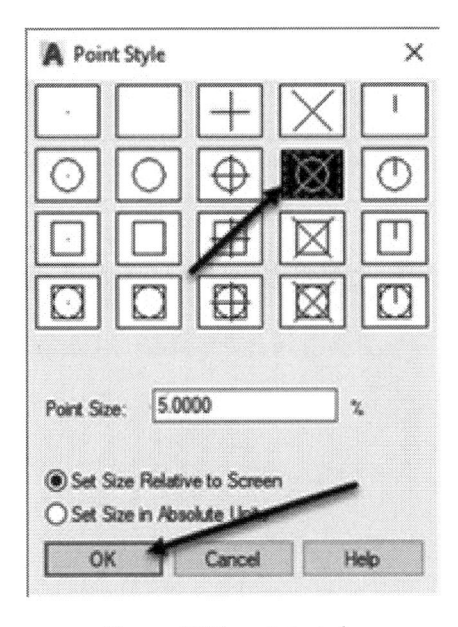

Figure 109: point style

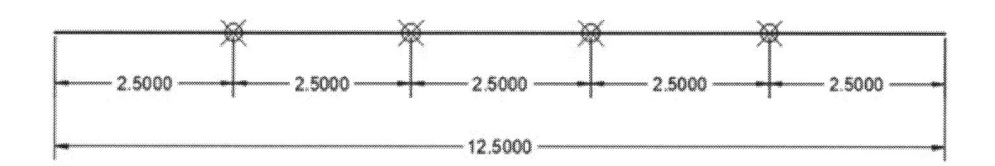

Figure 110: use of divide

When do we use MEASURE?

When we need to place points at specific required intervals along the line, polyline, arc or circle we use the command measure.

Step 1: Ribbon: Home tab ➢ Draw panel ➢ Measure

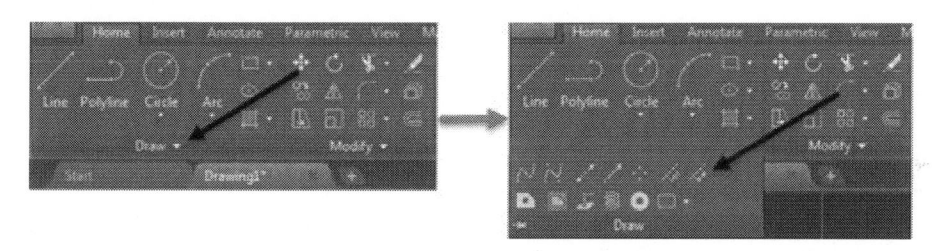

Figure 111: Measure tool icon

Command: ME

Step 2: Select object to measure: Select object

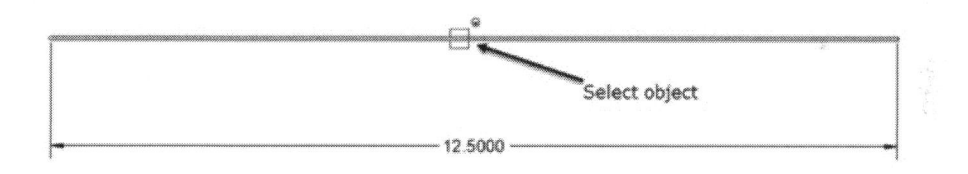

Figure 112: Select line

Step 3: Specify length of segment or [Block]: **3**
Step 4: Command: PTYPE (**Select any point style and OK)**

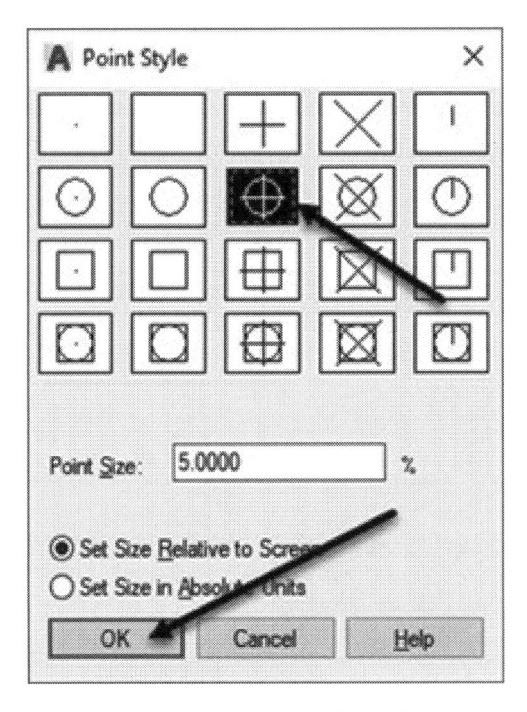

Figure 113: point style option

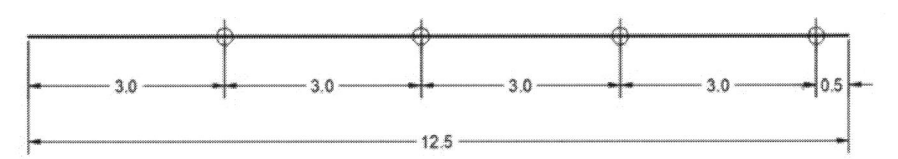

Figure 114: use of measure

What do you mean by REGION?

By using the command region, it converts a set of objects into a region object. Region is a 2D area made by different objects like arc, circle or line. It is used to convert 2d to 3d object.

Step 1: Ribbon: Home tab ➤ Draw panel ➤ Region

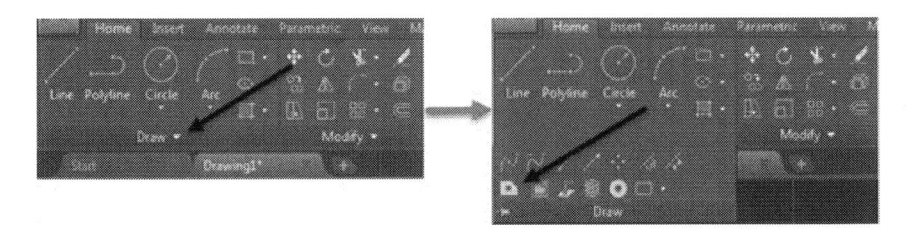

Figure 115: region tool icon

Draw Tools 47

OR

Command: REG

Step 2: Select object: select first object and second object then Enter

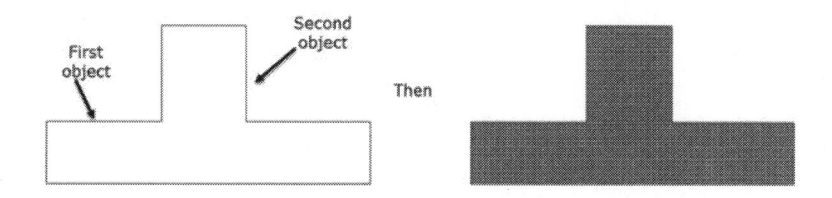

Figure 116: use of region

What do you mean by WIPEOUT?

It is used to hideout an object whenever needed. It can be of any cross-section area made by bounded sides such as polygon, rectangle, etc. The wipe-out area can be TURN ON for editing and TURNOFF for plotting.

Step 1: Ribbon: Home tab ➢ Draw panel ➢ Wipeout

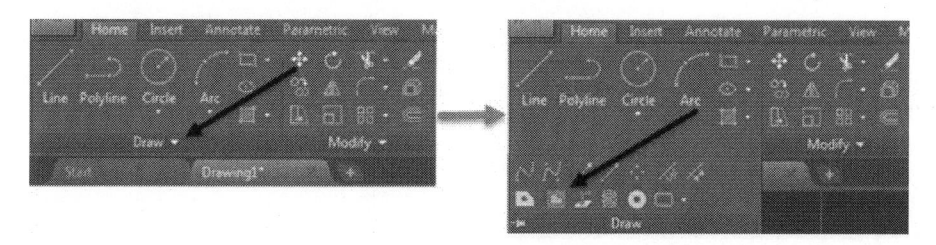

Figure 117: wipeout tool icon

OR

Command: WIP

Step 2: Specify first point or [Frames/Polyline]: **Pick 1 point**
Step 3: Specify next point: **Pick 2 point**
Step 4: Specify next point or [Undo]: **Pick 3 point**
Step 5: Specify next point or [Undo/Close]: **Pick 4 point**
Step 6: Specify next point or [Undo/Close]: **C**

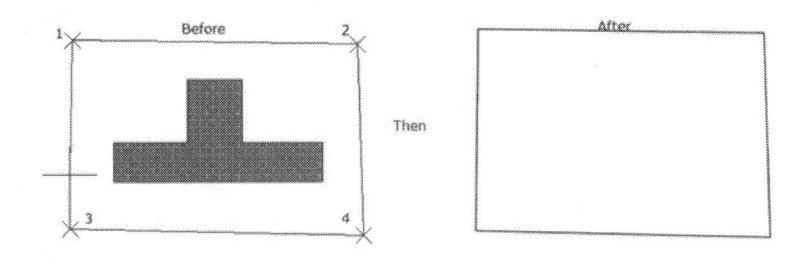

Figure 118: use of wipeout

What do you mean by 3D POLYLINE?

A 3D polyline is a connected sequence of straight line segments created as a single object. 3D polylines can be non-coplanar; however, they cannot include arc segments.

Step 1: Ribbon: Home tab ➤ Draw panel ➤ 3D polyline

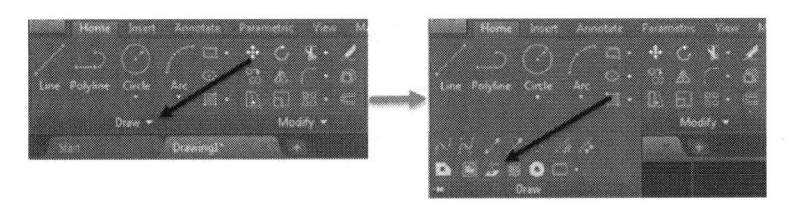

Figure 119: 3d polyline tool icon

OR

Command: 3DPOLY

Step 2: Specify start point of polyline: **Pick 1 point**
Step 3: Specify end point of line or [Undo]: **Pick 2 point**
Step 4: Specify end point of line or [Undo]: **Pick 3 point**
Step 5: Specify end point of line or [Close Undo]: **Pick 4 point**

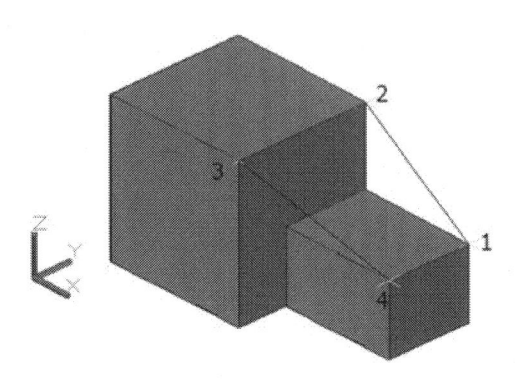

Figure 120: use of 3D polyline

What do you mean by HELIX?

Helix command creates a spring. Firstly give base radius, top radius and height as well as turns to the use of helix.

Step 1: Ribbon: Home tab ➤ Draw panel ➤ Helix

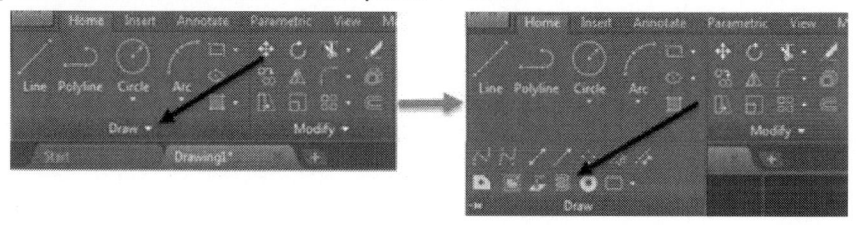

Figure 121: helix tool icon

OR

Command: HELIX

Step 2: Specify center point of base: **Pick 1 point**
Step 3: Specify base radius or [Diameter]: **20**
Step 4: Specify top radius or [Diameter]: **10**
Step 4: Specify helix height or [Axis endpoint Turns Turn height tWist]: **T** (T for turns)
Step 4: Enter the number of turns: **10**
Step 4: Specify helix height or [Axis endpoint Turns Turn height tWist]: **15**

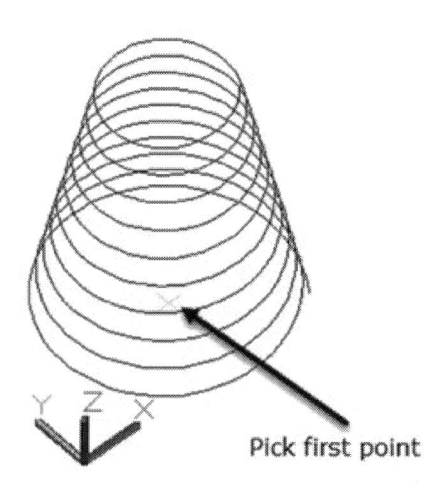

Figure 122: use of helix

What do you mean by REVISION CLOUD?

It is a command to highlight the area of the revision cloud. It is a series of arc formed to create a revision cloud.

Step 1: Ribbon: Home tab ➤ Draw panel ➤ Revision Cloud

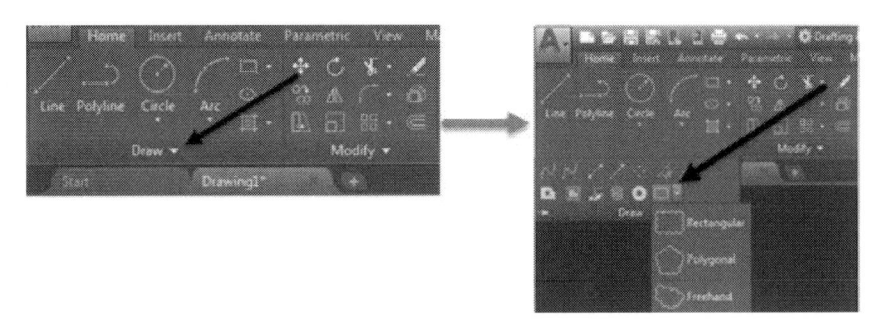

Figure 123: revision cloud tool icon

OR

Command: REVCLOUD

Step 2: F Enter for freehand option.

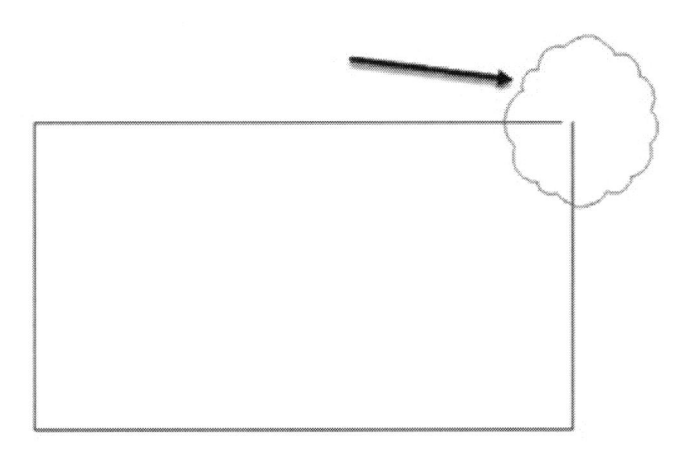

Figure 124: use of revision cloud

What do you mean by SOLID?

It is a command to create 2d filled polygons.

Step 1: Command: **SO**
Step 2: Specify first point: **Specify a point (1)**
Step 3: Specify second point: **Specify a point (2)**
Step 4: Specify third point: **Specify a point (3)**
Step 5: Specify fourth point or <exit>: **Specify a point (1)**

Draw Tools 51

Step 6: Specify third point: **Specify a point (4)**
Step 7: Specify fourth point or <exit>: **Specify a point (3)**

Figure 125: use of solid

What do you mean by Fill?

It is used to control the filling of an object such as in the hatch, 2d solid and wide polylines. Then we need to use regenerate command to refresh the object. It is a "mode" command by which we can view the filling through on and no filling of objects through off mode.

Command: FILL

FILL enter mode [ON/OFF]: Enter option

ON

By turning the fill mode on, the complete solid object is displayed. For the filling of a 3D object to be visible, its extrusion direction must be parallel to the current viewing direction, and hidden lines must not be suppressed.

Figure 126" fill on

OFF

By turning the fill mode off, only the outlines of objects are displayed. Changing Fill mode affects existing objects after the drawing is regenerated. The display of line weights is not affected by the Fill mode setting.

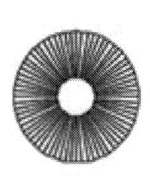

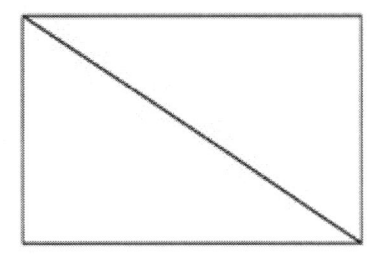

Figure 127: fill off

CHAPTER-4

Modify Tools

What do you mean by MOVE?

By using move we select an object, then select its base point and move it to the required position and direction.

Step 1: Ribbon: Home tab ➤ Modify panel ➤ Move

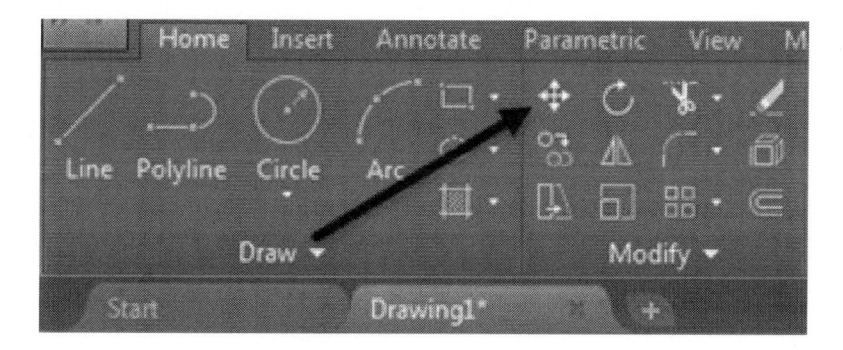

Figure 128: move tool icon

OR

Command: M

Step 2: Select object

Step 3: Specify base point or [Displacement]: Pick base point

Step 4: Specify second point or <use the first point as displacement>: **Give direction then 50**

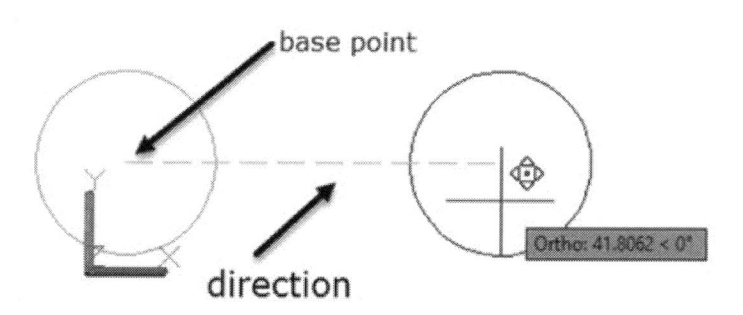

Figure 129: use of move tool

What do you mean by COPY?

When we need the same object at more than one place, we draw an object once and then use the command 'copy' to use the same object at other places.

Step 1: Ribbon: Home tab ➢ Modify panel ➢ Copy

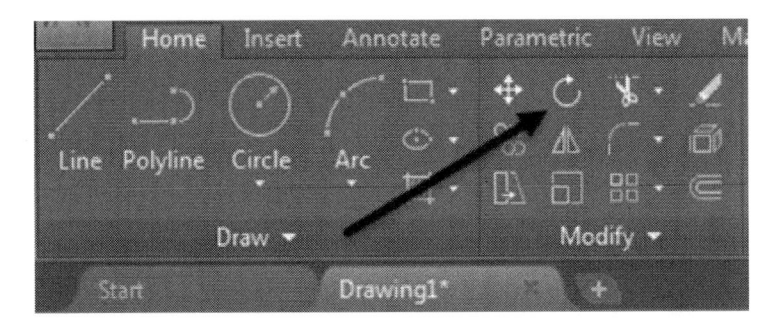

Figure 130: copy tool icon

OR

Command: CO

Step 2: Select object
Step 3: Specify base point or [Displacement/mOde]: Specify a base
Step 4: Specify second point or [Array]: **Pick first point**
Step 5: Specify second point or [Array]: **Pick second point**
Step 6: Specify second point or [Array]: **Give direction then 50**

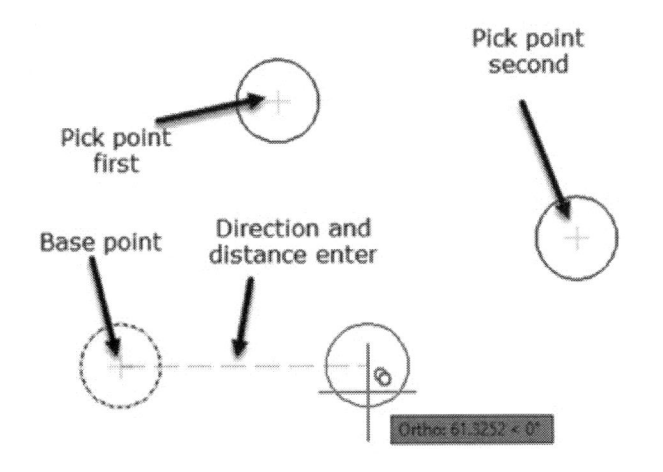

Figure 131: use of copy tool

What do you mean by STRETCH?

Command stretch allows us to move a portion of a drawing without distorting

Modify Tools

their connections with other parts of the drawing. But we cannot stretch Blocks, Hatch patterns, or Text entities.

Step 1: Ribbon: Home tab ➤ Modify panel ➤ Stretch

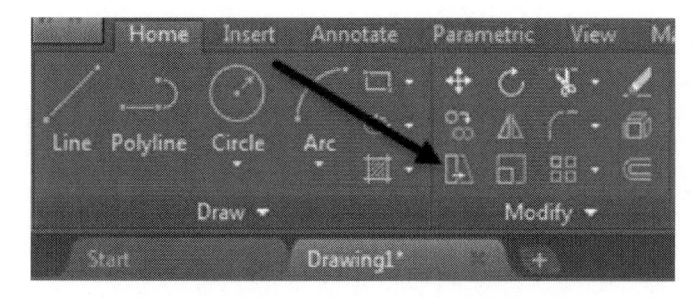

Figure 132: stretch tool icon

OR

Command: S

Step 2: Select object then

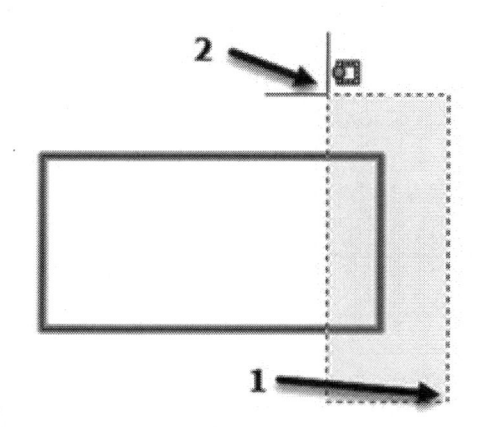

Figure 133: use of stretch

Step 3: Specify base point or [Displacement]: **Pick first point**

Pick first point   Direction

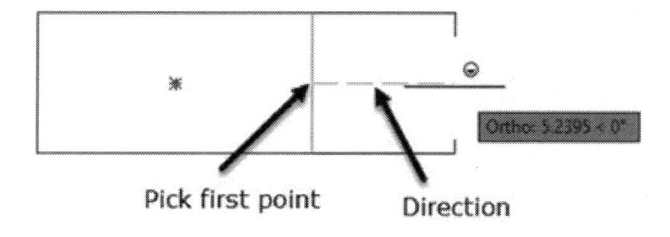

Figure 134: Stretch

What do you mean by ROTATE?

By using the command rotate, we can give inclination to an object from an axis.

Step 1: Ribbon: Home tab ➢ Modify panel ➢ Rotate

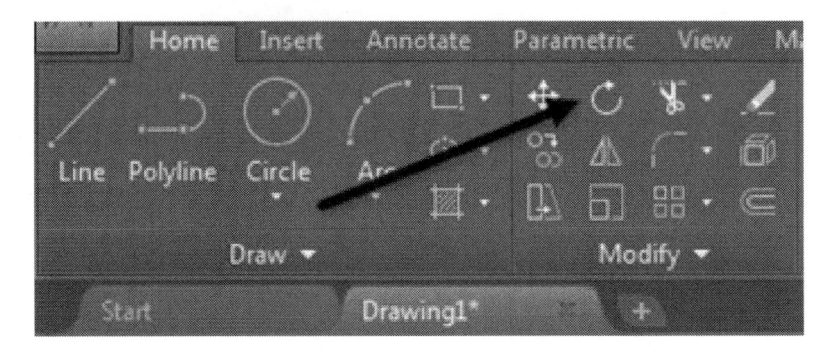

Figure 135: rotate tool icon

OR

Command: RO

Step 2: Select object then

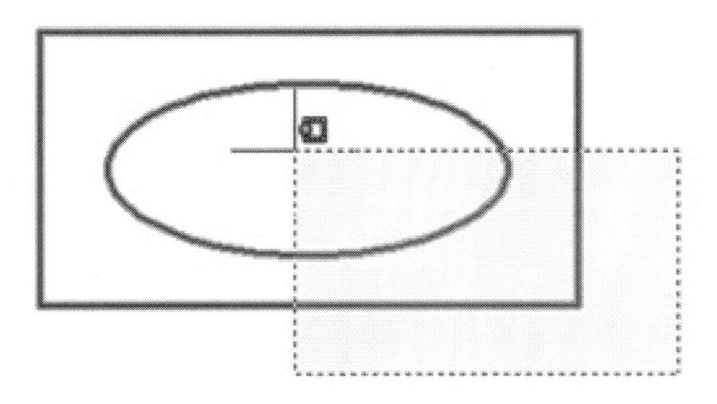

Figure 136: select object for rotate

Step 2: Specify base point: Pick point
Step 3: Specify rotation angle or [Copy/Reference]: 90

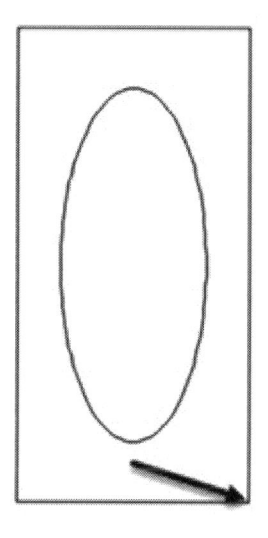

Figure 137: use of rotate

What do you mean by MIRROR?

We use the mirror command to create a reflection of a designated objected about a specified axis.

Step 1: Ribbon: Home tab ➤ Modify panel ➤ Mirror

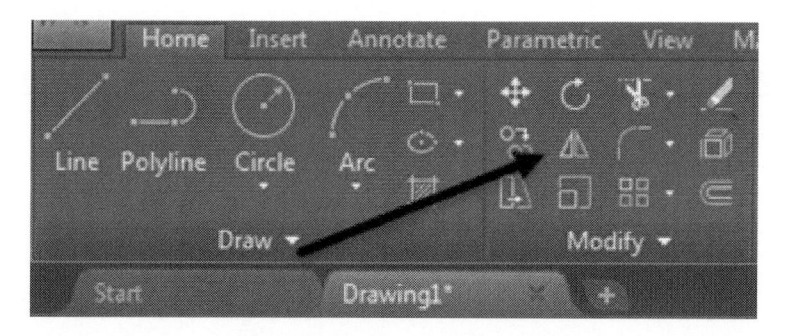

Figure 138: mirror tool icon

OR

Command: MI

Step 2: Select object then

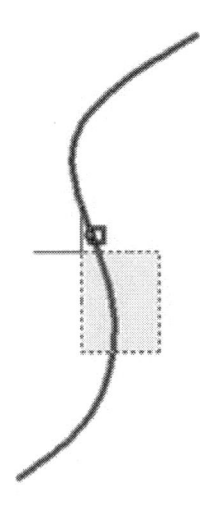

Figure 139: select object

Step 3: Specify first point of mirror line: **Pick first point**
Step 4: Specify second point of mirror line: **Pick second point**
Step 4: Erase source objects? [Yes/No]: **N**

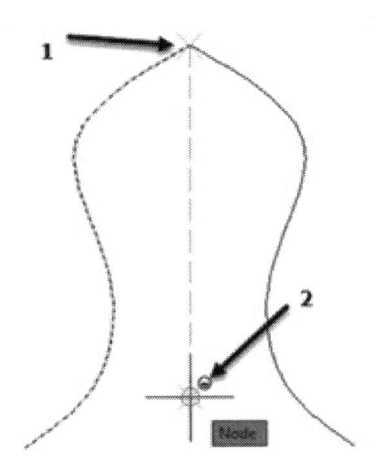

Figure 140: mirror axis point

What do you mean by SCALE?

By using command scale, we can alter the size of an object proportionally.
Step 1: Ribbon: Home tab ➤ Modify panel ➤ Scale

Modify Tools 59

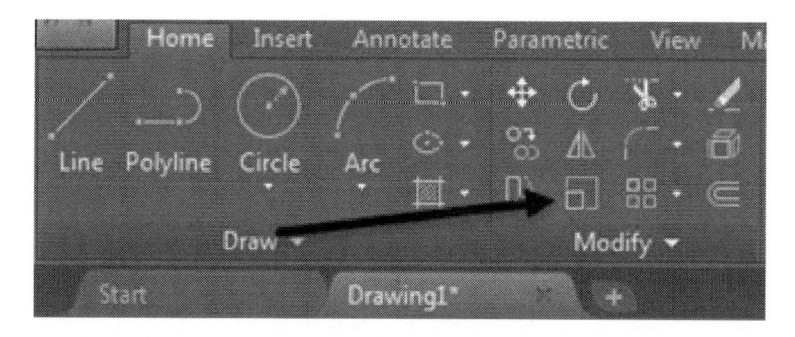

Figure 141: scale tool icon

OR

Command: SC ⏎

Step 2: Select object then
Step 3: Specify base point: **Pick base point**

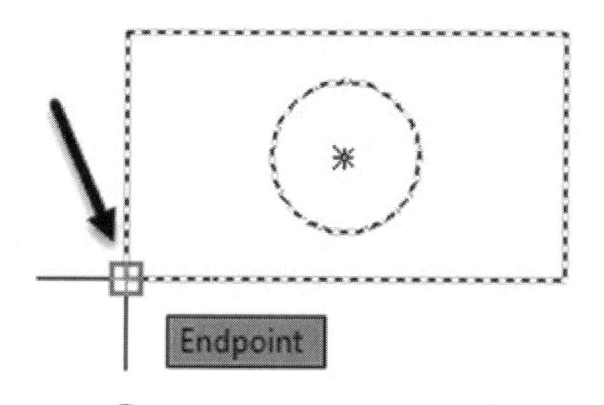

Figure 142: pick point

Step 4: Specify scale factor or [Copy/Reference]: **R** ⏎ **(R enter for reference)**
Step 5: Specify reference length: **1** ⏎
Step 6: Specify new length or [Point]: **2** ⏎

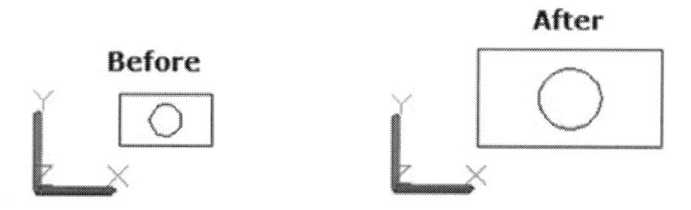

Figure 143: use of scale

What do you mean by TRIM?

We use command trim to erase a portion of the selected object that crosses a specified edge. In other words, we can use command trim on an object to meet edges of another object.

Step 1: Ribbon: Home tab ➢ Modify panel ➢ Trim

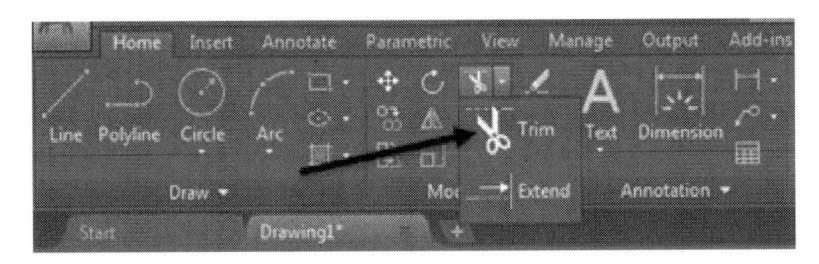

Figure 144: trim tool icon

OR

Command: TR

Step 2: Select object or <select all>: **Select reference object then**

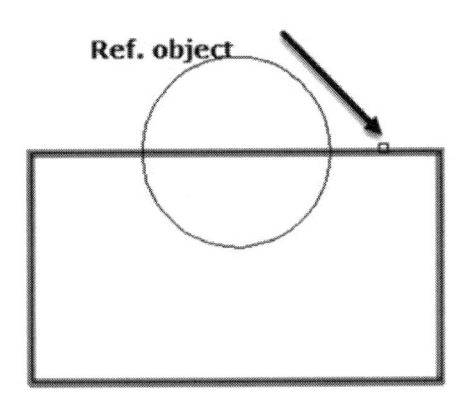

Figure 145: select ref. object

Step 3: Trim [Fence/Crossing/Project/eRase/Edge/Undo]: **Select trim object**

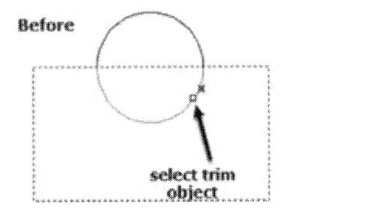

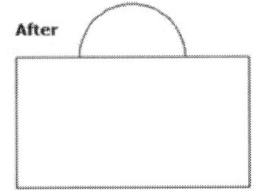

Figure 146: after trim

What do you mean by EXTEND?

By using the command extend, we can elongate or say lengthen a line, arc or polyline to meet a specified boundary edge.

Step 1: Ribbon: Home tab ➢ Modify panel ➢ Extend

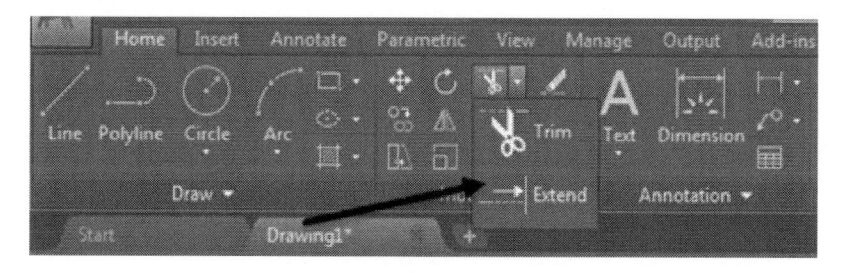

Figure 147: extend tool icon

OR

Command: EX

Step 2: Select object or <select all>: **Select reference object then**

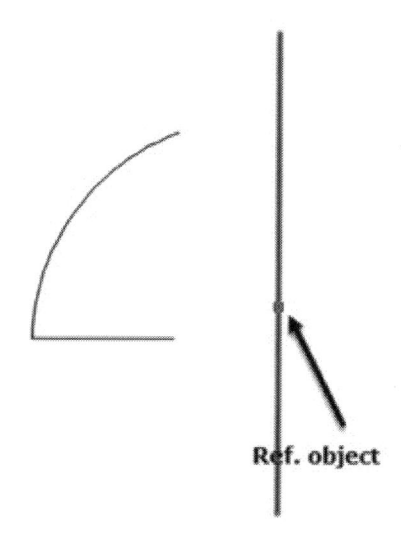

Figure 148: select ref. object

Step 3: Extend [Fence/Crossing/Project/Edge/Undo]: **Select Extend object**

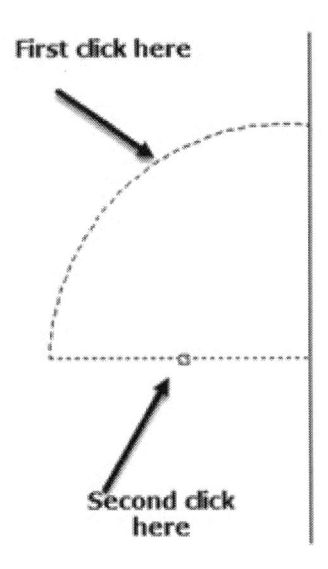

Figure 149: after extend

What do you mean by FILLET?

We use the command fillet when need to construct an arc of specified radius between two lines, arcs, circles or vertices of polylines.

Step 1: Ribbon: Home tab ➢ Modify panel ➢ Fillet

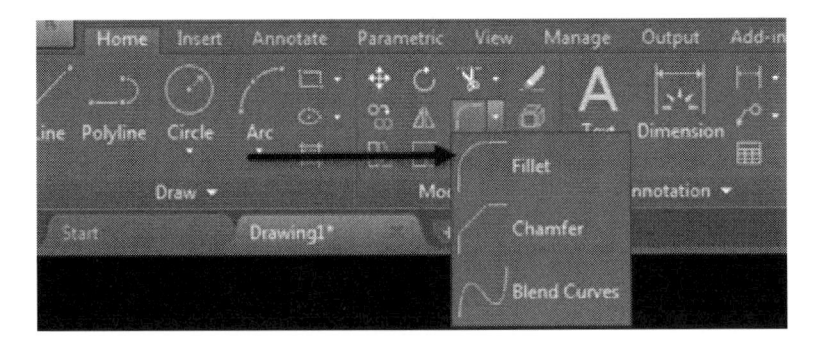

Figure 150: fillet tool icon

OR

Command: F

Step 2: Select first object or [Undo/Polyline/Radius/Trim/Multiple]: **R** **(R for fillet radius)**

Step 3: Specify fillet radius: **5**

Step 4: Select first object or [Undo/Polyline/Radius/Trim/Multiple]: **Select first object**

Modify Tools 63

Step 5: Select second object or shift-select to apply corner or [Radius]: **Select second object**

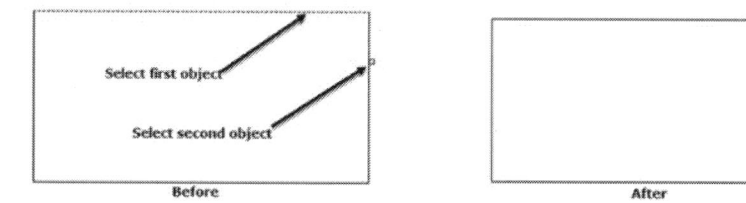

Figure 151: after fillet

What do you mean by CHAMFER?

A chamfer is an angled line connection, by using command chamfer we create an angled connection at the intersection of two lines.

Step 1: Ribbon: Home tab ➤ Modify panel ➤ Chamfer

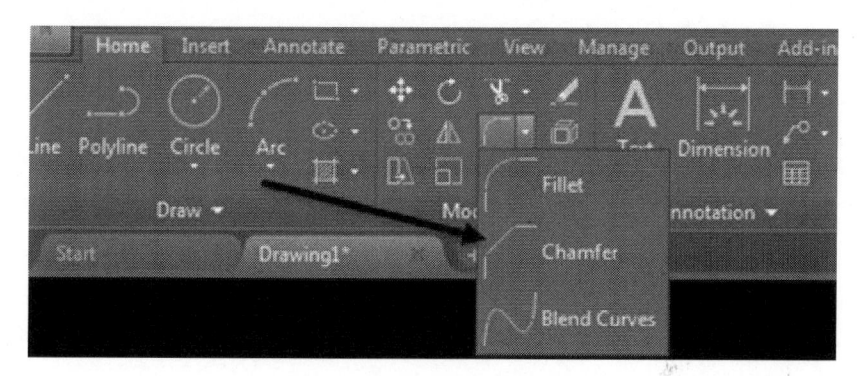

Figure 152: chamfer tool icon

OR

Command: CHA

Step 2: Select first line or [Undo/Polyline/Distance/Angle/Trim/mEthod/Multiple]: **D** (D enter for Distance)

Step 3: Specify chamfer length on the first line: **5**

Step 4: Specify chamfer length on the first line: **10**

Step 5: Select first line or [Undo/Polyline/Distance/Angle/Trim/mEthod/Multiple]: **Select first object**

Step 6: Select second line or shift-select to apply corner or [Distance/Angle/Method]: **Select second object**

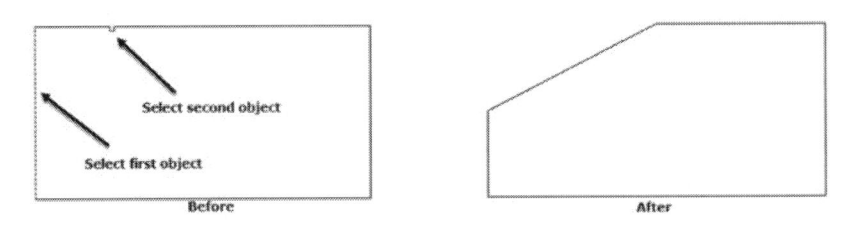

Figure 153: after chamfer

When do we use BLEND CURVES?

When we need to join two lines or curves, we use blend curves. It creates a spline between the selected object, shape of the spline depends upon specified points while the length of the selected object remains unchanged.

Step 1: Ribbon: Home tab ➤ Modify panel ➤ Chamfer

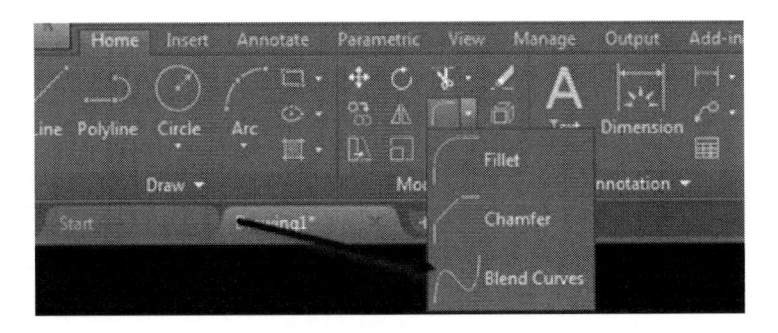

Figure 154: blend tool icon

OR

Command: BLEND

Step 2: Select first object or [CONtinuity]: **Select first object**
Step 3: Select second object: **Select second object**

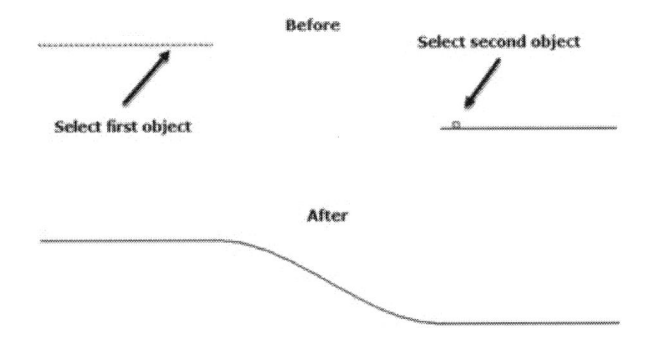

Figure 155: use of blend

Modify Tools 65

What do you mean by ARRAY?

We use command array for creating a series of object in a continuous manner and the required number of rectangular, polar (circular) or any selected path.

Ribbon: Home tab ➢ Modify panel ➢ Array

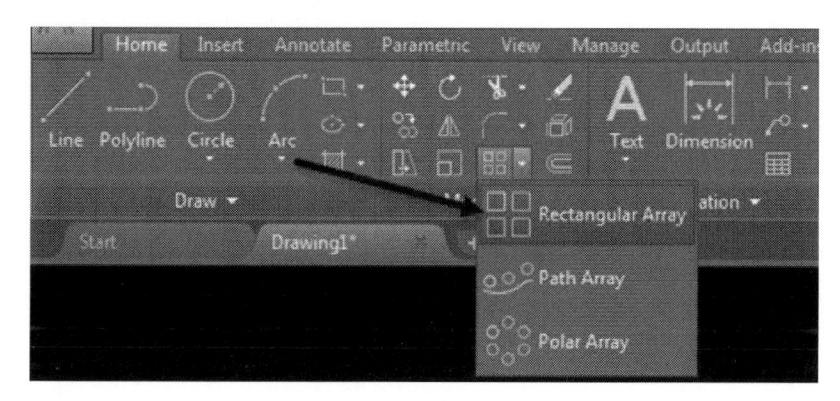

Figure 156: array tool icon

Rectangular

Rectangular Array can be copied to multiple objects. Rectangular Array object is a copy of the row and column where we can give the distance between rows and columns.

Step 1: Command: **AR**

Step 2: Select object: **Select rectangle**

Step 3: Enter array type [Rectangular/PAth/POlar]: **R**

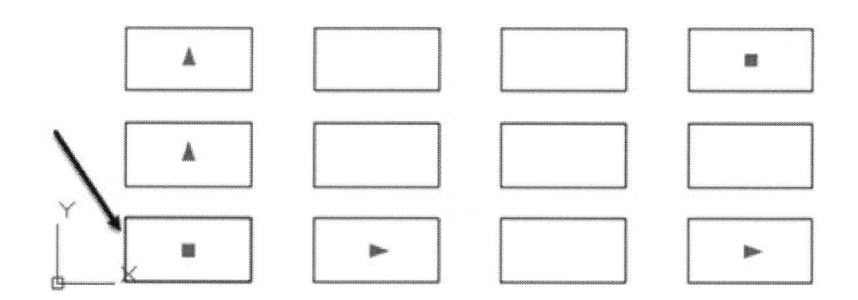

Figure 157: use of rectangle array

If you want to change the column distance and row distance or number

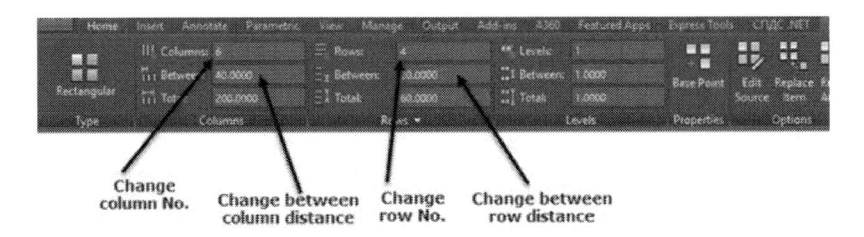

Figure 158: rectangle array setting

Then

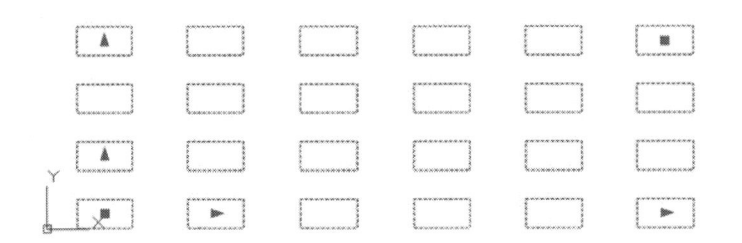

Figure 159: after editing

Path

Polar Array of objects in multiple copies can be made in a circular pattern. Polor Array by the center point and the number and angle of the object copy is given to the use of Polor Array. Copy of which may be circular object.

Step 1: Command: **AR**

Step 2: Select object: **Select object**

Step 3: Enter array type [Rectangular/PAth/POlar]: **PA**

Step 4: Select curve path: **Select path**

Figure 160: use of path array

If you want to change the distance or number

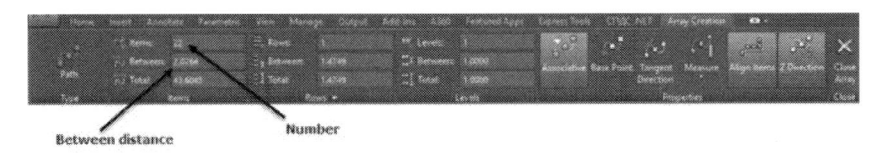

Figure 161: path array setting

Modify Tools 67

Then

Figure 162: use of path array

Polar

Array path, the path of an object like any other object copies. The second object path which does work. The Curve is the path.

Step 1: Command: **AR**

Step 2: Select object: **Select object**

Step 3: Enter array type [Rectangular/PAth/POlar]: **PO**

Step 4: Specify center point of array [Base point Axis of rotation]: Pick center point

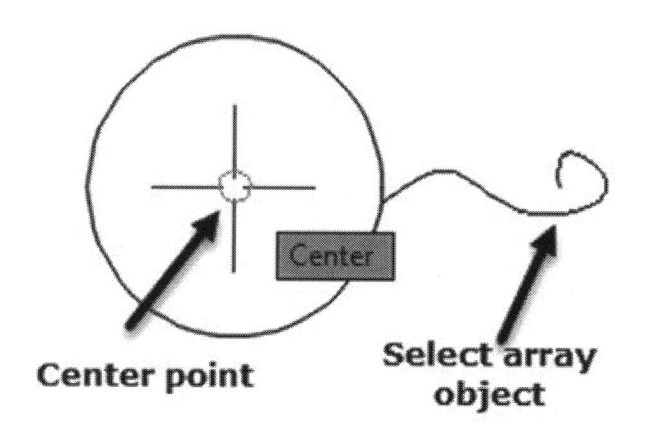

Figure 163: use of polar array

If you want change Angle or number

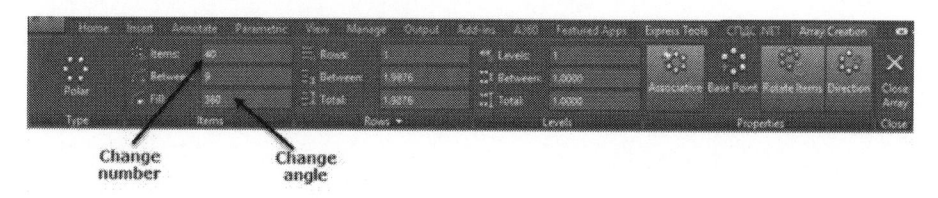

Figure 164: polar array setting

Then

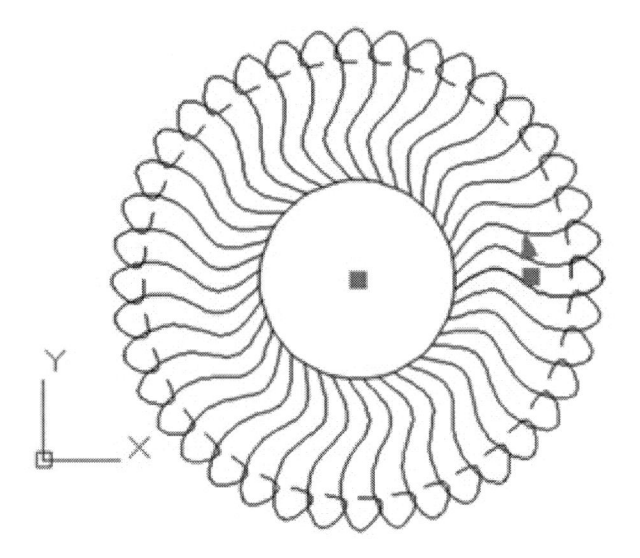

Figure 165: after polar array editing

What do you mean by EXPLODE?

Command Explode breaks a block, hatch pattern or dimension into its constituent entities and polyline into a series of straight lines. By using explode, we can also modify the properties of a particular object in block, etc.

Step 1: Ribbon: Home tab ➢ Modify panel ➢ Explode

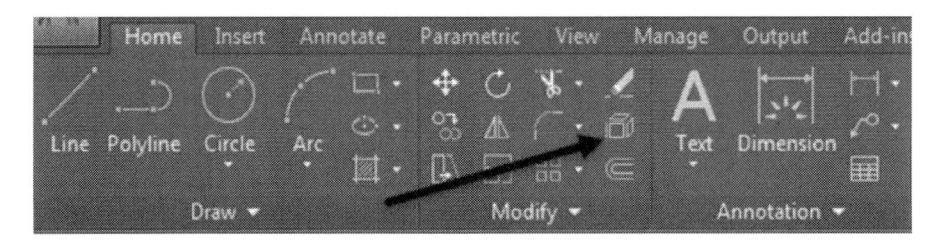

Figure 166: explode tool icon

OR

Command: X

Step 2: Select object then

Modify Tools

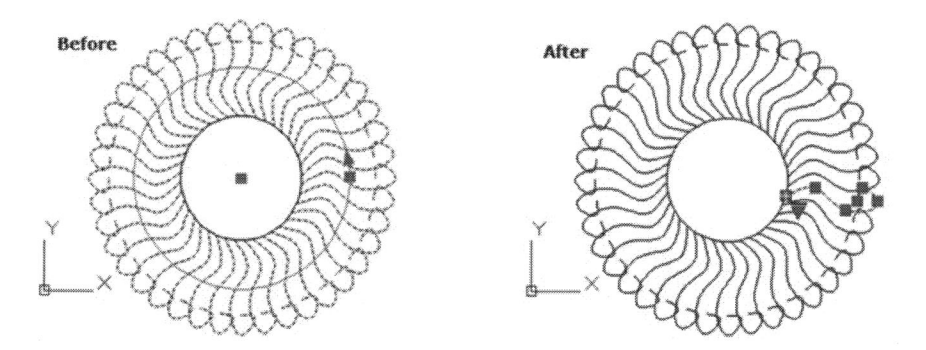

Figure 167: after explode

What do you mean by OFFSET?

By using the command offset, we can create a new line, polyline, and arc or circle parallel to the object and at a specified distance from it.

Step 1: Ribbon: Home tab ➢ Modify panel ➢ Offset

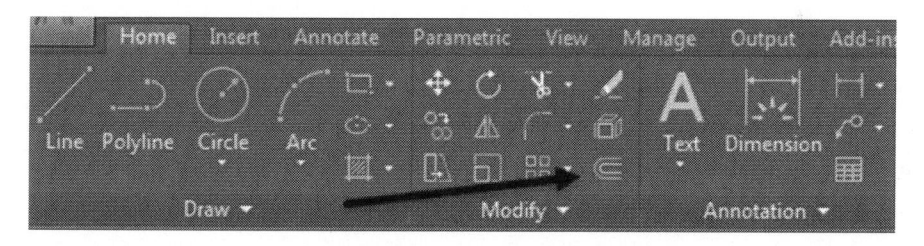

Figure 168: offset tool icon

OR

Command: O

Step 2: Specify offset distance or [Through/Erase/Layer]: **1**
Step 3: Select object to offset or [Exit/Undo]: **Select object**

Figure 169: select object

Step 4: Specify point on side to offset or [Exit/Multiple/Undo]: **Pick a side**

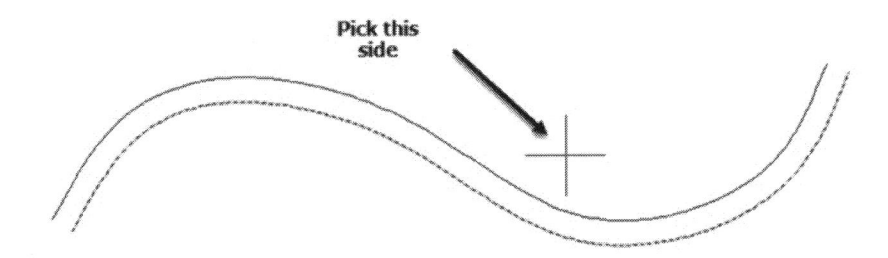

Figure 170: specify side

What do you mean by LENGTHEN?

Command LENGTHEN Changes the length of an object and the included angle of arcs. We can specify changes as the final length, an increment or angle. LENGTHEN can be used as an alternative tool instead off TRIM or EXTEND.

Step 1: Ribbon: Home tab ➤ Modify panel ➤ Lengthen

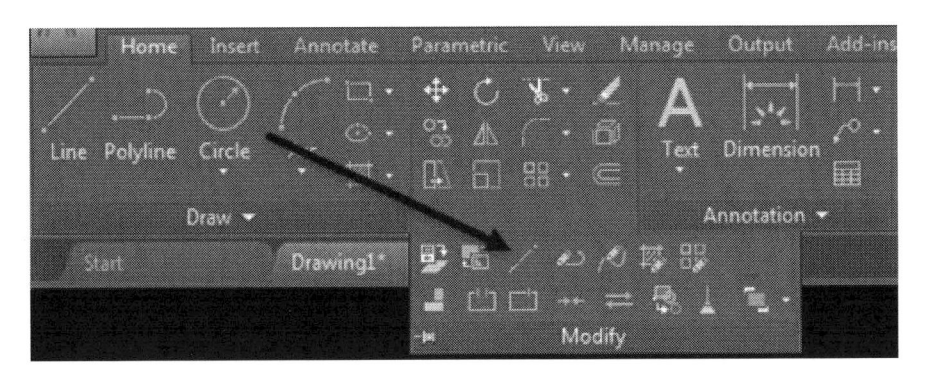

Figure 171: Lengthen tool icon

OR

Command: LEN

Step 2: Select an object to measure or [DElta Percent Total DYnamic]: **select object then P**

Step 3: Enter percentage length: **150**

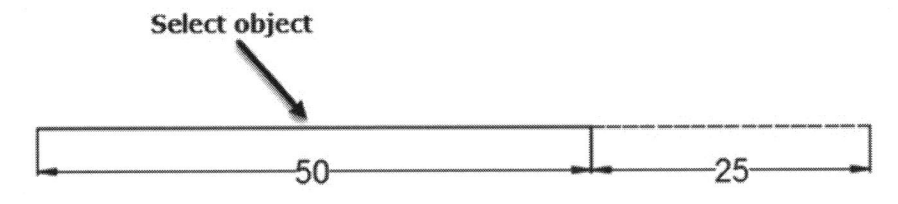

Figure 172: use of lengthen

What do you mean by ALIGN

We use command Align when we need to keep an object in scale with another object i.e. it usexd for aligning one or more point of an object called source point with the points of other object called definition point.

Step 1: Ribbon: Home tab ➤ Modify ➤ panelAlign

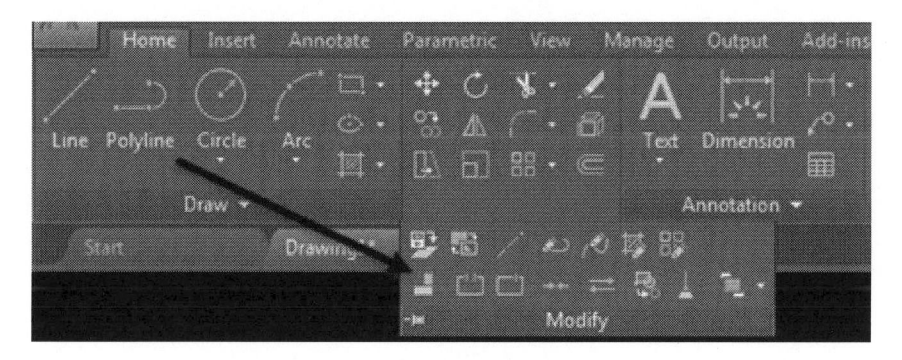

Figure 173: align tool icon

OR

Command: AL

Step 2: Select object: **Select source object**

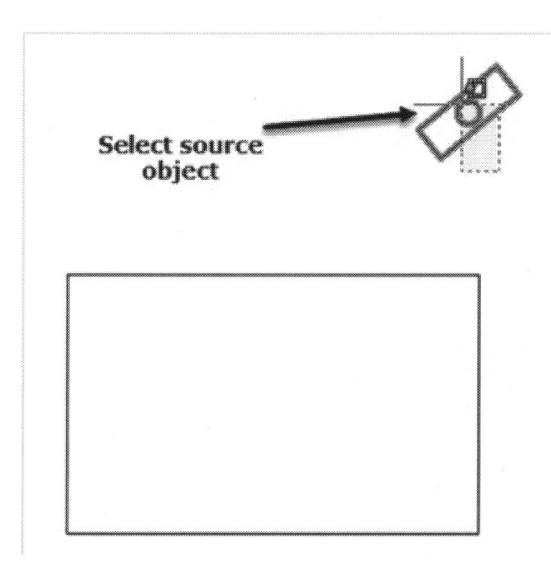

Figure 174: Select source object

Step 3: Specify first source point: **Pick first point**
Step 4: Specify first destination point: **Pick second point**
Step 5: Specify second source point: **Pick third point**

Step 6: Specify second destination point: **Pick fourth point**
Step 7: Specify third destination point or <continue>: ⏎
Step 8: Scale objects based on alignment point? [Yes/No]: **Y** ⏎

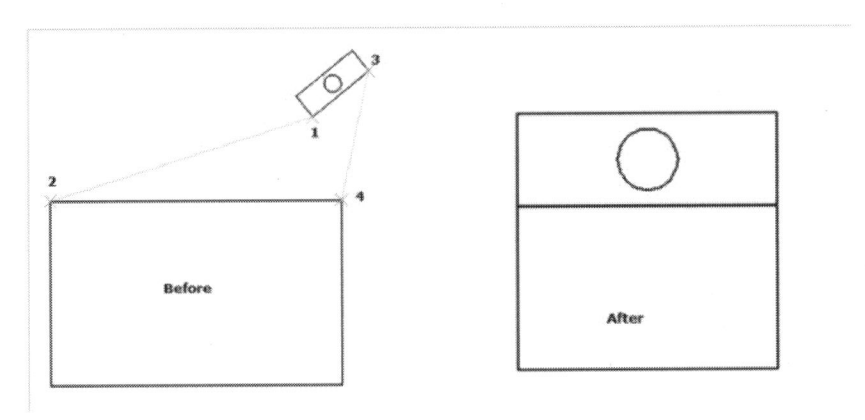

Figure 175: Use of align

What do you mean by BREAK?

By using command break, we can erase part of the line, arc or a circle or used to split it into two lines or arc. Generally, we use it for creating a gap between lines for writing text.

Step 1: Ribbon: Home tab ➤ Modify panel ➤ Break

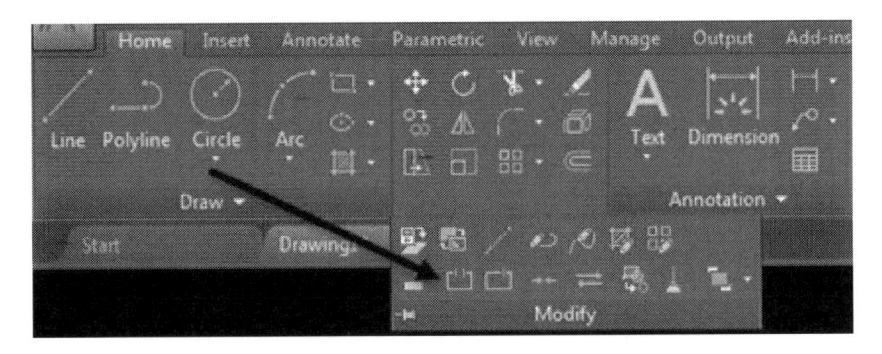

Figure 176: break tool icon

OR

Command: BR ⏎

Step 2: Select object
Step 3: Specify second break point or [First point]: **F** ⏎
Step 4: Specify first break point: **Pick first point**
Step 5: Specify second break point: **Pick second point**

Modify Tools   73

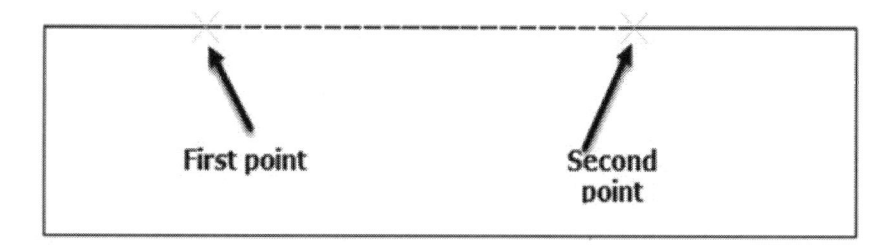

Figure 177: use of break

What do you mean by JOIN?

By using Command join, we can attach two objects lying in the same plane.
Step 1: Ribbon: Home tab ➤ Modify panel ➤ Join

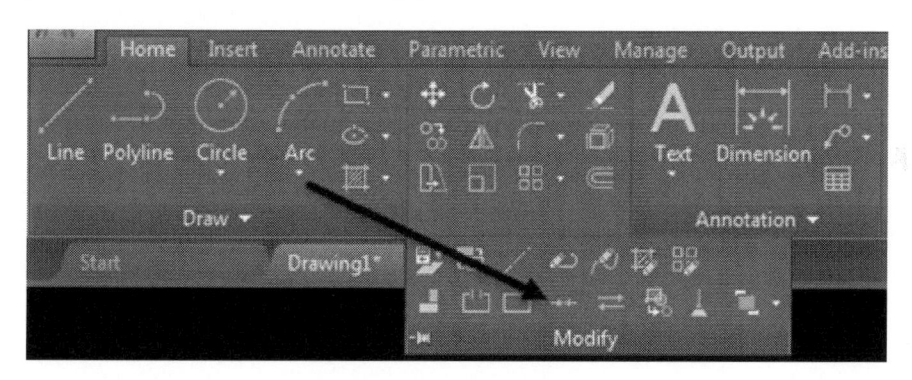

Figure 178: join tool icon

OR

Command: J

Step 2: Select source object or multiple objects to join at once: **Select first line**
Step 3: Select objects to join: **Select second line then**

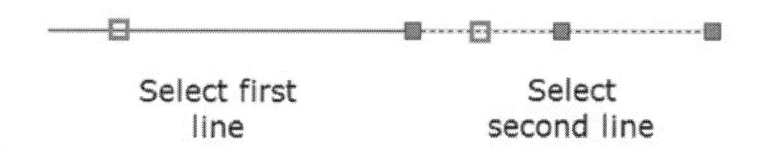

Figure 179: use of join

What do you mean by DELETE DUPLICATE OBJECT?

This command removes duplicate or overlapping lines, arcs, and polylines. Also, combines partially overlapping or contiguous ones.

Step 1: Ribbon: Home tab ➤ Modify panel ➤ Delete duplicate object

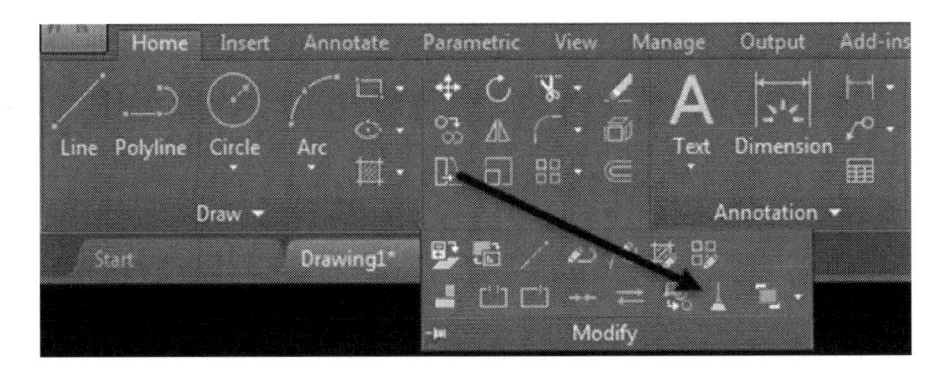

Figure 180: delete duplicate object tool icon

OR

Command: OVERKILL

Step 2: Select object then

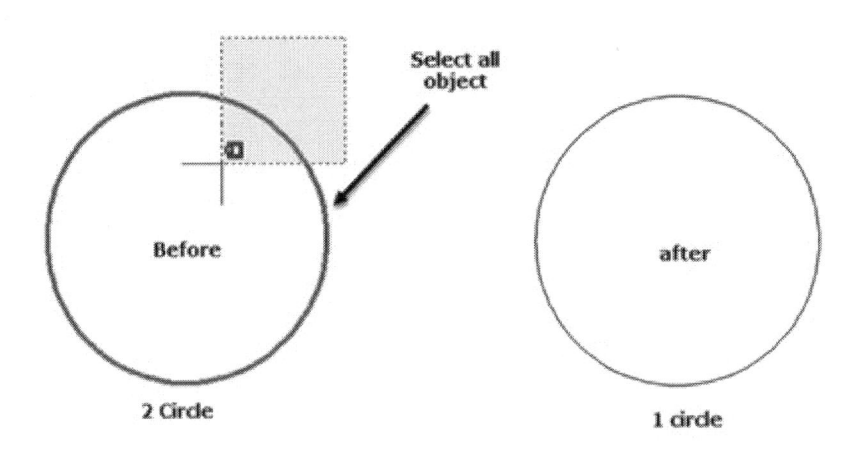

Figure 181: use of overkill command

Step 3: Select all Radio Button and click Ok

Modify Tools

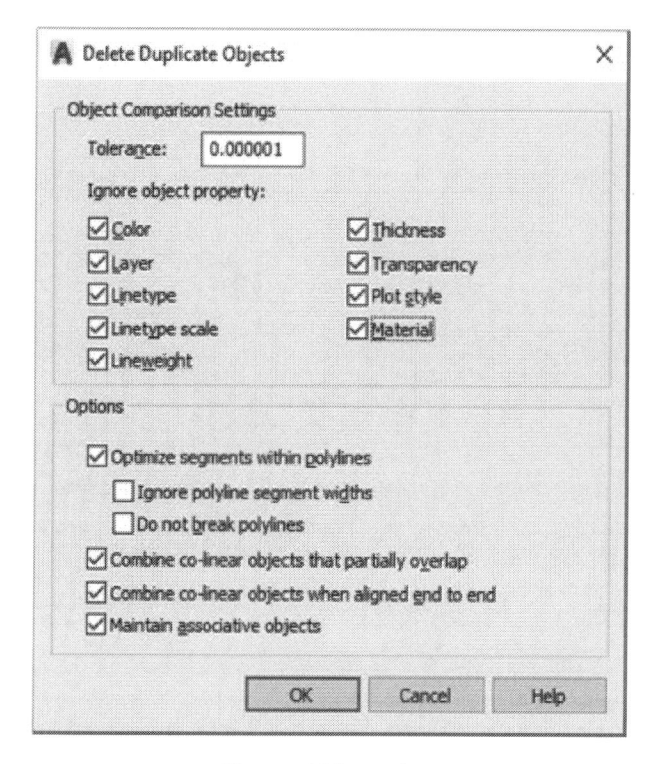

Figure 182: option

What do you mean by DRAW ORDER?

Several options are available that control the order in which overlapping objects are displayed. In addition to the DRAWORDER command, the TEXTTOFRONT command brings all text, dimensions, or leaders in a drawing in front of other objects, and the HATCHTOBACK command sends all hatch objects behind other objects.

Select Objects

Specifies the objects for which you want to change the draw order. For the above and under options, an additional prompt displays in which you select the reference objects that the originally selected objects should be above or under.

Above Objects

Moves the selected object above the specified reference objects.

Under Objects

Moves the selected objects below the specified reference objects.

Front

Moves the selected objects to the top of the order of objects in the drawing.

Back

Moves the selected objects to the bottom of the order of objects in the drawing.

Step 1: Ribbon: Home tab ➢ Modify panel ➢ Draw order

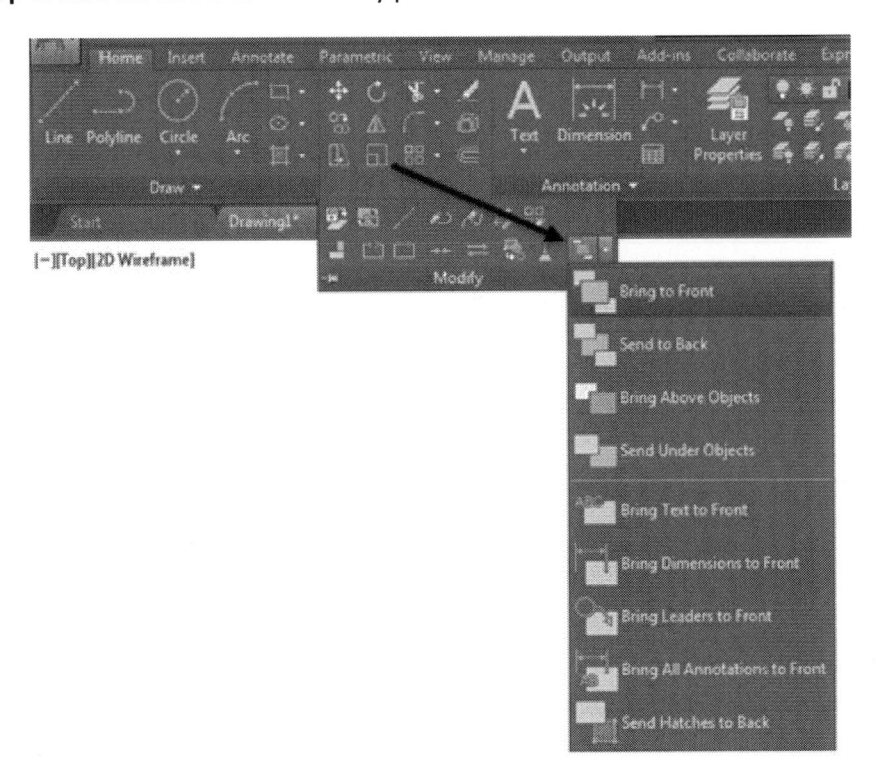

Figure 183: draw order tool icon

OR

Command: DR

Step 2: Select object then

Step 3: Enter object ordering option [Above objects Under objects Front Back]: **B**

Before   After

Figure 184: use of draw order

Modify Tools   77

What do you mean by BLOCKS?

It is used to create a block by selecting that object and giving it an insertion point and then save it by the name of itself. These blocks are saved in the design centre toolbar and the tool palettes.

Ribbon: Insert tab ➢ Block panel ➢ Create block

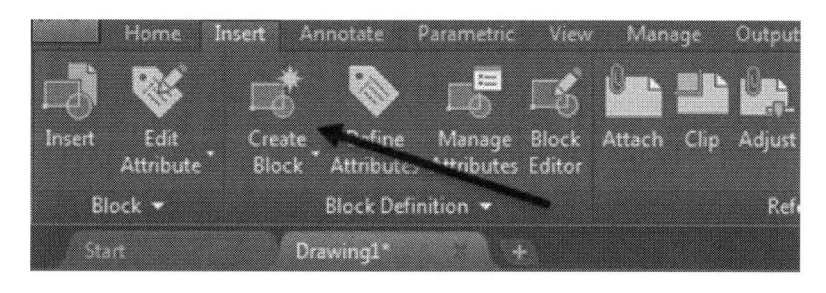

Figure 185: block tool icon

OR

Command: B

Step 1: Give the command 'B' and press Enter, A block definition tab appears.

Step 2: Give a name to your block followed by selecting the option of "select object" and select the object you want to convert to blocks.

Step 3: Select the base point by clicking "pick points" and give the values of X, Y and Z coordinates.

Step 4: Click OK.

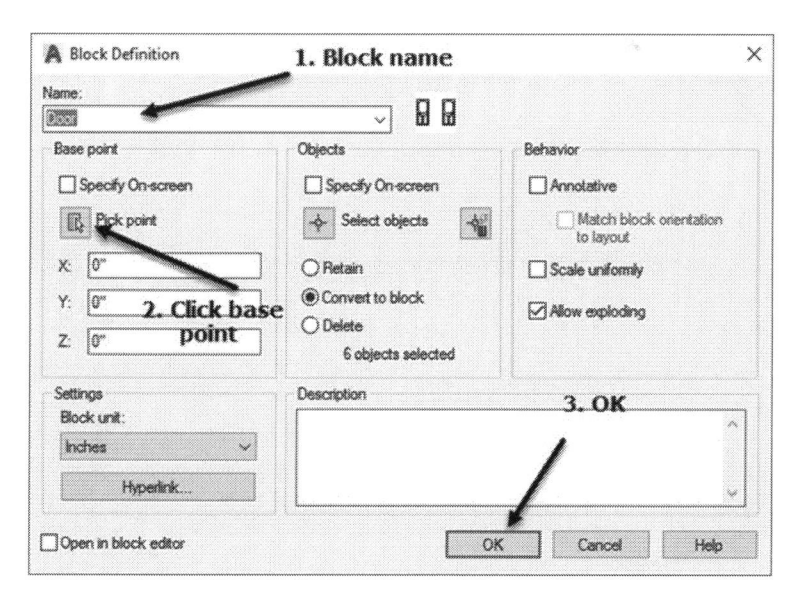

Figure 186: block setting tab

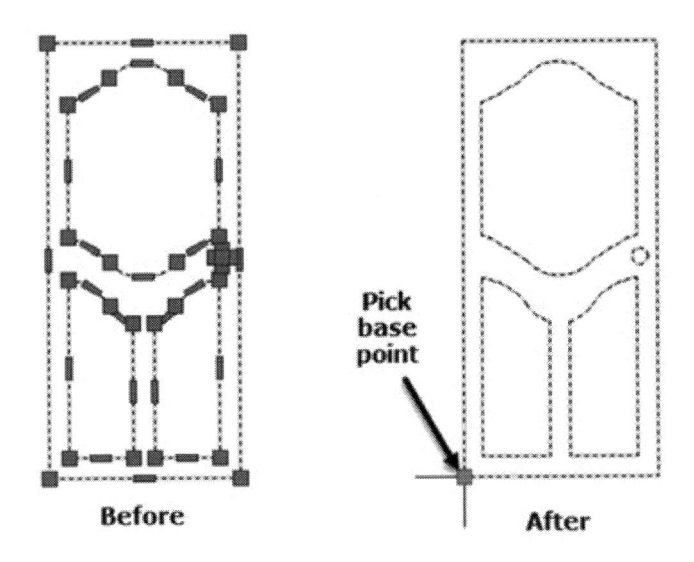

Figure 187: use of block

CHAPTER-5

Annotation

What do you mean by TEXT?

It is a command to create a single-line text object. It is sometimes used to define different line text objects which we can modify, relocate.

Step 1: Ribbon: Annotation tab ➤ Text ➤ Single line text

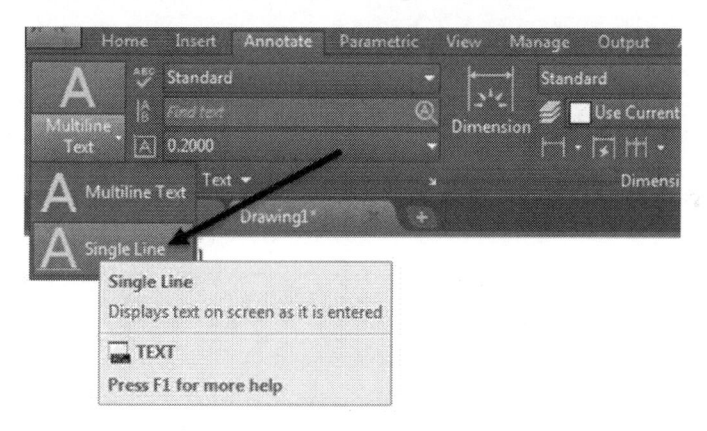

Figure 188: text tool icon

OR

Command: DT

Step 2: Specify start point of text or [Justify/Style]: **Pick Start point**
Step 3: Specify the height: **2**
Step 4: Specify rotation angle of the text: **30**
Step 5: Type any text Ex: **AutoCAD 2019 By Linkan Sagar** then

Figure 189: text

What do you mean by MULTILINE TEXT?

It is a used to create multiline text objects such as paragraphs. It can also be modified, relocate. Using this command, we can format text appearance, boundaries and columns.

Step 1: Ribbon: Annotation tab ➤ Text ➤ Multiline text

Figure 190 mtext tool icon

OR

Command: MT

Step 2: Specify first corner: **Pick first corner**

Step 3: Specify opposite corner or [Height/Justify/Line spacing/Rotation/Style/Width/Columns]: **Pick second corner**

Figure 191: pick corner

Step 4: Type any text and text formatting, click Close **X**

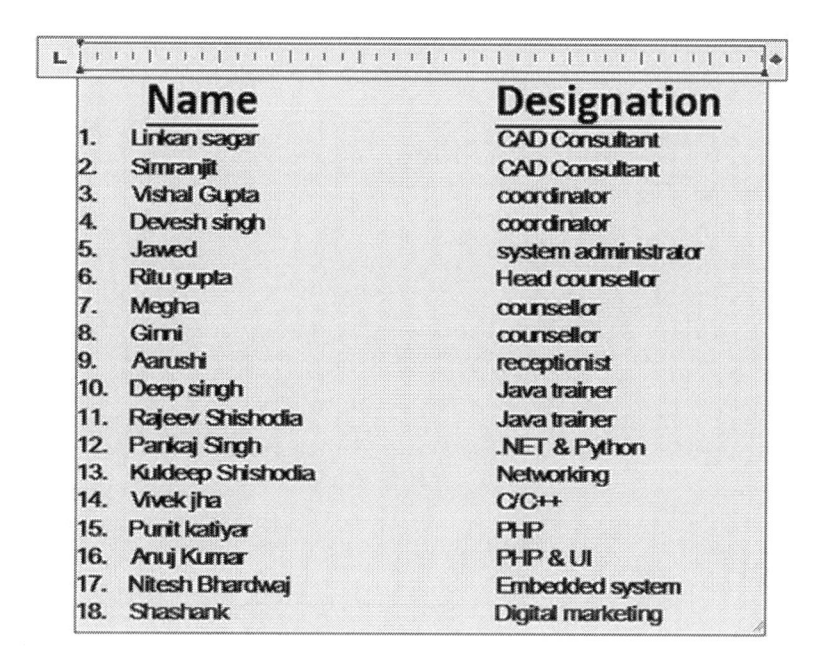

Figure 192: mtext

What do you mean by TEXT STYLE?

It is used to change text style like text height, text font.
Step 1: Ribbon: Annotation tab ➤ Text Text ➤ style

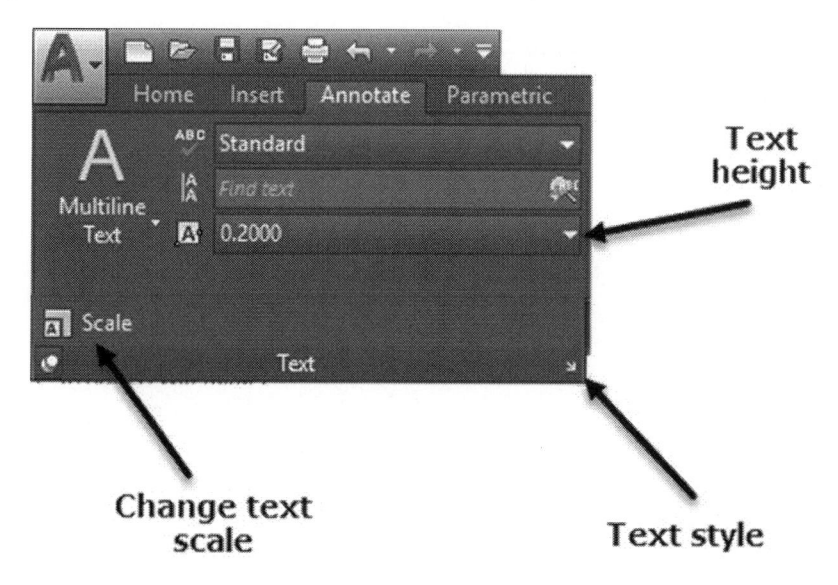

Figure 193: text style tool icon

Text style

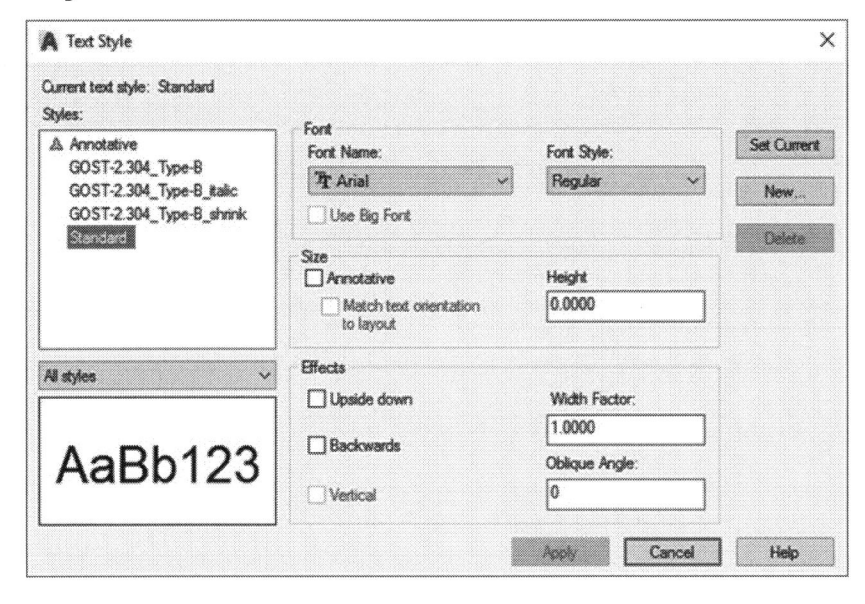

Figure 194: text style option

What do you mean by DIMENSIONING?

It is a command with the help of which we can draw the current viewport, change current text style, undo the recently created objects, etc.

Command: DIM & DIM1

Dimensioning mode command equivalents	
Dimensioning mode Command	**Equivalent Command**
ALIGNED	DIMALIGNED
ANGULAR	DIMANGULAR
BASELINE	DIMBASELINE
CENTER	DIMCENTER
CONTINUE	DIMCONTINUE
DIAMETER	DIMDIAMETER
HOMETEXT	DIMEDIT Home
HORIZONTAL	DIMLINEAR Horizontal
LEADER	LEADER
JOG	DIMJOGGED
NEWTEXT	DIMEDIT New
OBLIQUE	DIMEDIT Oblique
ORDINATE	DIMORDINATE

OVERRIDE	DIMOVERRIDE
RADIUS	DIMRADIUS
RESTORE	-DIMSTYLE Restore
ROTATED	DIMLINEAR Rotated
SAVE	-DIMSTYLE Save
STATUS	-DIMSTYLE Status
TEDIT	DIMTEDIT
TROTATE	DIMEDIT Rotate
UPDATE	-DIMSTYLE Apply
VARIABLES	-DIMSTYLE Variables
VERTICAL	DIMLINEAR Vertical

What do you mean by LINEAR?

We use linear command, to create a linear dimension with a vertical, horizontal, or rotated dimension line.

Step 1: Ribbon: Annotate tab ➤ Dimensions panel ➤ Linear

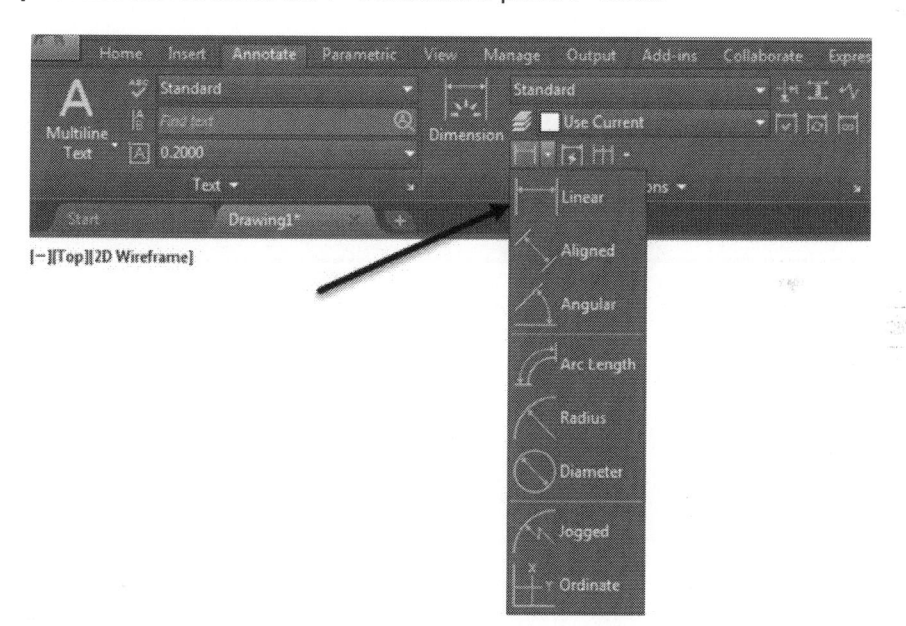

Figure 195: linear dimension tool icon

OR

Command: DIMLIN

Step 2: Pick first point and Pick second point then give direction and click.

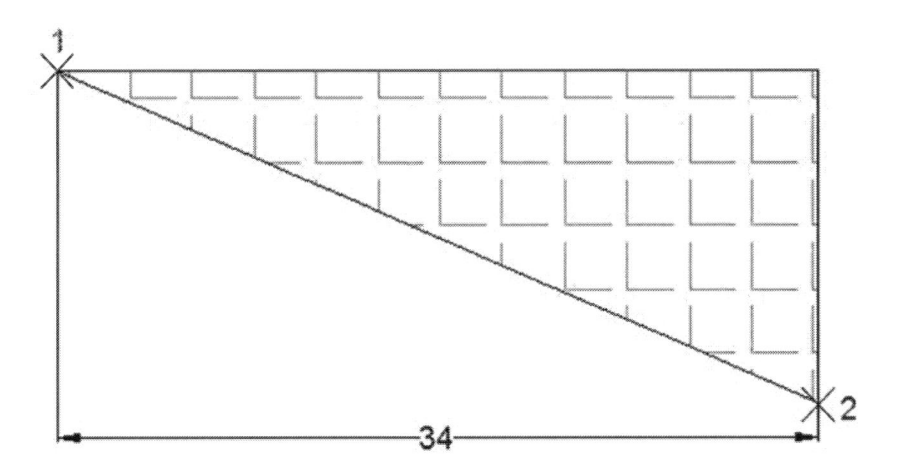

Figure 196: use of linear dim

What do you mean by ALIGNED?

It is a command to create a linear dimension in aligned position.

Step 1: Ribbon: Annotate tab ➢ Dimensions panel ➢ Aligned

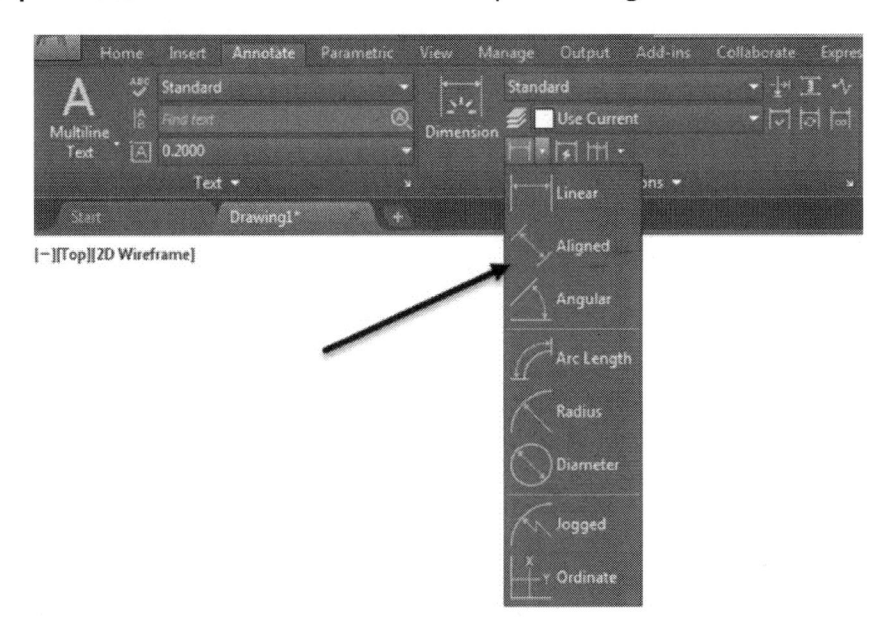

Figure 197: aligned dimension tool icon

OR

Command: DIMALI

Step 2: Pick first point and Pick second point then give direction and click.

Annotation 85

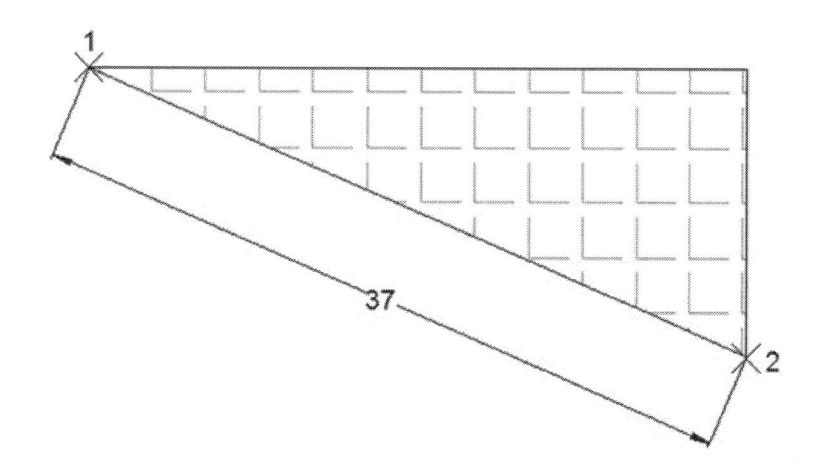

Figure 198: use of aligned dim

What do you mean by ANGULAR?

It is a command to measure Angle of object.

Step 1: Ribbon: Annotate tab ➤ Dimensions panel ➤ Angular

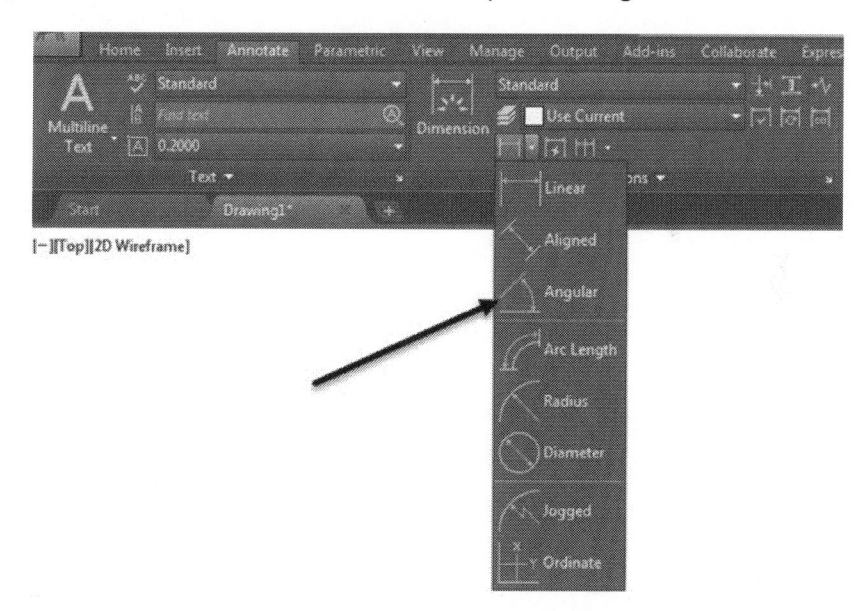

Figure 199: angular dimension tool icon

OR

Command: DIMANG

Step 2: Select first object and select second object then click.

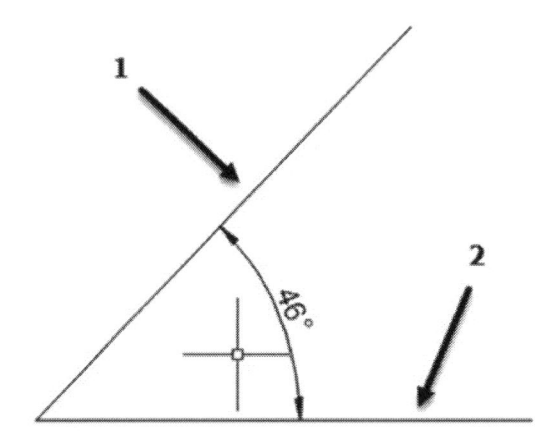

Figure 200: use of angular dim

What do you mean by ARC LENGTH?

It is a command to measure the length of a simple arc or polyline arc.

Step 1: Ribbon: Annotate tab ➢ Dimensions panel ➢ Arc length

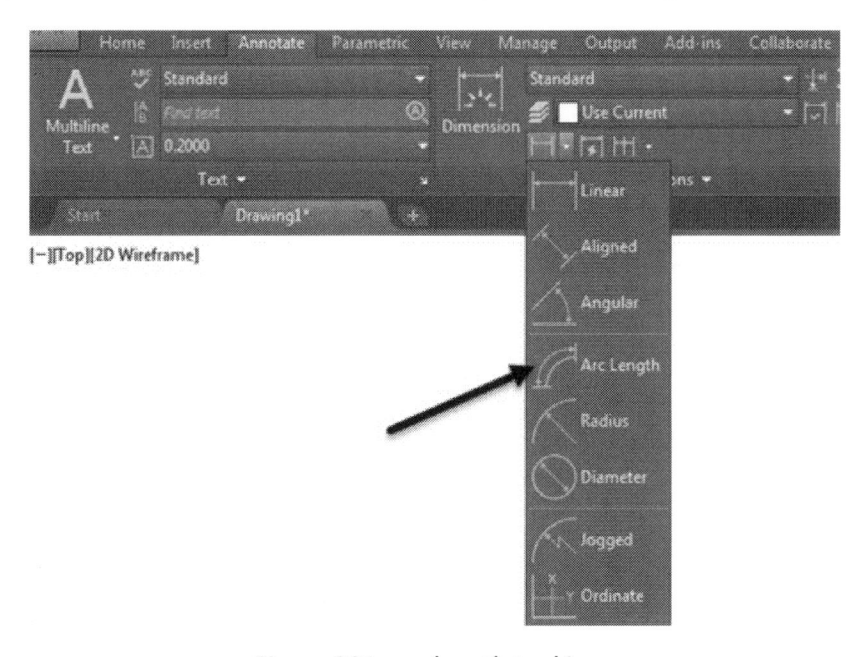

Figure 201: arc length tool icon

OR

Command: DIMARC

Step 2: Select Arc then give direction and click.

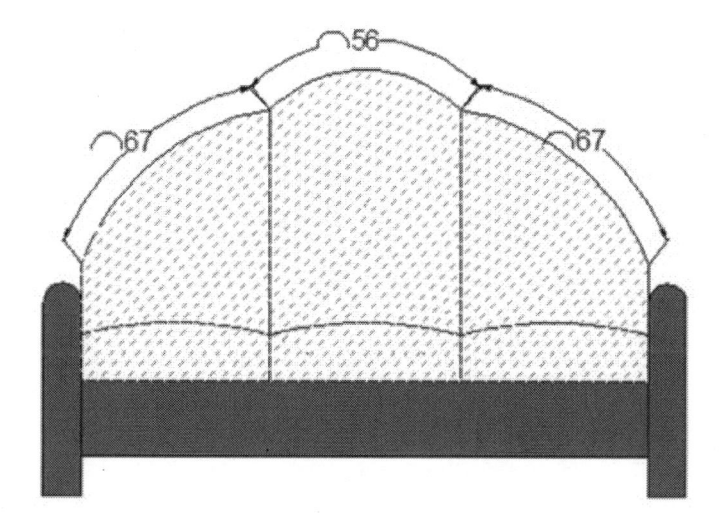

Figure 202: use of arc length

What do you mean by RADIUS?

As we all know, radius is the distance between the centre point and the point on the circle or the half of the diameter. It is a command to measure the radius of a selected circle or arc and display the dimension text having a radius symbol in front of it.

Ribbon: Annotate tab ➤ Dimensions pane ➤ Radius

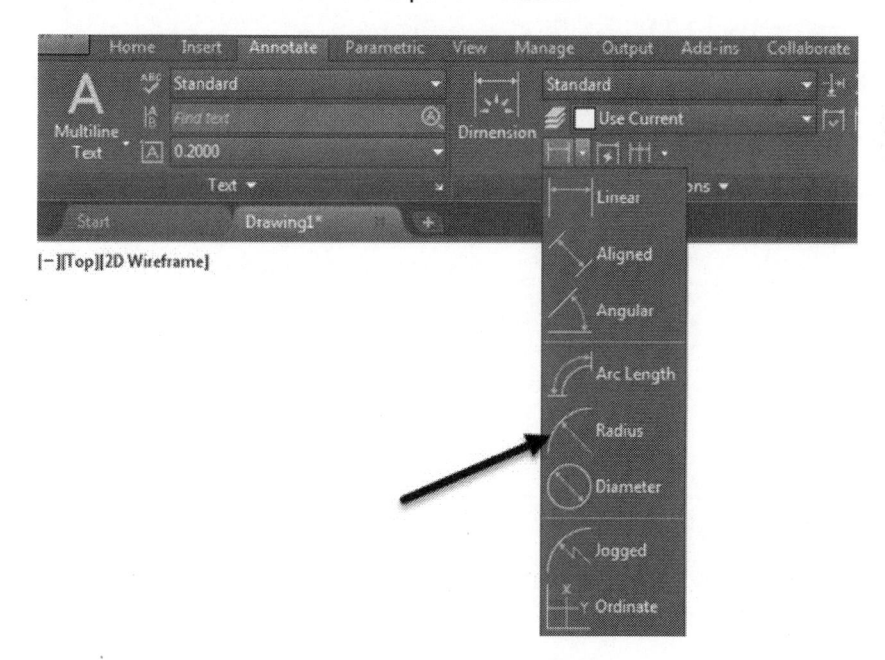

Figure 203: radius tool icon

OR

Command: DIMRAD

Step 2: Select Circle or Arc and give direction then click.

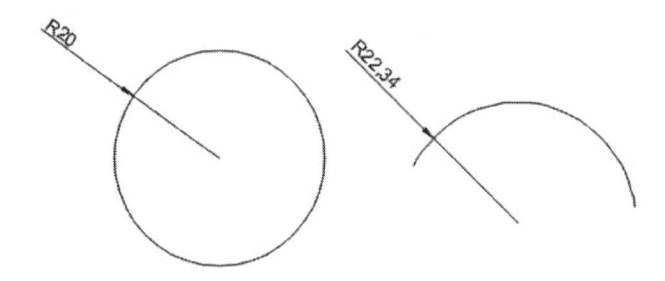

Figure 204: use of radius dim

What do you mean by DIAMETER?

It is a command to measure the diameter of the selected circle or arc, display the dimension text with diameter symbol in front of it and can relocate the resulting diameter dimension.

Step 1: Ribbon: Annotate tab ➢ Dimensions panel ➢ Diameter

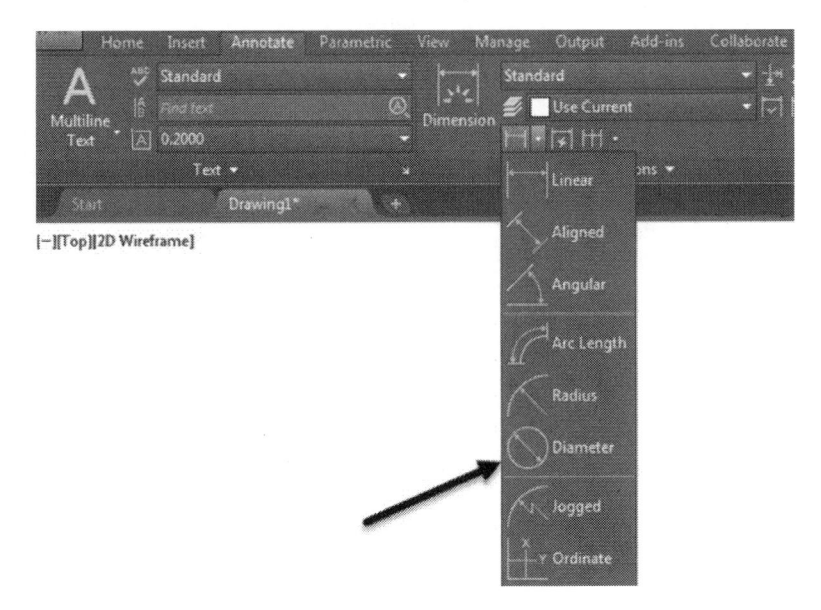

Figure 205: diameter tool icon

OR

Command: DIMDIA

Step 2: Select Circle or Arc and give direction then click.

Annotation 89

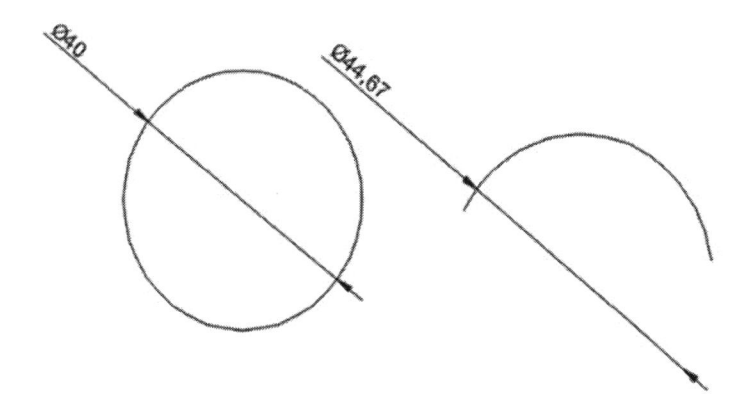

Figure 206: use of diameter

What do you mean by JOGGED RADIUS DIMENSION?

It is a command that measures the radius of the selected object and displays a radius symbol with dimension text.

Step 1: Ribbon: Annotate tab ➢ Dimensions panel ➢ Jogged

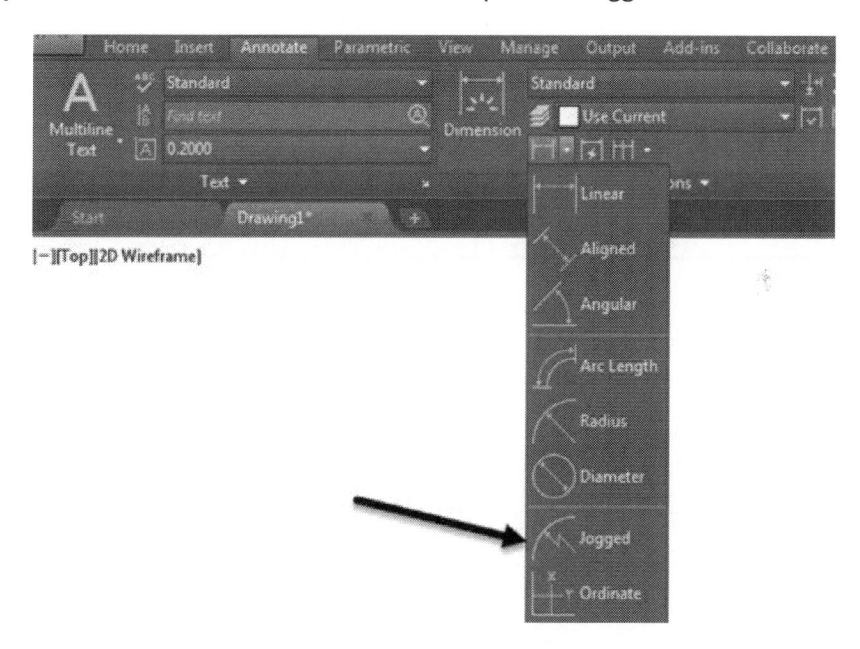

Figure 207: jogged tool icon

OR

Command: DIMJOGGED

Step 2: Pick first arc then pick second point override center.
Step 3: Pick third point for text location then pick fourth point for direction.

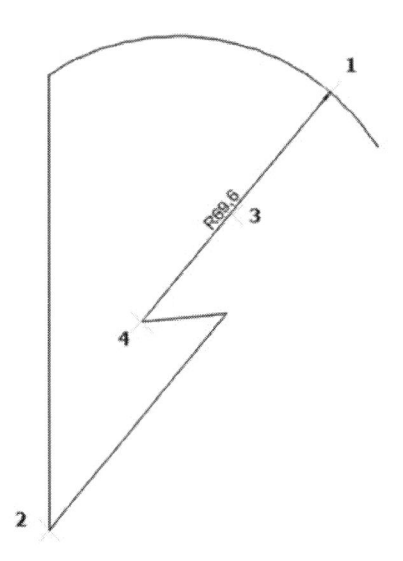

Figure 208: use of jogged

What do you mean by ORDINATE?

It is a command to measure horizontal or vertical distance from the point of origin (0, 0).

Step 1: Ribbon: Annotate tab ➢ Dimensions panel ➢ Ordinate

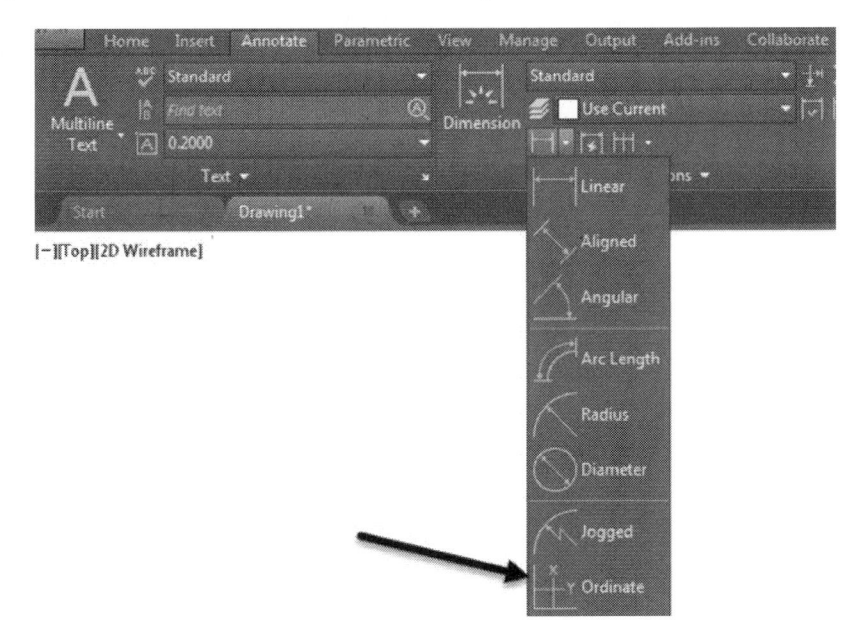

Figure 209: ordinate tool icon

OR

Command: DIMORD

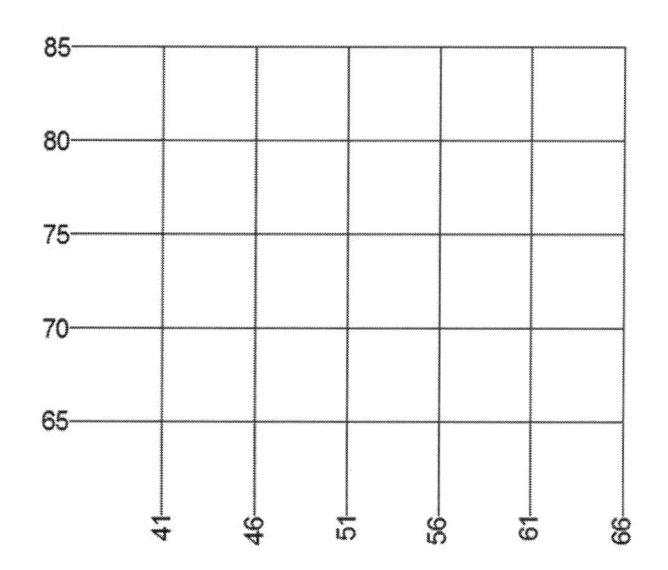

Figure 210: use of ordinate

What do you mean by QUICK DIMENSION?

It is a command which quickly creates multi-dimensions of the selected objects, particularly useful for dimensioning a series of circles and arcs, for creating a series of baseline.

Continuous

Creates a series of continued dimensions.

Ordinate

Creates a series of ordinate dimensions.

Staggered

Creates a series of staggered dimensions.

Radius

Creates a series of radius dimensions.

Edit

Edit a series of dimensions. When we are ready to add or remove points from existing dimensions.

Baseline

Creates a series of baseline dimensions.

Datum Point

Sets a new datum point for baseline and ordinate dimensions.

Diameter

Creates a series of diameter dimensions.

Settings

Sets the default object snap for specifying extension line origins. We get the following prompt:

Step 1: Ribbon: Annotate tab ➤ Dimensions panel ➤ Quick Dimension

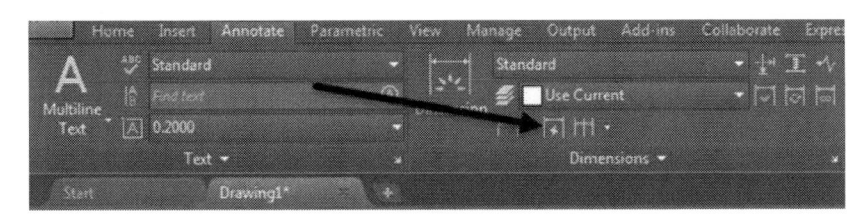

Figure 211: quick dim tool icon

OR

Command: QDIM

Step 2: Select geometry to dimension: **Select all object then**

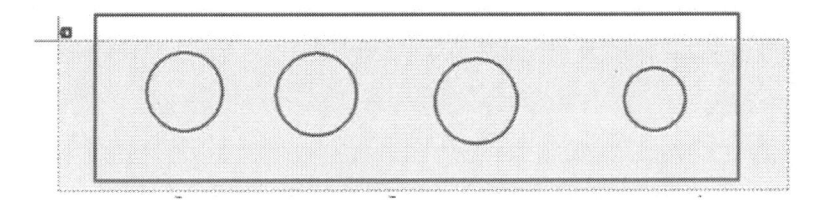

Figure 212: select all object

Step 3: Specify dimension line position, or [Continuous/ Staggered/ Baseline/ Ordinate/ Radius/ Diameter/ datumPoint/ Edit/ seTtings]: **Give direction and click**

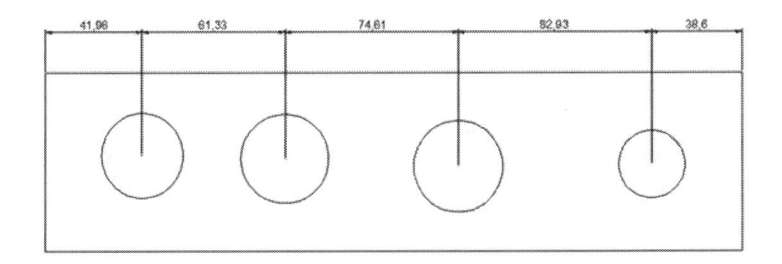

Figure 213: use of quick dim

What do you mean by CONTINUE?

It is a command to create an extension line automatically from the last selected linear, angular or ordinate dimension.

Step 1: Ribbon: Annotate tab ➤ Dimensions panel ➤ Continue

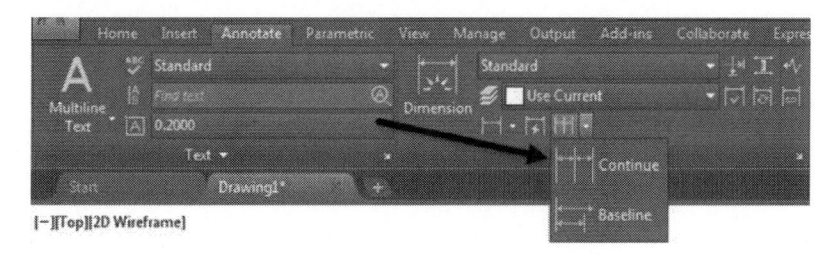

Figure 214: continue dim tool icon

OR

Command: DIMCONT

Step 2: Pick third point, pick fourth point and pick fifth point.

(First of all use different dimension command like aligned then use continue dimension)

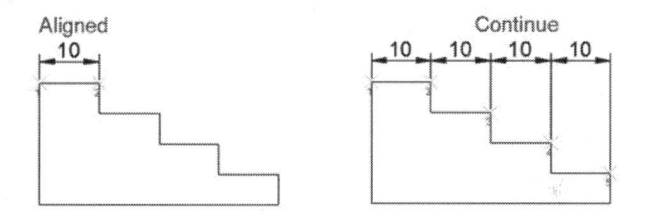

Figure 215: use of continue dim

What do you mean by BASELINE?

It is a command to create angular, linear and ordinate dimension from the baseline of the selected dimension.

Step 1: Ribbon: Annotate tab ➤ Dimensions panel ➤ Baseline

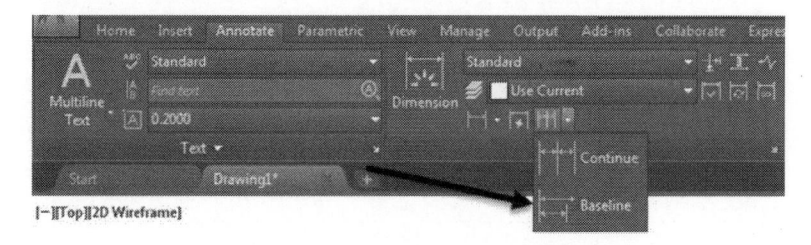

Figure 216: baseline dim tool icon

OR

Command: DIMBASE

Step 2: Select base dimension line and then click next point.

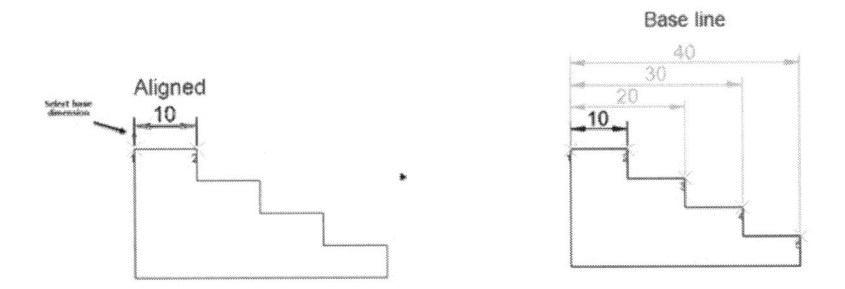

Figure 217: use of baseline dim

What do you mean by CENTRE MARK?

It is a command to create a centre point in a circle or arc.

Step 1: Ribbon: Annotate tab ➢ Centerlines ➢ Center Mark

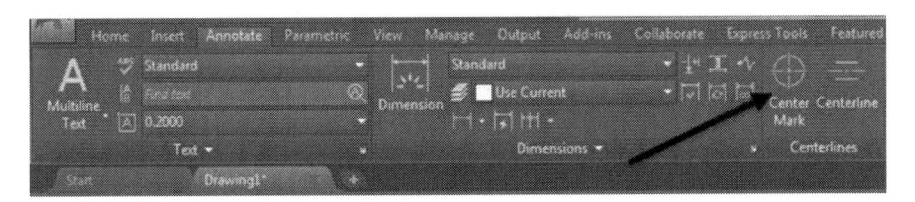

Figure 218: center mark tool icon

Step 2: Select arc or circle: **Select circle**

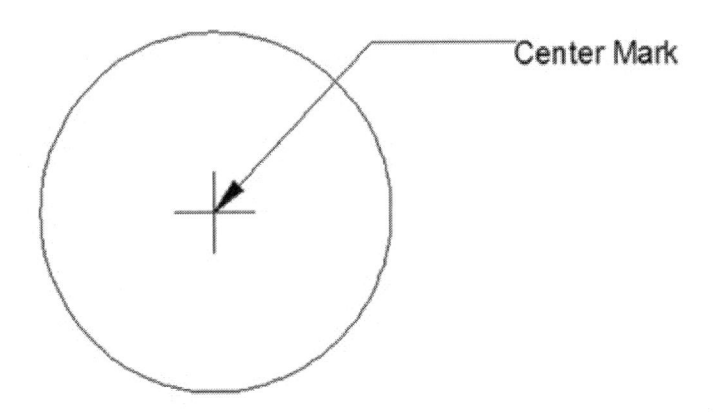

Figure 219: use of center mark

What do you mean by CENTRE LINE?

It is a command to create a centerline in a line.

Step 1: Ribbon: Annotate tab ➤ Centerlines ➤ Center Line

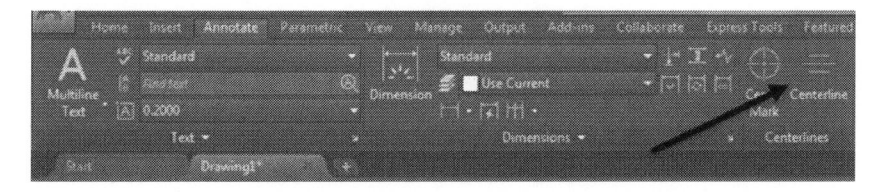

Figure 220: center line tool icon

Step 2: Select first line then select second line.

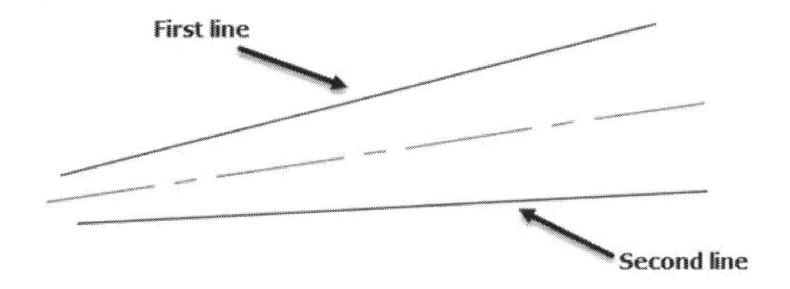

Figure 221: use of center line

What do you mean by INSPECTION DIMENSION?

It is a command to inspect the dimension given I the drawing so as to maintain the standard of the dimensions.

Step 1: Ribbon: Annotate tab ➤ Dimensions panel ➤ Inspect

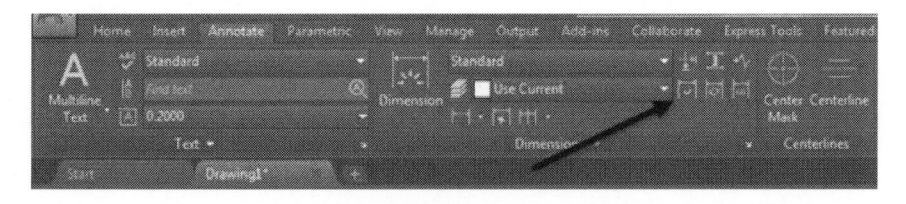

Figure 222: inspection tool icon

OR

Command: DIMINSPECT

Step 2: Select dimension then and set inspection rate.

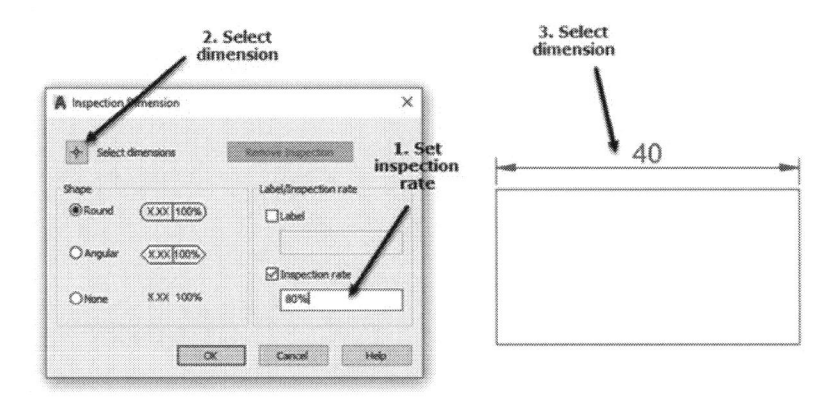

Figure 223: inspection dimension setting tab

Then click OK

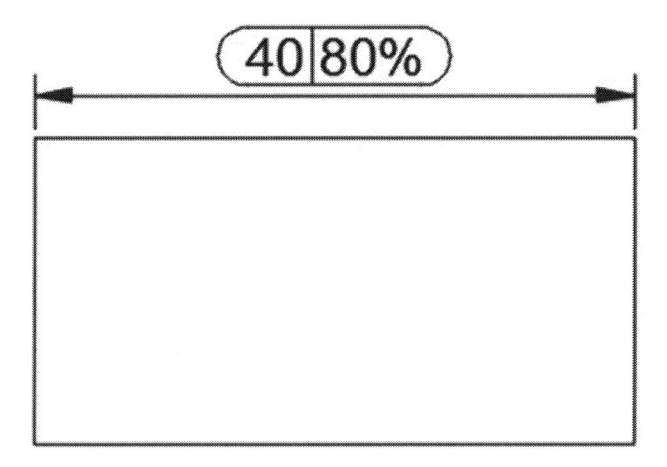

Figure 224: use of inspection dim

What do you mean by DIMENSION BREAK?

It is a command to break or restore the dimension or extension lines when they cross each other.

Step 1: Ribbon: Annotate tab ➤ Dimensions panel ➤ Break

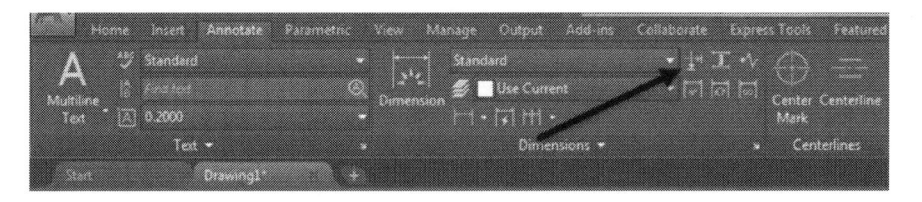

Figure 225: break dimension tool icon

Annotation 97

OR

Command: DIMBREAK

Step 2: Select dimension then

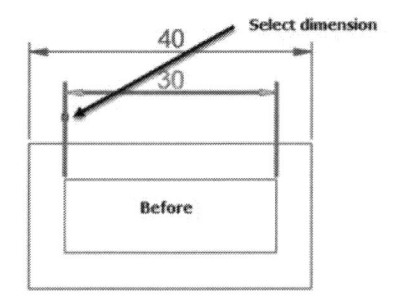

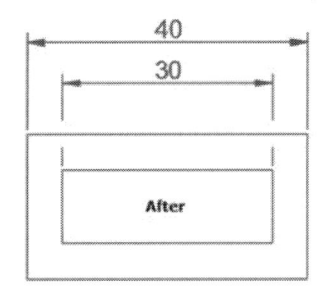

Figure 226: use of break dim

What do you mean by DIMENSION SPACE?

It is a command to adjust the spacing or distance between linear or angular dimensions.

Step 1: Ribbon: Annotate tab ➤ Dimensions panel ➤ Adjust Space

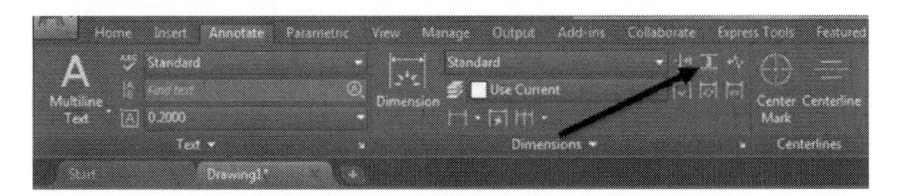

Figure 227: dimension space tool icon

OR

Command: DIMSPACE

Step 2: Select first reference dimension and select second dimension then

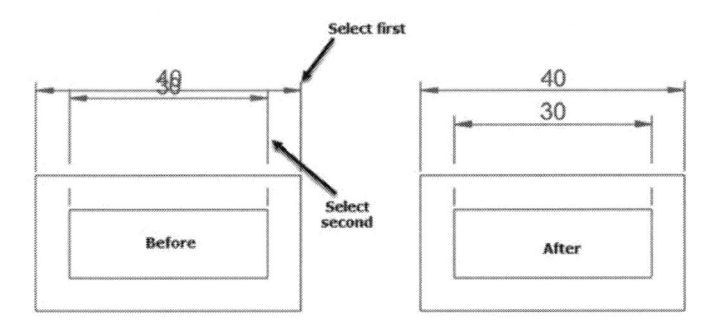

Figure 228: use of dimension space

When do we use DIM STYLE?

When we need to change the dimension setting and have control over the dimension used in the drawing, we use 'DIM Style". It stands for Dimension Style, by using 'dimstyle' we can create dimension styles and specify the format of dimensions quickly.

Like: Text height, Arrow size and precision etc.

Step 1: Ribbon: Annotate tab ➢ Dimensions panel ➢ Dimension Style

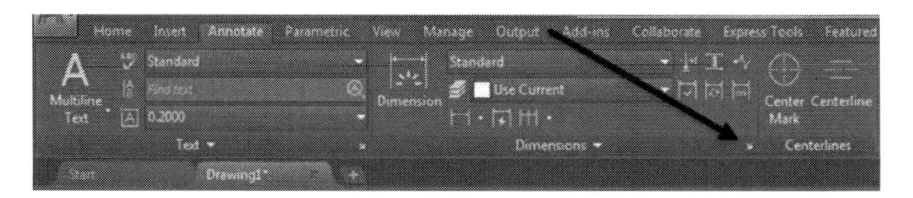

Figure 229: dimension style tool icon

OR

Command: D

Step 2: Click modify button then select any tab like text, arrow etc.

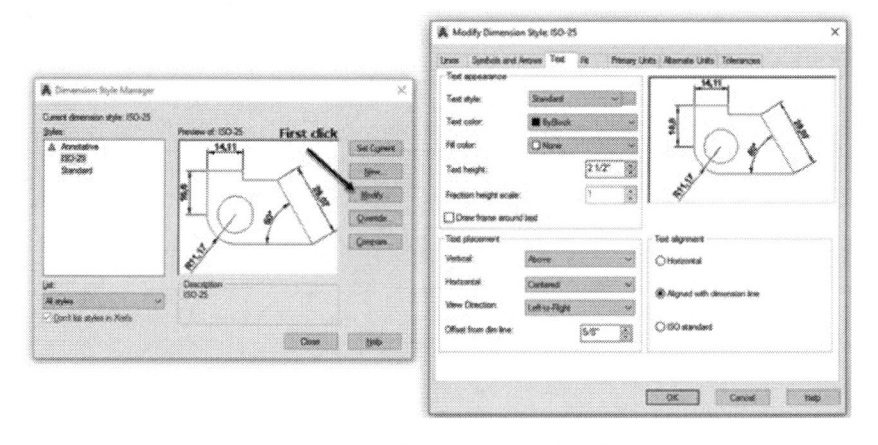

Figure 230: dimension style tab

What do you mean by QLEADER?

We use 'QLeader' to create leader annotation. By its help we can set location of set multiline text annotation and specify leader format

You can use QLEADER to

- Set the location where leaders attach to multiline text annotation
- Specify leader annotation and annotation format
- Constrain the angle of the first and second leader segments.

Annotation

- Limit the number of leader points

Step 1: Command: LE
Step 2: Specify first leader point, or [Settings]: **First point**
Step 3: Specify next point: **Second point**
Step 4: Specify text width: **0**
Step 5: Enter first line of annotation text: **Wall 4.5"**

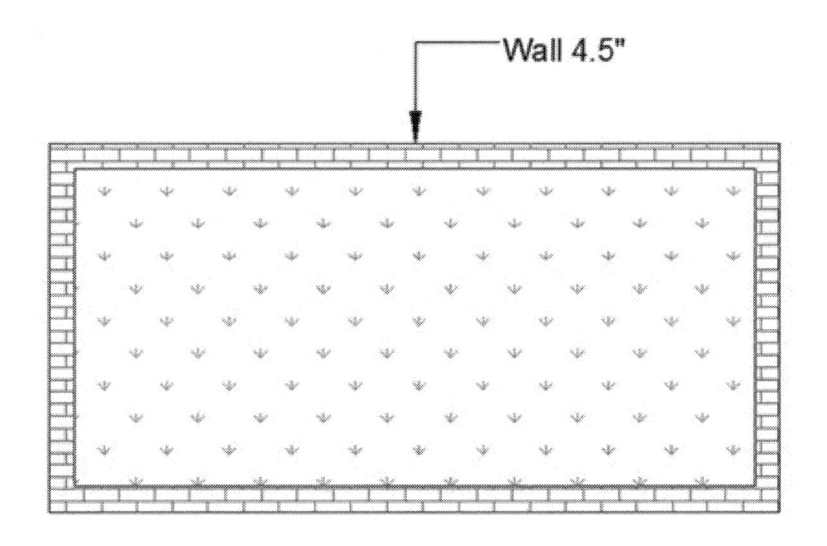

Figure 231: use of qleader

What do you mean by LEADER?

It is a command to create a line that can be connected to a feature by annotation. It also draws a leader line segment to the point specified.

Step 1: Command: LEAD
Step 2: Specify leader start point: **Pick first point**
Step 3: Specify next point: **Pick second point**
Step 4: Specify next point or [Annotation/Format/Undo]: **Pick third point**
Step 5: Specify next point or [Annotation/Format/Undo]: **Pick fourth point**
Step 6: Specify next point or [Annotation/Format/Undo]: **A**
Step 7: Enter first line of annotation text or <option>: **Park**
Step 8: Enter next line of annotation text:

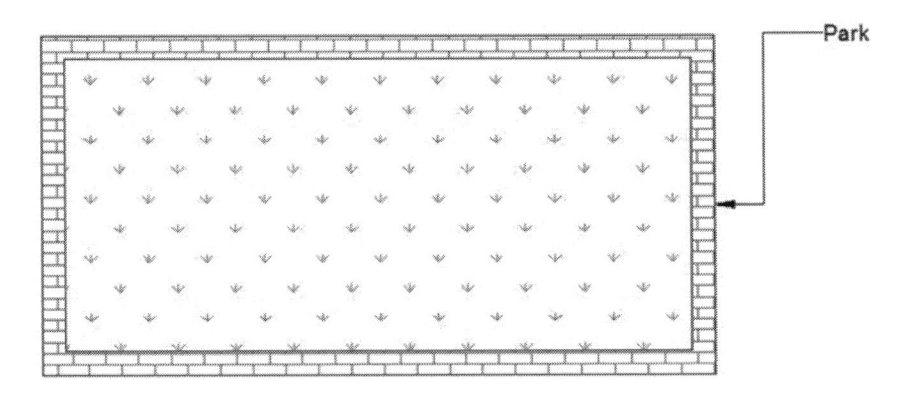

Figure 232: use of leader

What do you mean by TABLE?

It is a command to create several rows and columns in an empty table. We use table when we need to show the data input in tabular form.

Step 1: Ribbon: Home tab ➤ Annotation panel ➤ Tables

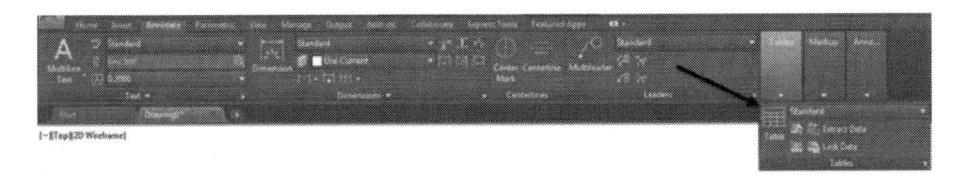

Figure 233: table tool icon

OR

Command: TB

Step 1: Give the command 'TB' and press Enter.. An insert Table tab appears.

Step 2: If we have a table in excel then click the option of "from a data link" and browse the file and upload it. Else to create a new table select "Start from an empty table"

Step 3: Specify the requirements of the table in columns and rows settings.

Step 4: Click "preview" if you want a preview of your table, else click OK.

Annotation

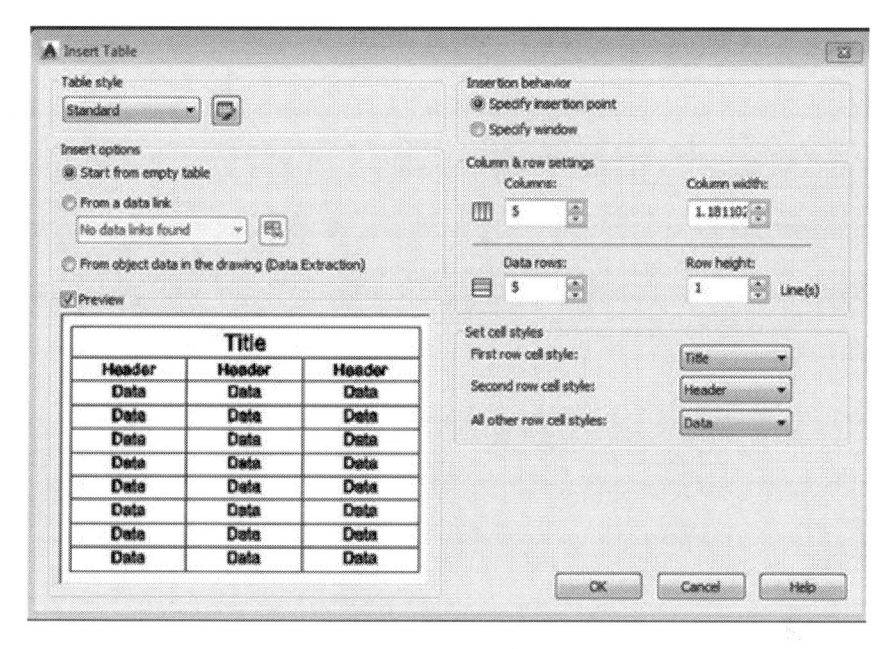

Figure 234: table tab

OR

Step 2: If you want link excel file so click from a data link.

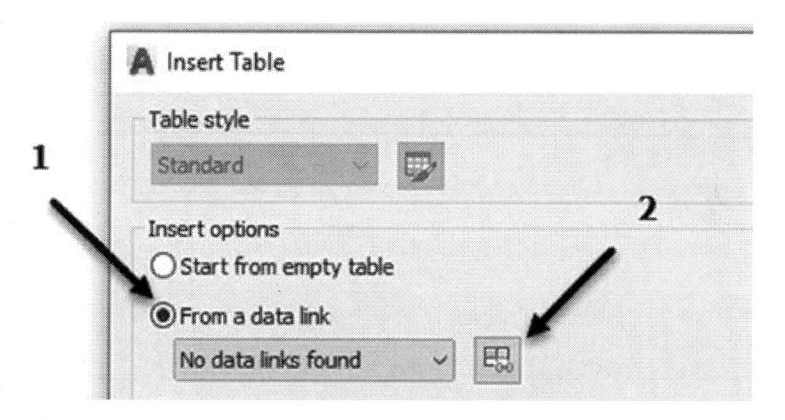

Figure 235: insert data link tab

Step 3: Create a new excel data link. Then give name and press OK.

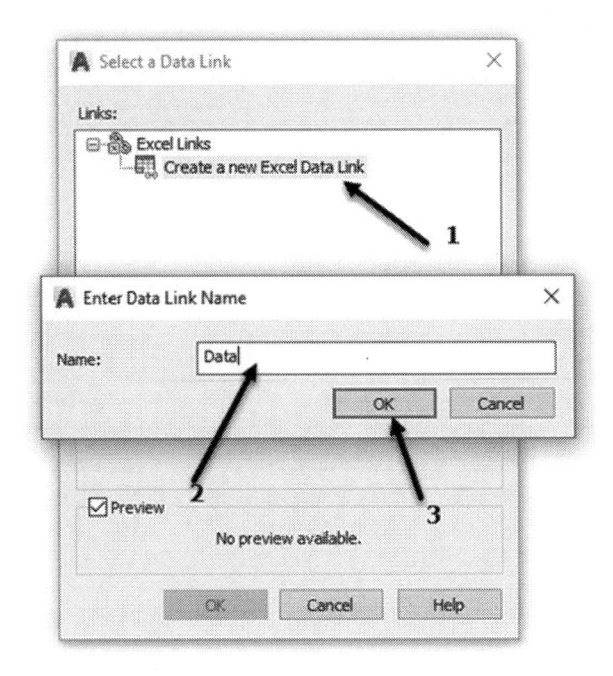

Figure 236: enter data link name

Step 4: Click browse then OK.

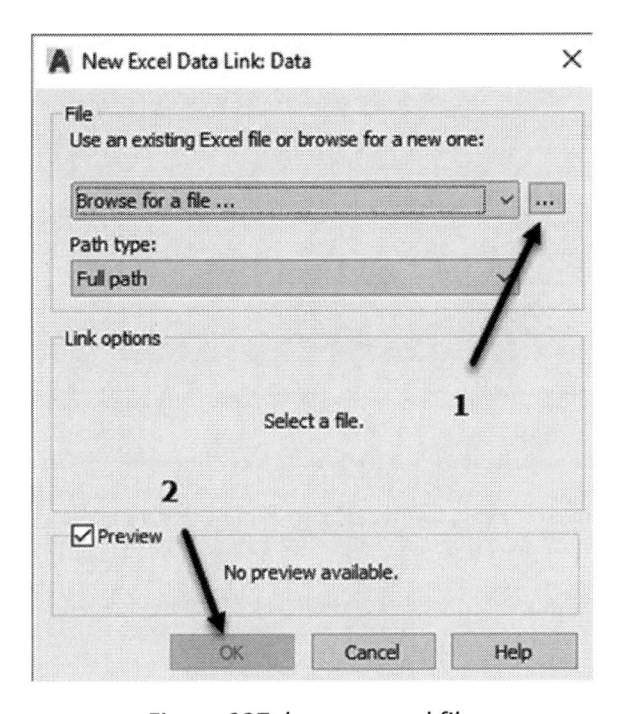

Figure 237: browse excel file

Step 5: Select Excel file then ok.

	A	B
1	Name	Designation
2	Linkan sagar	CAD Consultant
3	Simranjit	CAD Consultant
4	Anuj Kumar	PHP&UI
5	Nitish Bhardwaj	Embedded system
6	Vishal Gupta	coordinator
7	Devesh singh	coordinator
8	Mohammad Jawed Ali	system administrator
9	Ritu gupta	Head counsellor
10	Megha	counsellor
11	Ginni	counsellor
12	Aarushi	receptionist
13	Deep singh	Java trainer
14	Rajeev Shishodia	Java trainer
15	Pankaj Singh	.NET & Python
16	Kuldeep Shishodia	Networking
17	Vivek jha	C/C++
18	Punit katiyar	PHP
19	Shashank	Digital marketing

Figure 238: insert excel data

What do you mean by Smart Dimension?

Smart Dimension tool is recently introduce in AutoCAD 2017.

This tool is use to show the dimension of an object. This tool has an existing feature by which you can check any dimension of an object. While in normal dimension tool, the dimensions of an object is different like aligned, linear, radius etc. but Smart dimension lonely work on behalf of all dimension.

Step 1: Ribbon: Annotate ➤ Dimensions ➤ Dimension.

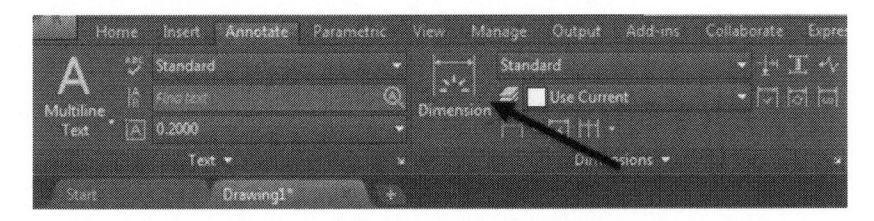

Figure 239: smart dimension tool icon

Step 2: Select object.

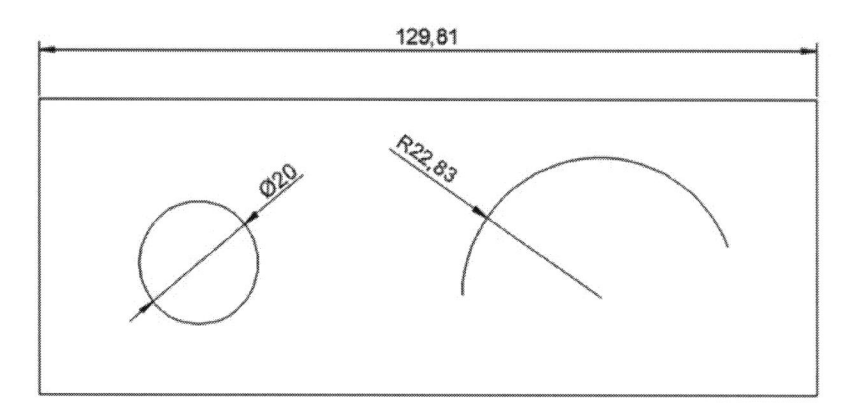

Figure 240 all dimension use

CHAPTER-6

Inquiry

What do you mean by LIST?

When we need to know the all properties of an object, we use command LIST. It lists all information of the selected objects such as what type of object it is (whether it is a circle, arc, block etc.), what is its color, its axis, its thickness, location of its end points, elevation from z-axis.

Following information we can get through command LIST:

- Line weight, Color, line type.
- How thick the object is..?.
- Z Coordinate elevation.
- Extrusion direction (UCS coordinates), with different Z (0, 0, 1) axis.
- Information related to a particular object type such as for dimensional constraint objects, name, and value; LIST displays the constraint type, reference type (yes or no), expression.

Step 1: Select object then LI

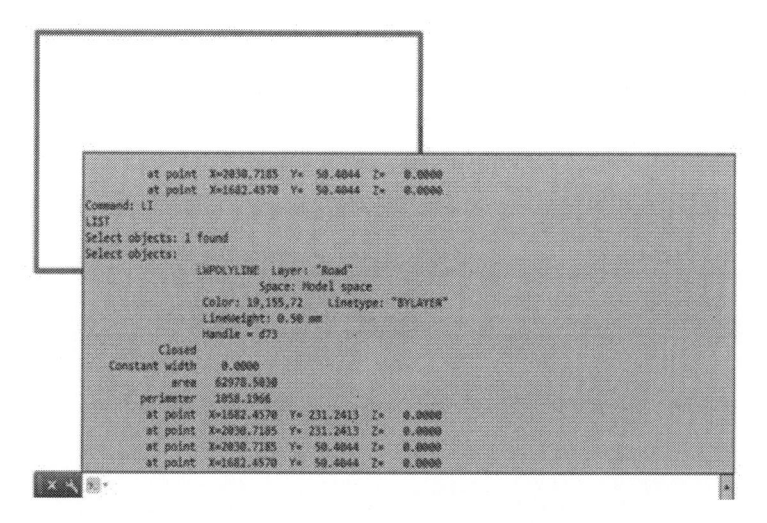

Figure 241: rectangle list and detail

What do you mean by ANGLE?

We use command ANGLE to know the angle between points, circle, or arc.

Step 1: Ribbon: Home tab ➤ Utilities panel ➤ Angle

Step 2: Select arc, circle, line or <Specify vertex>: **Select arc Angle=1300**

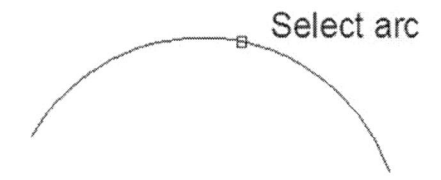

Figure 242: select arc

What do you mean by DIST?

DIST is an inquiry command which lists the distance between any two selected points in our command bar.

Step 1: DI ⏎ then click first point.
Step 2: Click second click.

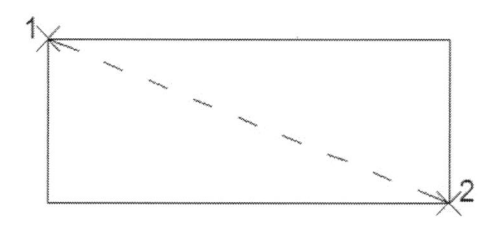

Figure 243: pick point

And press F2 key

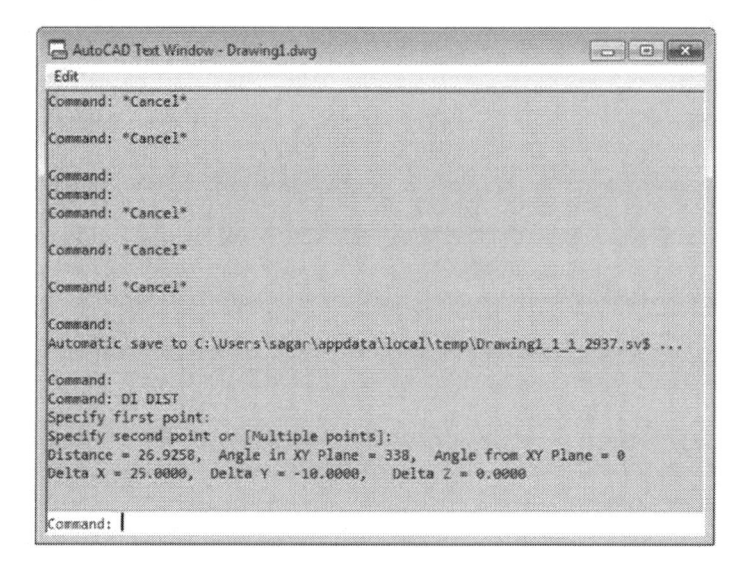

Figure 244: List detail tab

Inquiry

What do you mean by VOLUME?

We use volume command, to compute volume of a defined object.

Step 1: Ribbon: Home tab ➢ Utilities panel ➢ Volume
Step 2: Click first point.
Step 3: Click second point.
Step 4: Click third point.
Step 5: Click forth point.
Step 6: T Enter for total.
Step 7: 5 Enter for height.

Figure 245: use of volume tool

Volume=1250.00

What do you mean by AREA?

We use the command area to calculate the area of an object or shape. Using this command, we can calculate the area of the object such as circle or by selecting the various points of a given object etc.

Step 1: AA Enter.
Step 2: Click first point.
Step 3: Click second point.
Step 4: Click third point.
Step 5: Click forth point.
Step 6: T Enter for total.

Figure 246: use of area tool

And press F2 key

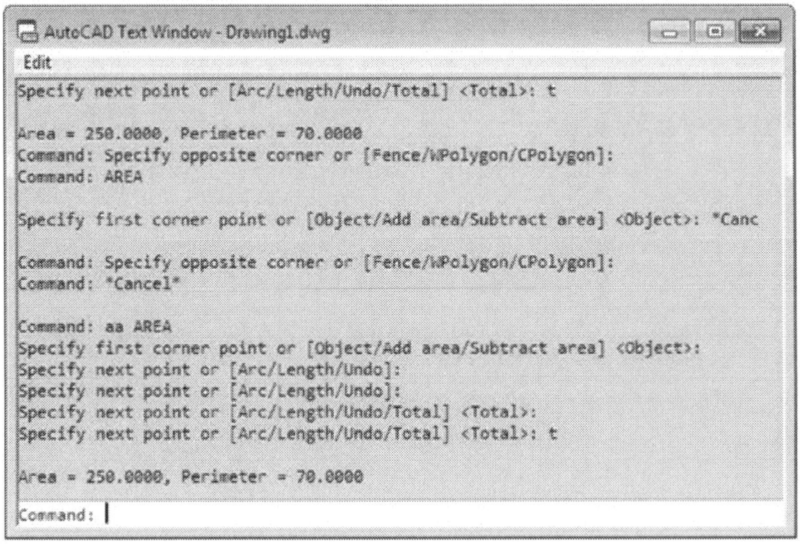

Figure 247: area list tab

CHAPTER-7

Parametric

What is meant by PARAMETRIC DRAWINGS?

By using Parametric constraints, we can force an object to behave the way we want it to. If we need an object to behave the same way as other we need to set a constraint on it to do the same. For example, if we need a pair of line to always remain parallel to one another we can select constraint parallel, then even if we change the position of any one object the other will also change accordingly being always parallel to the first.

In the Parametric tool panels, Constraints are divided into three sections:

GEOMETRIC CONSTRAINTS

DIMENSIONAL CONSTRAINTS

MANAGE

Ribbon: Parametric

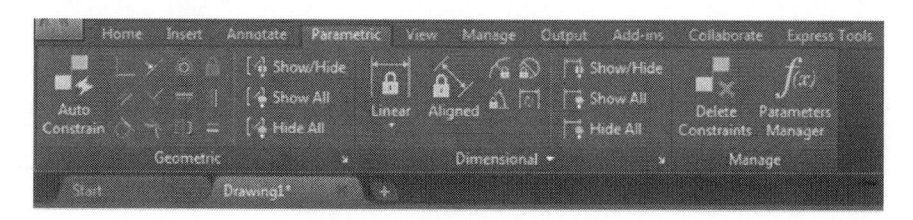

Figure 248: parametric tab

Menu: Parametric

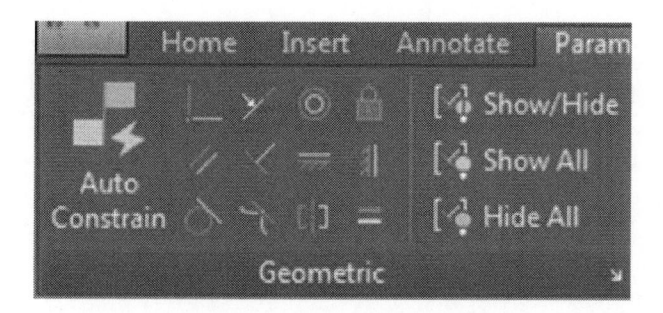

Figure 249: geometric panel

Geometric Constraints: Constrains a object based on geometric properties : Vertical, horizontal, etc.

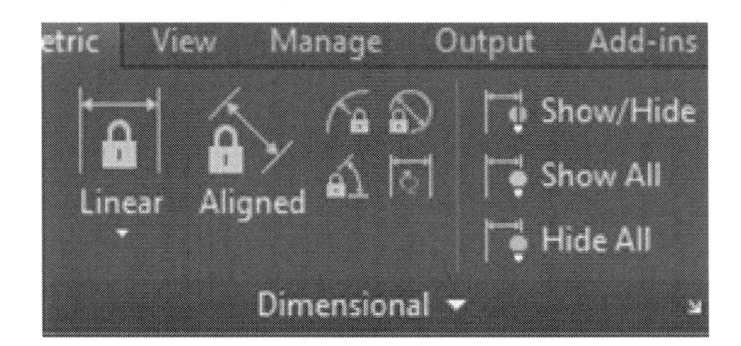

Figure 250: dimensional panel

Dimensional Constraints: Dimensional Constraints an object based on a set length or radius.

GEOMETRIC CONSTRAINTS

Ribbon: Parametric ➢ Geometric

Menu: Parametric ➢ Constraints

Geometric constraints associate geometric objects together. For example, If we have a symmetric drawing and later we make a change in the drawing, now the work will no longer remain symmetric, to maintain symmetricity of the drawing we apply the constraints symmetry and select the objects that we require to keep symmetrical.

Let's say we have a rectangle. As for rectangle, sides have to be perpendicular to each other. But in case during the design, we may need to change the position of a vertex. If we extend one of the rectangle vertex, then it would not remain a rectangle anymore. As AutoCAD is not aware that we want to keep it as a rectangle.

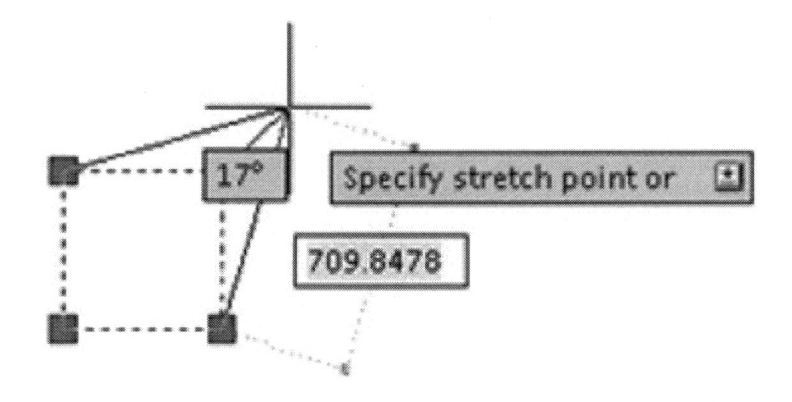

Figure 251: before geometric

To prevent this, in AutoCAD, we apply perpendicular constraints, ensuring that we

Parametric **111**

want them always perpendicular to each other. So now we add a perpendicular constraint to the two sides. Now, try to stretch the vertex again.

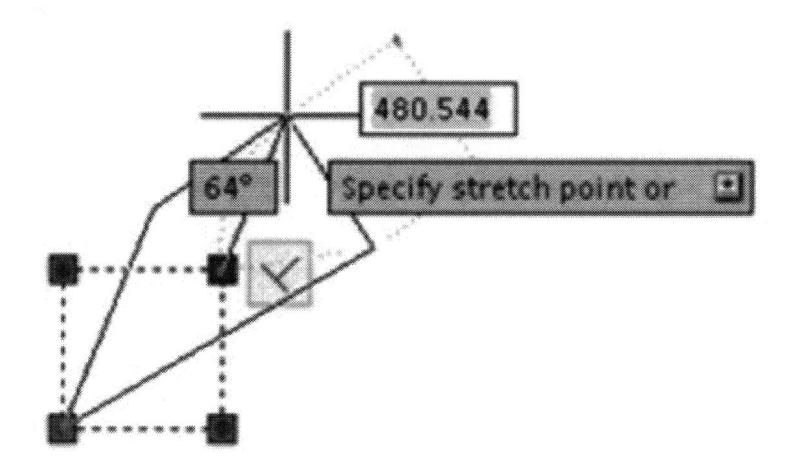

Figure 252: after geometric

As we can see, the two sides are perpendicular to each other. But the other edges don't. So, we need to add all constraint to keep it a rectangle.

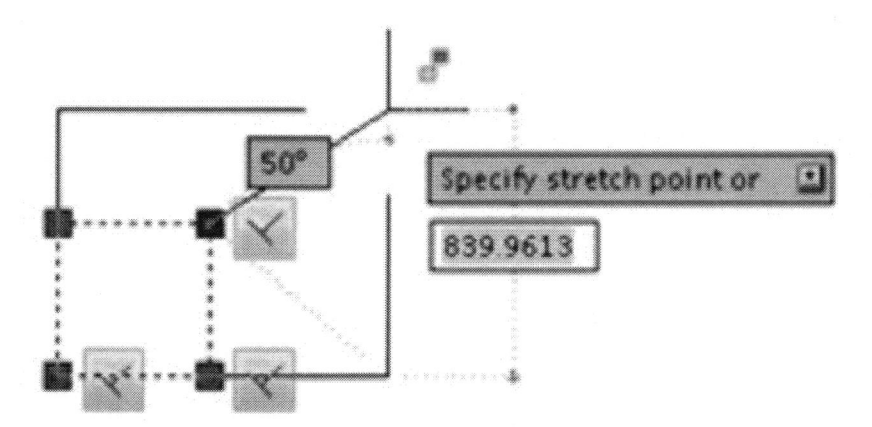

Figure 253: complete use geometric

Geometric tool	Before	After

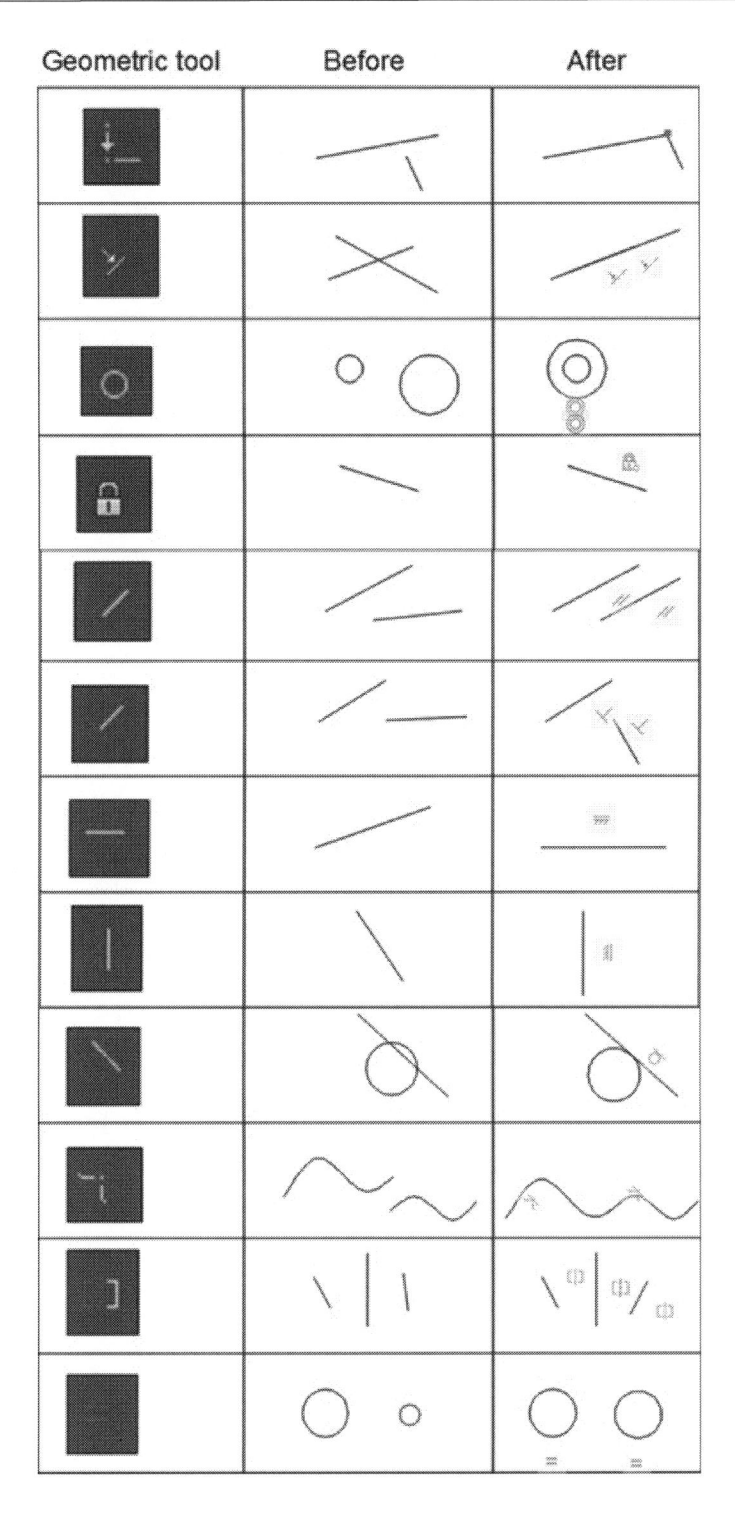

Figure 254: use of geometric

Parametric **113**

DIMENSIONAL CONSTRAINTS

Dimensional constraints are different to geometrical; these are used in making changes to what we have already worked with. If we have a drawing and we need to make amendments in the dimensions of the objects we use dimensional constraints

Instead of making a line vertical (for example), we can make a line 10 units long and make it stay that way until we change it. We can add more than one dimensional constraint on certain objects.

Draw a random angled line on the screen. Pick on the Aligned constraint icon. Pick two points on the line.

Notice that even if we have our Osnaps off, we can only pick the endpoints and midpoint on the line. After selecting the 2 points, we can now enter a length that we want the distance between those points to be.

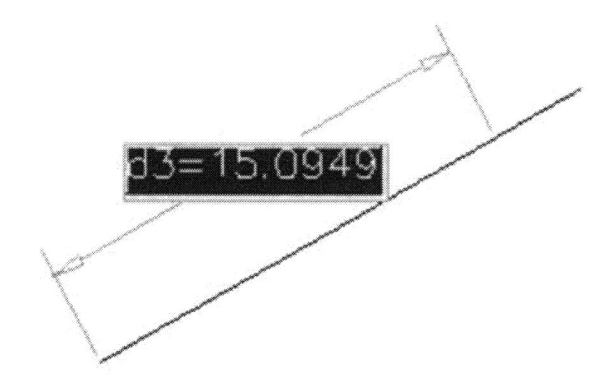

Figure 255: dimensional sample

With the constraint still highlighted, enter a number. D3 in this example refers to the 3rd dimensional constraint in the drawing. If we add a constraint from end to middle, add another from end to end (or vice versa). Notice that the constraint will be double the first one. If we change one, the other will change accordingly.

How to MANAGE CONSTRAINTS

In the third column of parametric toolbar we have 'manage' section. In this section we can perform two operations, we can use "parameters manager" to generate excel sheets of all the constraints used and secondly "delete constraints" to remove unnecessary constraints. By using Parameter manager, the excel sheet of parameter is generated, using this sheet we can also make changes in the sheet that are simultaneously applied on the objects in the drawing.

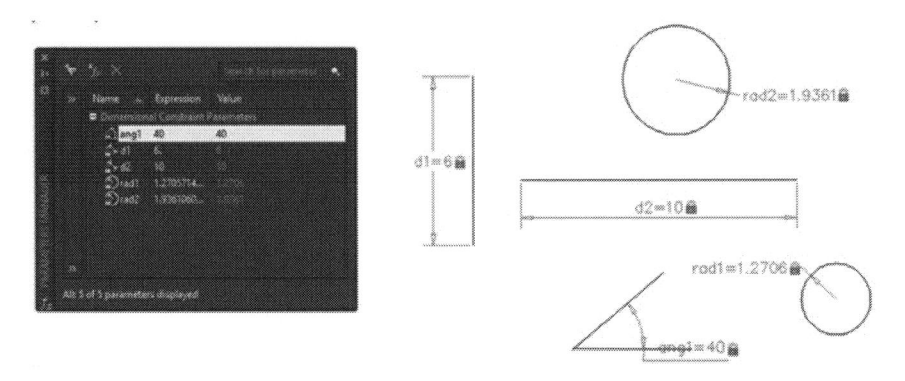

Figure 256: Manage option

CHAPTER-8

Setting & Option

What do you mean by INFER CONSTRAINT?

It a helping type of tool for applying geometrical constraints while creating and editing geometrical objects. We can also use it as parametric constraint and also creates line infer on and off.

INFER CONSTRAINT command automatically applies constraints between the object or points associated with object snaps and the object we are creating or editing.

Similarly AUTOCONSTRAIN command, constraints are applied only if the objects meet the constraint conditions.

With Infer Constraints turned on, to infer geometric constraint we specify the object snap while creating geometry. However, the following object snaps are not supported: Apparent Intersection, and Quadrant, Extension, Intersection

The following constraints cannot be implied:
- Smooth
- Symmetric
- Equal
- Concentric
- Fix
- Collinear

Toolbar: Status bar ➤ Infer

Create a line infer off and create a line infer on.

Infer off

Infer on   Infer constraints

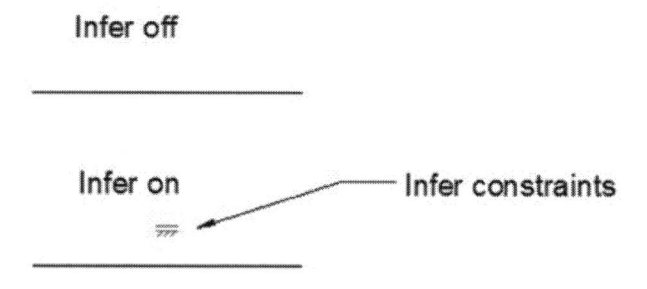

Figure 257: use of infer

Right click for Infer setting

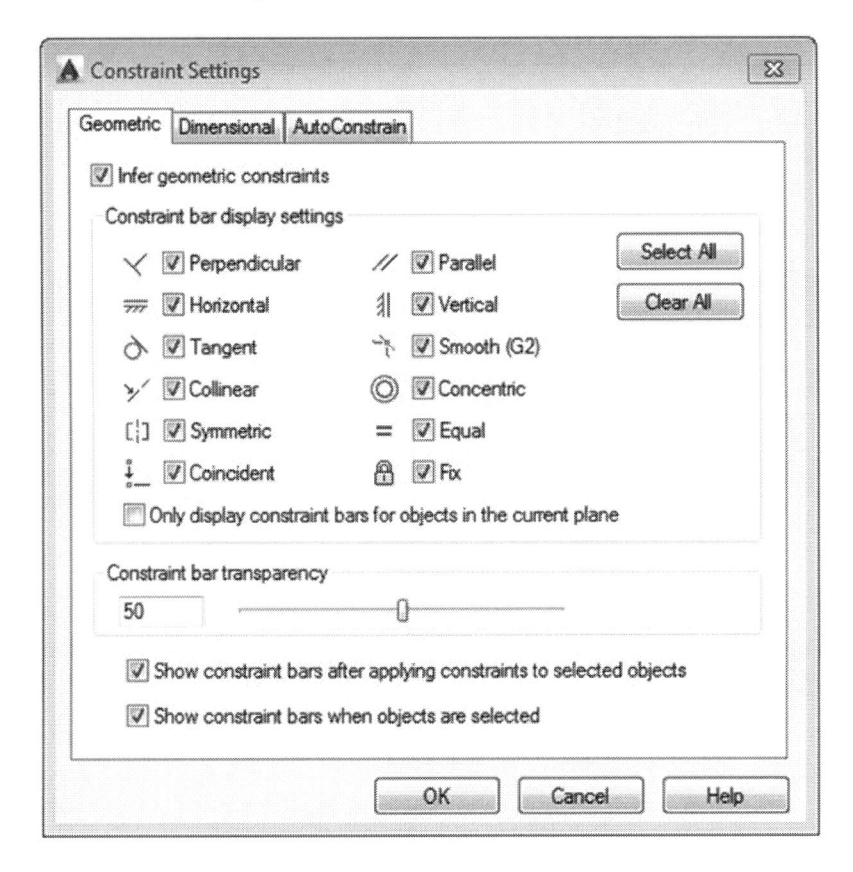

Figure 258: infer option

What do you mean by GRID & SNAP?

The grid is a pattern of straight lines that crosses over each other, forming square. In AutoCAD it is infinite in the given workspace. Grid helps us in aligning objects and visualizing the distances between them. Horizontal lines are said to be minor grid lines and vertical lines are said to be major grid lines.

Snap mode limits the movement of the crosshairs since it is defined. With Snap mode on, the cursor will follow an invisible rectangular grid. Snap is helpful in specifying precise points with the arrow keys.

Both are independent to each other but sometimes we use them simultaneously.

Toolbar: Status bar ➢ Grid or Snap

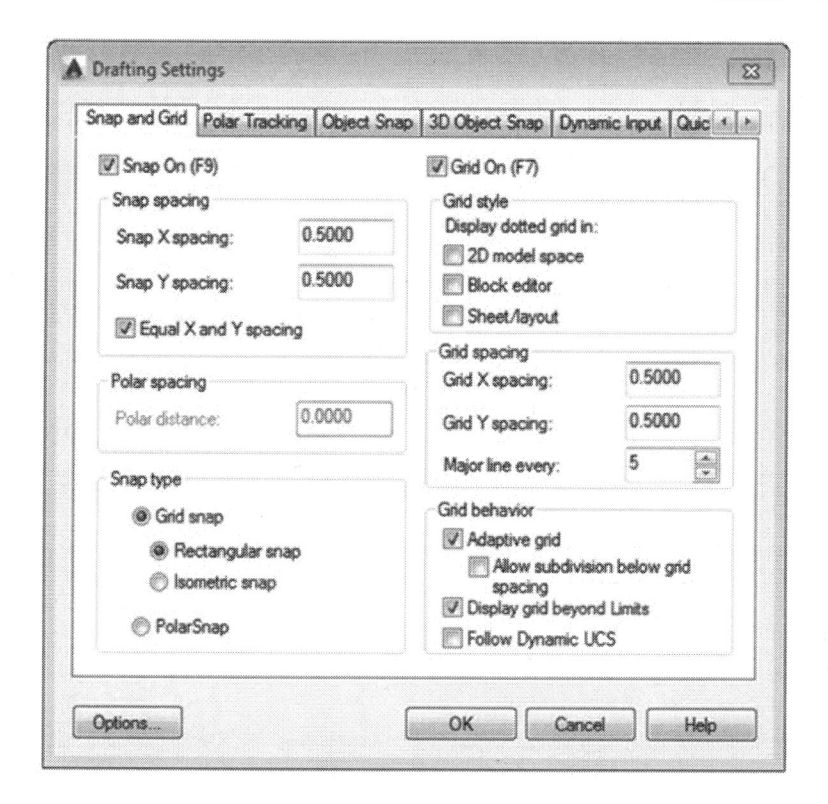

Figure 259: grid and snap setting

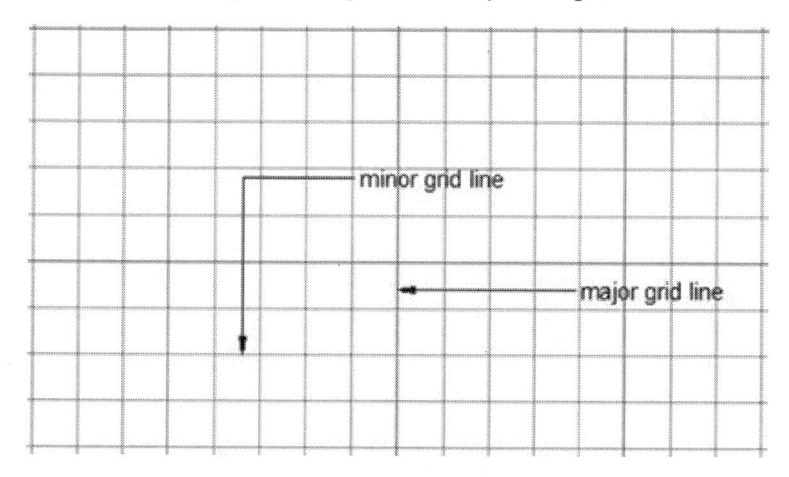

Figure 260: grid

What do you mean by OSNAP?

"OSNAP" means object snap. The Object Snaps are drawing tool that help us in drawing accurately. Osnap specifies us to snap onto a particular point location while picking a point. For example, using Osnap we can sharply pick the end point of a line or the center of a circle. Osnap in AutoCAD is so essential that we cannot draw faultlessly without them.

Toolbar: Status bar ➤ Osnap

ENDPOINT: The Endpoint command snaps to the end points of arcs, line and to polyline vertices.

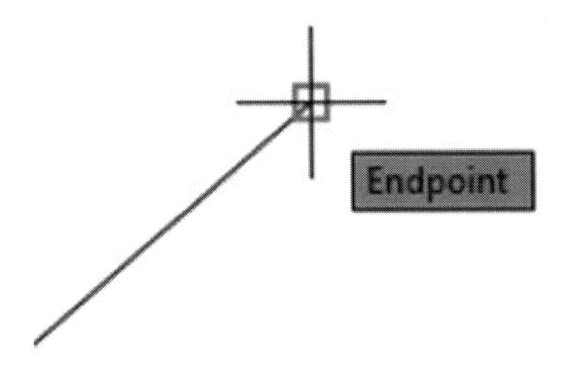

Figure 261: endpoint

MIDPOINT: The Midpoint command snaps to the mid-point of lines and arcs and to the mid-point of polyline segments.

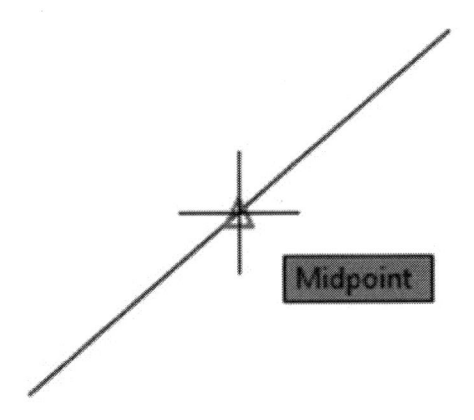

Figure 262: midpoint

INTERSECTION: The Intersection command snaps to the physical intersection of any two drawing sheet.

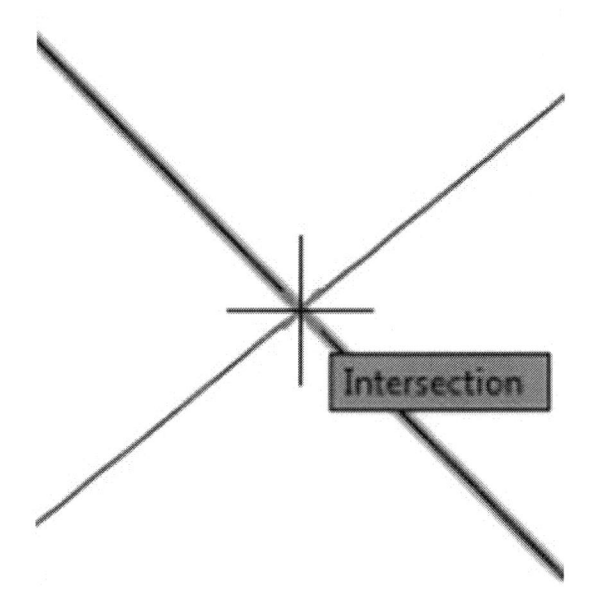

Figure 263: intersection

APPARENT INTERSECT: Apparent Intersection command snaps to the point where objects seems to intersect in the current view.

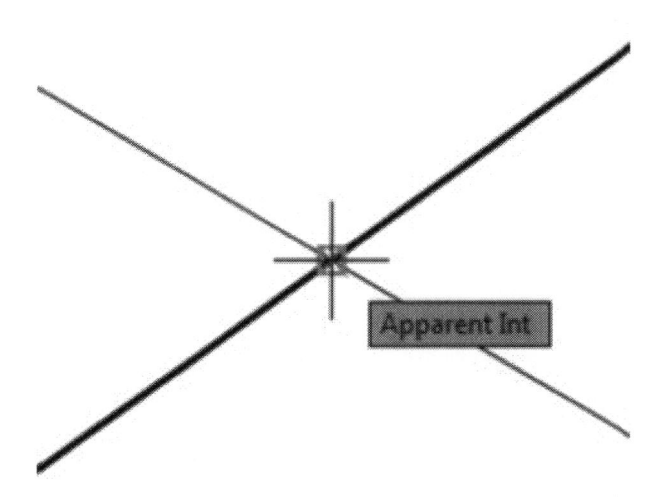

Figure 264: APPARENT INTERSECT

EXTENSION: The Extension command helps to snap to some point along the imaginary extension of the arc, the line, or polyline segment.

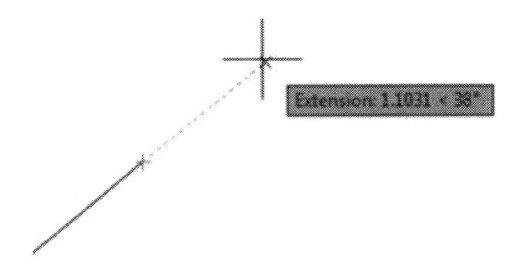

Figure 265: EXTENSION

CENTRE: The Centre command snaps to the center of a circle, arc, an object or polyline arc segment.

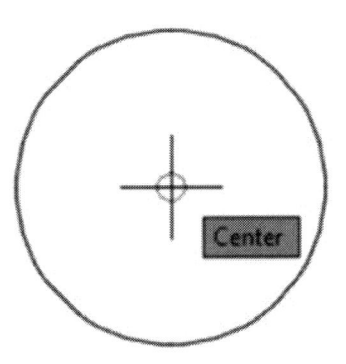

Figure 266: CENTRE

QUADRANT: The Quadrant command locates the four circle quadrant points located at east, north, west and south or 0, 90, 180 and 270 degrees respectively.

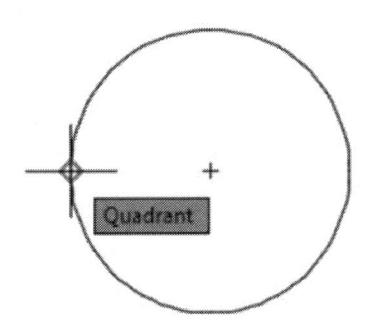

Figure 267: QUADRANT

TANGENT: The Tangent command snaps to a tangent point on a circle.

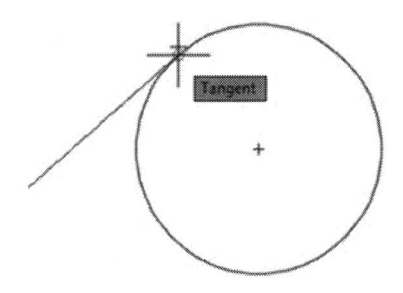

Figure 268: TANGENT

PERPENDICULAR: The Perpendicular command snaps to a point where it forms a perpendicular line with the selected object.

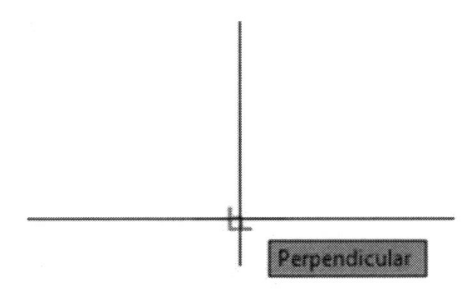

Figure 269: PERPENDICULAR

PARALLEL: The parallel command is used to draw a line parallel to a line segment.

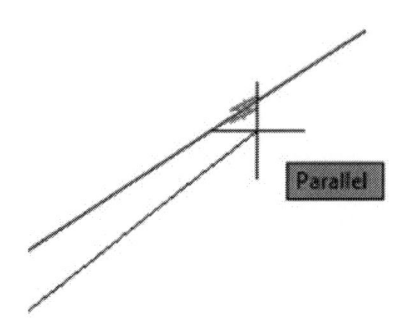

Figure 270: PARALLEL

INSERT: The Insert command snaps to the insertion point of the text, block or image.

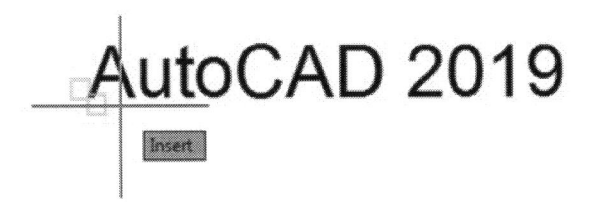

Figure 271: insert

NODE: The Node command snaps to the centre of a Point object.

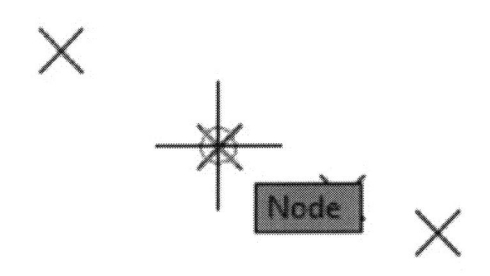

Figure 272: node

NEAREST: The nearest command snaps the nearest point on the drawing sheet.

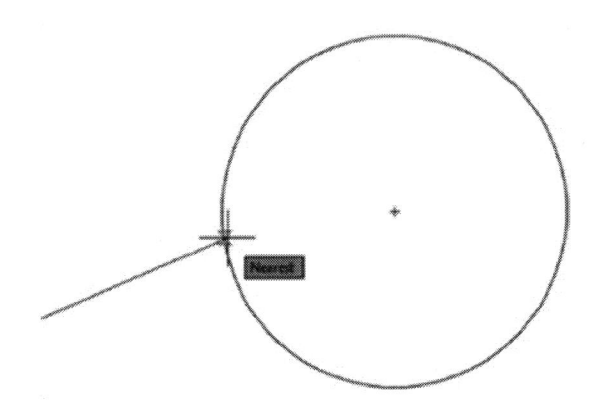

Figure 273: NEAREST

Geometric Center: Snaps to the Geometric center point of polyline, 2D polyline and 2D spline.

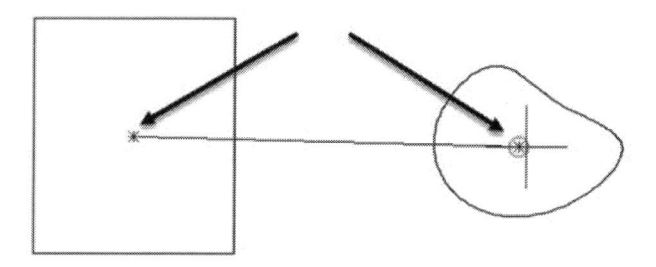

Figure 274: Geometric Center

What do you mean by POLAR?

It is a helping type of tool used to define an angle and to draw using angles. It setting contains two types of angles:
- INCREMENT ANGLE
- ADDITIONAL ANGLE

Increment angle is the angle that is shown in the drawing as a multiple of it, but additional angle we take more than one and they can be easily seen in the drawing.

Toolbar: Status bar ➤ Polar

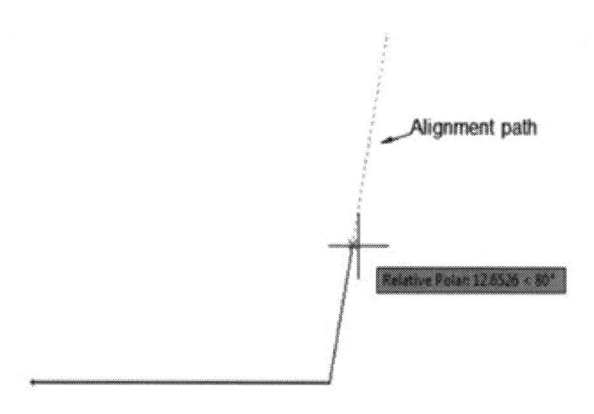

Figure 275: polar

What do you mean by ORTHO?

It is a setting by which cursor movement is constrained to vertical and horizontal direction only. We use it often when we specify the distance and angle between two points.

Toolbar: Status bar ➢ Ortho

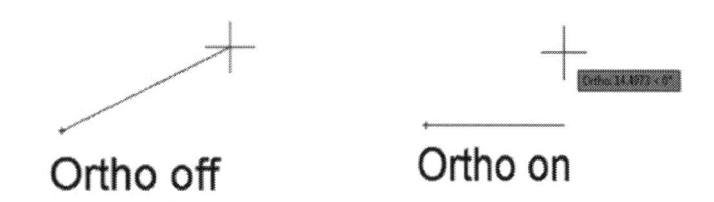

Figure 276: ortho

What do you mean by OTRACK?

It is a command that hover over the reference point until the Otrack box appears. Otrack point can be changed whenever needed.

Toolbar: Status bar ➢ **Otrack**

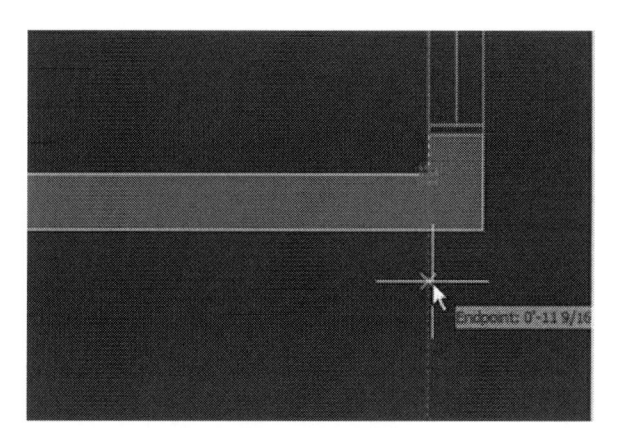

Figure 277: otrack

What do you mean by LWT?

It is a command used to increase and decrease the pixels of the line segment.

Toolbar: Status bar ➢ **Lwt**

Figure 278: use of LWT

What do you mean by DYN?

It is a setting in the status bar which acts as a command interface near the cursor so as to keep the focus in the drafting area.

Setting & Option **125**

Toolbar: Status bar ➤ **Dyn**

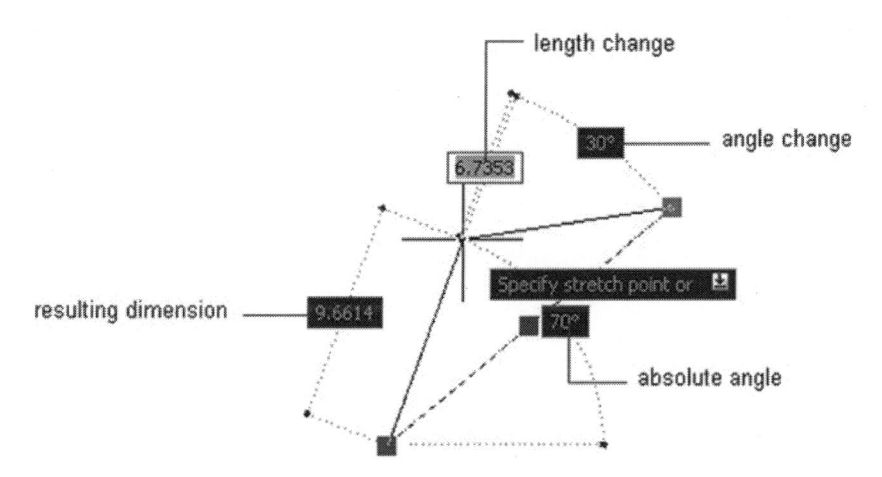

Figure 279: use of dyn

What do you mean by QP (Quick properties)?

It is used to observe the properties of the required object such as color, layer, linetype, centre x, centre y, circumference, area, diameter, radius.

Toolbar: Status bar ➤ **QP**

Select object then modify properties like radius, color etc.

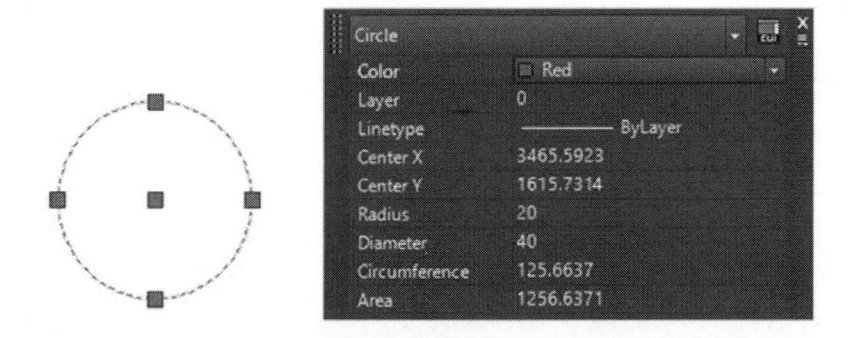

Figure 280: use of quick properties

What do you mean by COLOUR?

It is a display type of tool which is used in interface elements so that the elements used can be distinguished from one another.

Command: OP

1. Click display tab

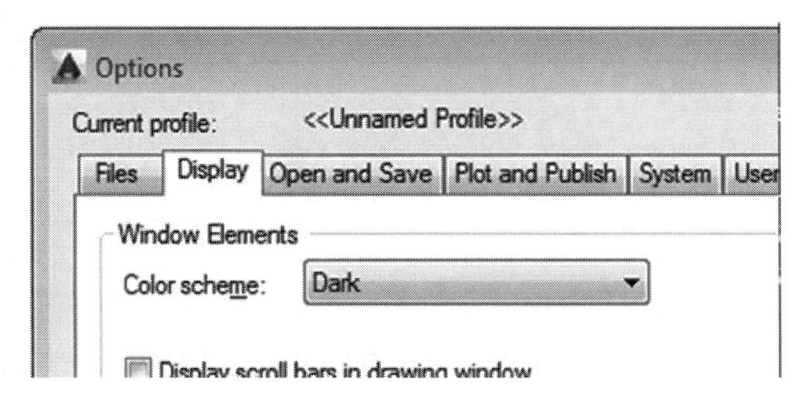

Figure 281: display tab

2. Click Colors

Figure 282: color tab

Setting & Option

3. **Chose interface element & color**

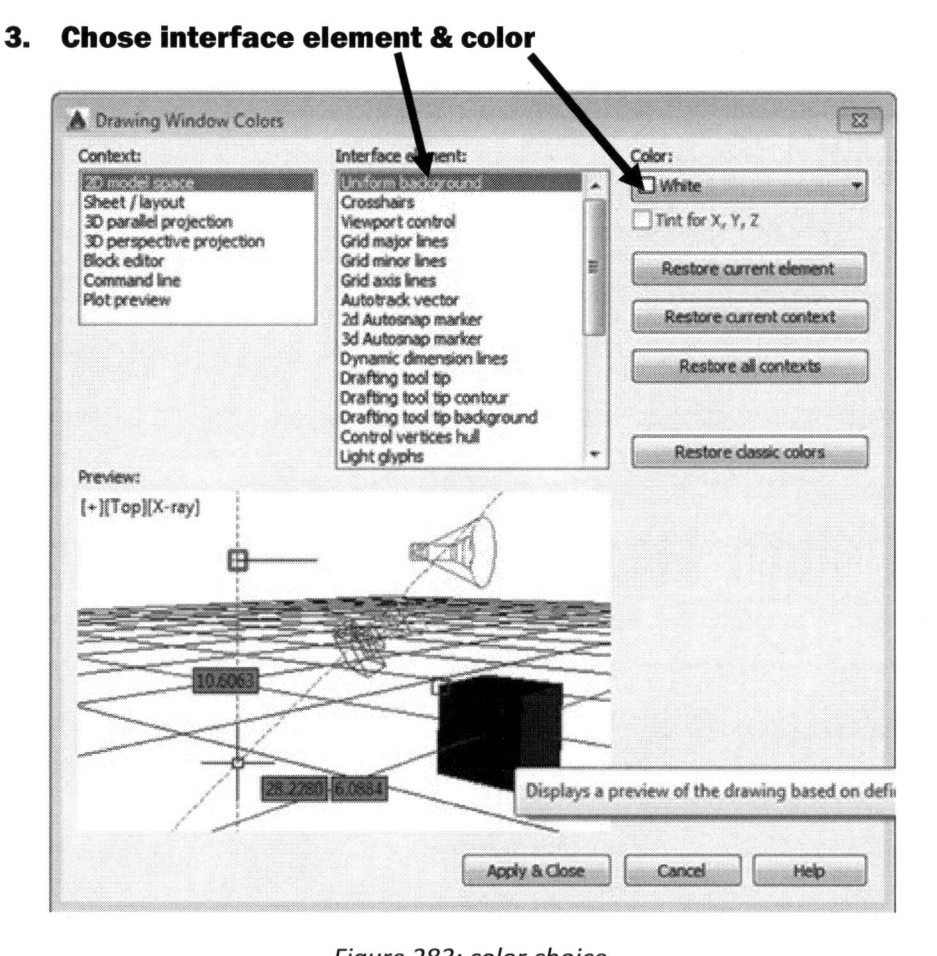

Figure 283: color choice

4. **Click apply & close**
5. **Click apply & ok**

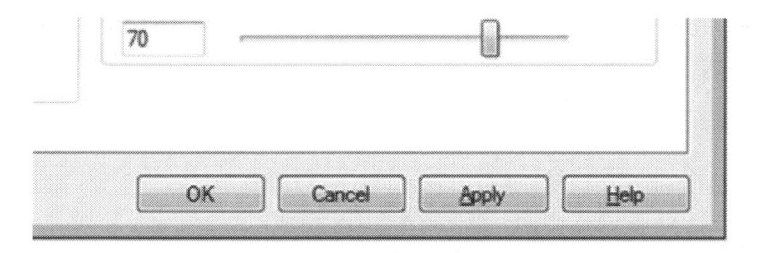

Figure 284: Click ok

What do you mean by UI COLOUR CHANGES

It is the latest setting in the AUTOCAD 2019 used to change the color to light and dark version so as to be identified easily in dark. It decreases the contrast between the elements used (tools) and workspace. It also helps in Lessing the strain on the user.

Command: OP

1. Click display & Chose color scheme.

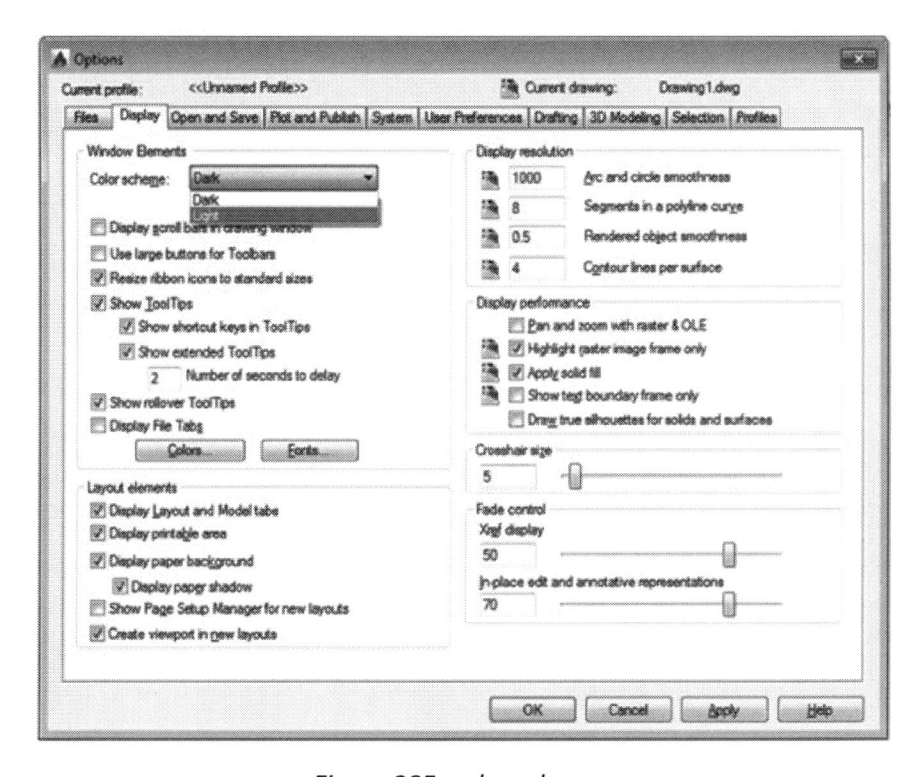

Figure 285: color scheme

Dark

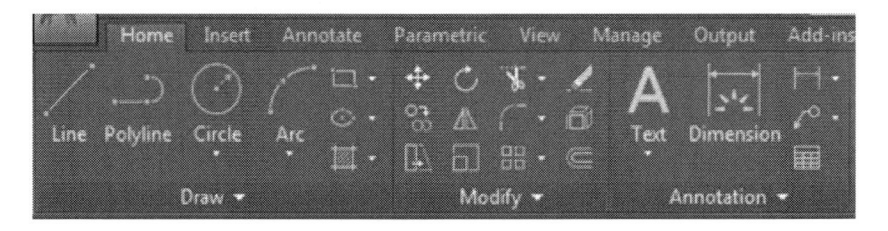

Figure 286: dark effect

Setting & Option 129

Light

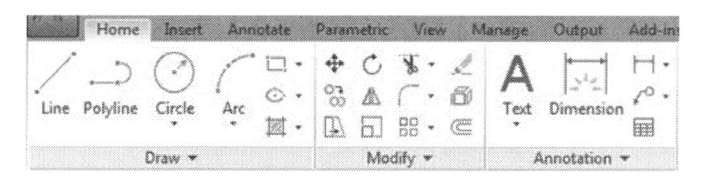

Figure 287: light affect

What do you mean by PAN?

It is a command to move view planar to the home screen.

Menu: View ➤ Zoom ➤ Pan

Command: P

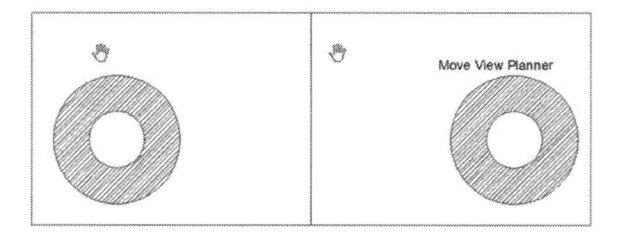

Figure 288: pan use

What do you mean by STEERING WHEELS?

It is a navigation wheel to have a watch on the drawing made in 2-d or 3-d. some of the tools in the navigation wheel are:

- **ZOOM:** To show a smaller area of an image at higher magnification or a larger area at a lower magnification.
- **REWIND:** It restores the most recent view. By clicking and dragging left or right, we can move backward or forward respectively.
- **PAN:** By panning we can reposition the current view.
- **ORBIT:** Rotates the current view around a fixed pivot point.
- **WALK:** Pretend walking through a model.
- **CENTRE:** To adjust the center of the current view by specifying a point on a model or change the target point used for some of the navigation tools.
- **UP/DOWN:** Slides the current view of a model along the Z axis of the model.

LOOK: Turns around the current view.

Figure 289: STEERING WHEELS icon

Command: WHEEL

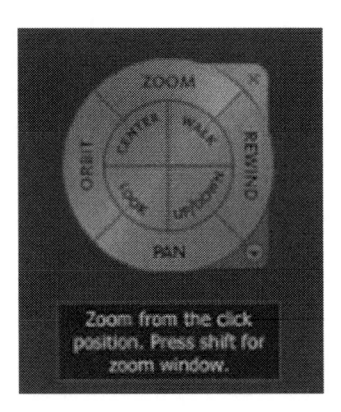

Figure 290: STEERING WHEELS

What do you mean by GRIPS EDITING?

It is an editing option for the grip in the line. In editing the grip, we can change the size and color of the grip.

Command: GR

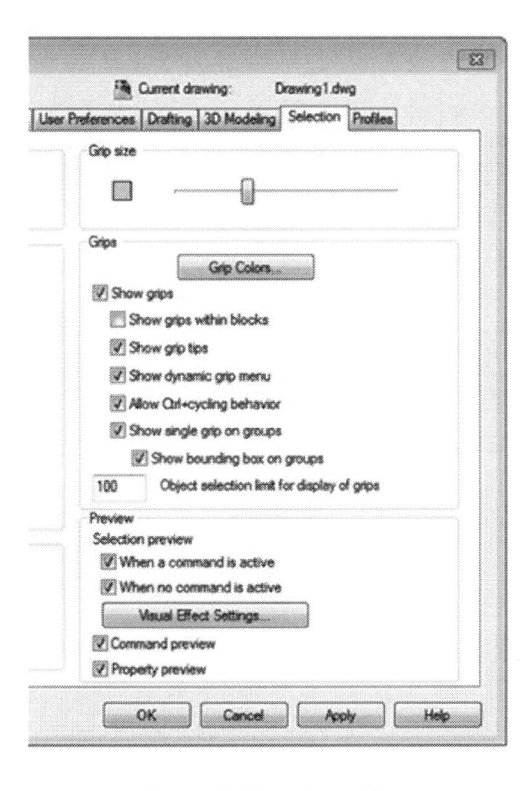

Figure 291: grip setting

Figure 292: grip

What do you mean by REGEN?

It is a command to regenerate the entire drawing in the current viewport.

Menu: View ➢ Regen

Command: RE

Before Regen   After Regen

Figure 293: use of regen

What do you mean by MULTLINE STYLE?

It is a command to set the elements and the properties of the new multiline style or it can change them for the existing multiline style.

Menu: Format ➢ Multiline Style

Command: MLSTYLE

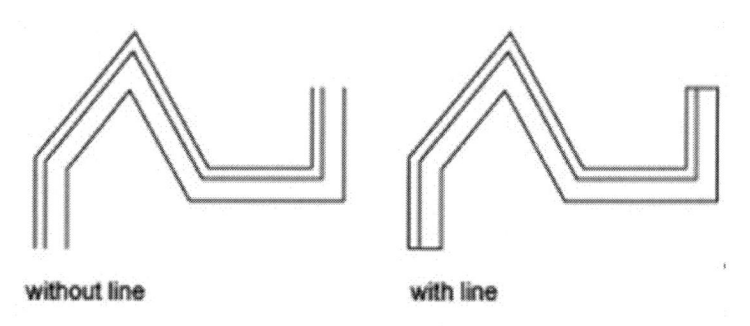

without line   with line

Figure 294: multiline style

What do you mean by POINTSTYLE?

It is a command that shows and can change the current point style and size of the point style.

Menu: Format ➤ Point Style

Command: PTYPE

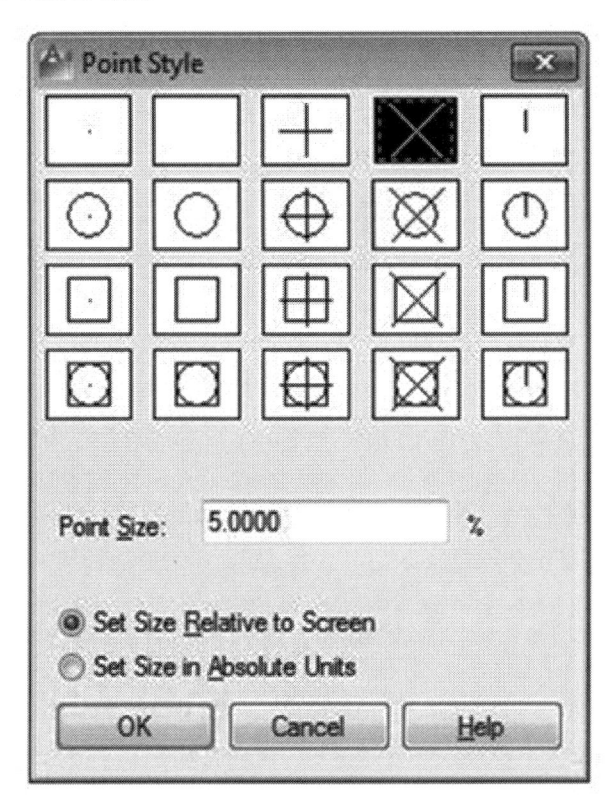

Figure 295: point style option

What do you mean by TABLESTYLE?

The overall look of the table is denoted by table style. We can use the default table style, STANDARD, or create own table styles.

When we create a new table style, we can specify a starting table. Once the table is selected, you can specify the structure and contents to copy from that table to the table style.

Ribbon: Annotate tab ➤ Tables panel ➤ Tables style

Menu: Format ➤ Tables style

Setting & Option 133

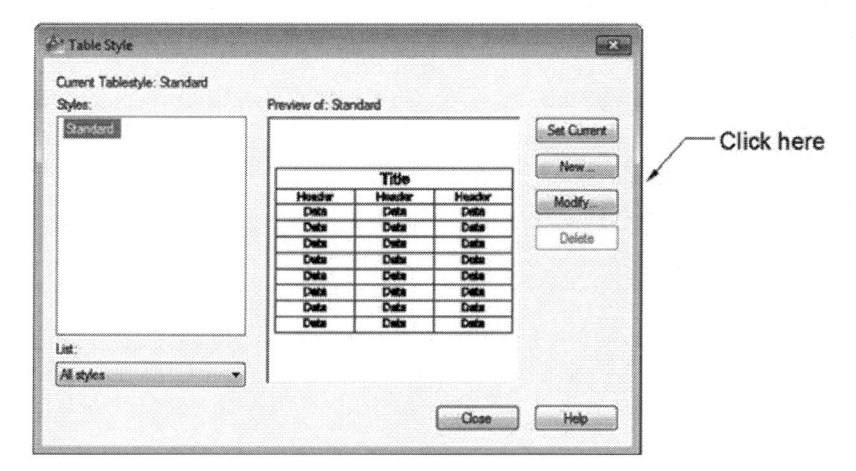

Figure 296: table style tab

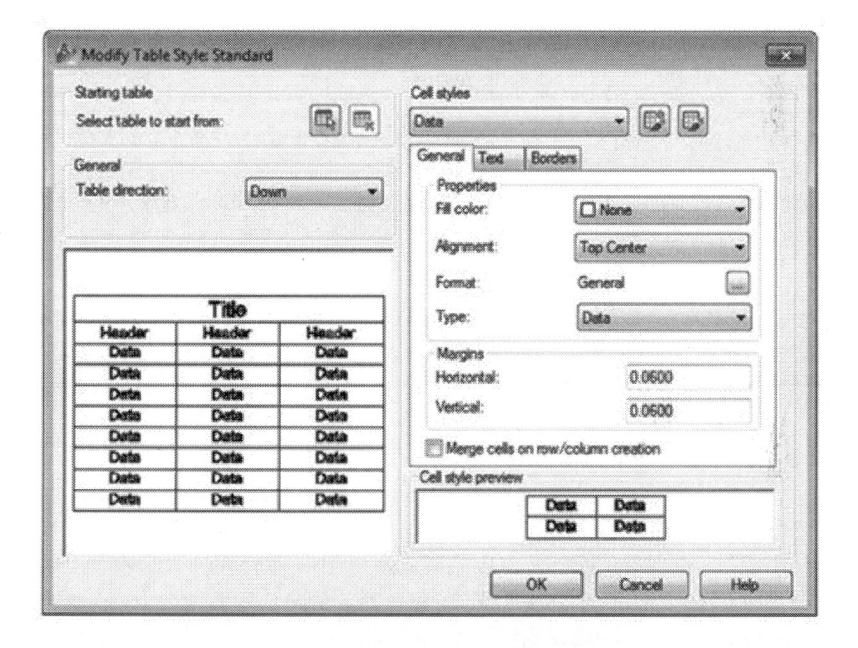

Figure 297: table modify tab

What do you mean by BACKGROUND MASK?

It is a command which is used for mtext for applying background mask. In background mask dialogue box, we can specify border offset and can fill color. It can also be applied in dimension objects.

Right click and click Background Mask.

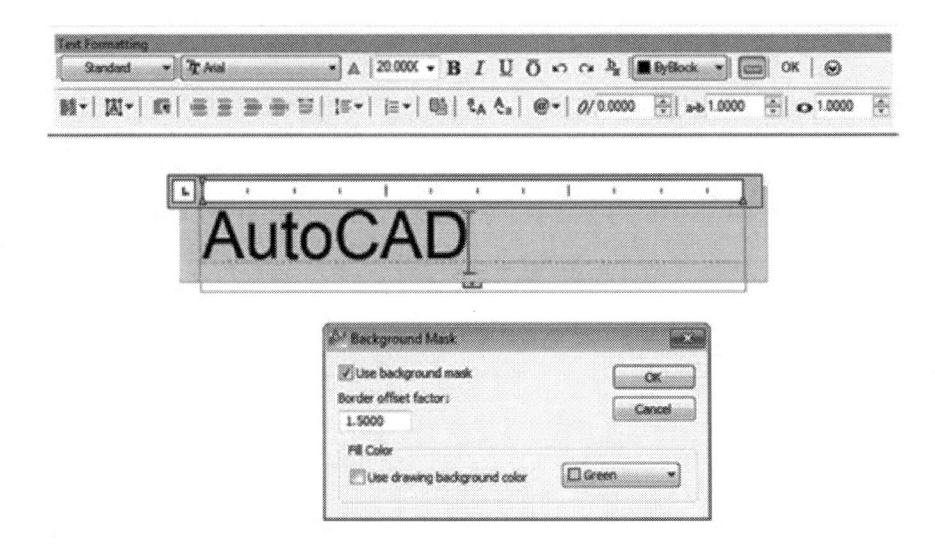

Figure 298: text background color

When do we use UNITS?

When we begin our new work we start by setting up the units of measurement in which we need to work. When we give the command for unit, we see the Drawing Units dialogue box. The dialogue box is divided into four main sections, namely 'Length,' 'Angle,' 'Insertion Scale.' In "Length" we select our linear units whereas in "Angles," we select our angular units. We can make amendments for linear units and angular units independently and in both sections we can also control the type and precision required. In the Angle section we can also specify the direction of angle as per our requirement and ease.

LINEAR UNITS

The default unit for length is "Decimal." The AutoCAD 2019 provides five different linear unit types in its box. Brief necessary description of the different units is provided in the table below.

Unit Type Units	1.5 Drawing Units	1500 Drawing	Description
Decimal	1.5000	1500.0000	Metric or SI units
Scientific	1.5000E+00	1.5000E+03	Decimal value raised to a power
Engineering	0'-1.5000"	125'-0.0000"	Feet and decimal inches
Architectural	0'-1 1/2"	125'-0"	Feet and fractional inches
Fractional	1 ½	1500	Whole numbers and fractions

Setting & Option

ANGULAR UNITS

As linear, the default angular unit is also decimal and in general circumstances it is not required to be changed. We will find five different angular units provided to us in the units dialogue box. Below is a table describing the necessary description of the types of angular units?

Unit Type	12.5 Angular Units	180 Angula Units	Description
Decimal Degrees	12.500	180.000	Metric units
Deg/Min/Sec	12d30'0"	180d0'0"	Degrees, Minutes and Seconds
Grads	13.889g	200.000g	400 grads = 360 degrees
Radians	0.218r	3.142r	2 Pi radians = 360 degrees
Surveyor	N 77d30'0" E	W	Compass bearings

What do you mean by LAYERS?

It is a command having large space where all types of object are placed, and the basic designing is done on it…

On starting AutoCAD default layer is only shown which is set current. The person using it defines the various different layers .the object defined is only seen on the layer, the layer itself is not seen. Layer is invisible matter…..

Ribbon: Home tab ➤ Layers panel ➤ Layer Properties Manager
Menu: Format ➤ Layer
Command: LA

1. **Choose:** Format, Layer.

Or

2. **Type:** LAYER at the command prompt.

Command: LAYER (or LA)

Or

3. **Pick:** the layers icon from the Layer Control box on the object properties toolbar.

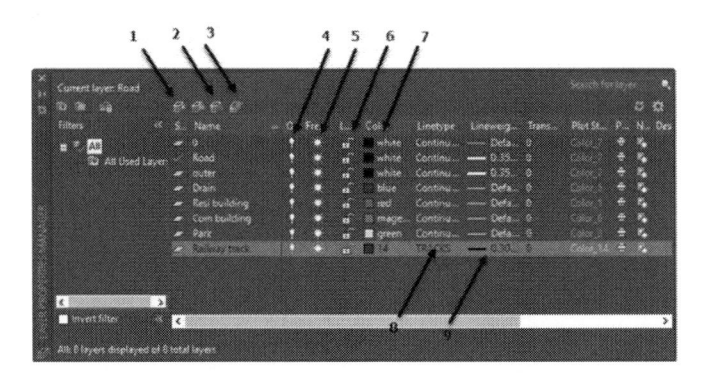

Figure 299: layer setting tab

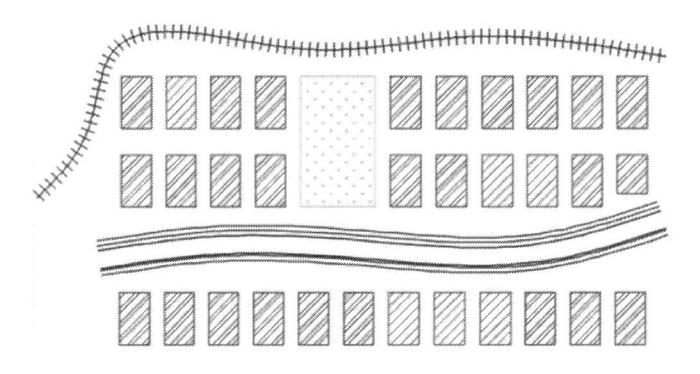

Figure 300: layer use

New	Creates new layers.
?	Lists layers, with states, colors and linetypes.
Make	Creates a new layer and makes it current.
Set	Sets current layer.
ON	Turns on specified layers.
OFF	Turns off specified layers.
Color	Assigns color to specified layers.
Ltype	Assigns linetype to specified layers.
Freeze	Completely ignores layers during regeneration.
Thaw	Unfreezes specified layers Ltype.
Lock	Makes a layer read only preventing entities from being Edited but available visual reference and osnap functions.
Unlock	Places a layer in read write mode and available for edits.
Plot	Turns a Layer On for Plotting
No Plot	Turns a Layer Off for Plotting
LWeight	Controls the line weight for each layer

Setting & Option **137**

TIP: Layers can be set using the command line prompts for layers. To use this, Type –LAYER or -LA at the command prompt

1. **Type** Command: **-LAYER** or **LA**
2. **Type** One of the following layer options ?/Make/Set/New/ON/OFF/Color/Ltype/Freeze/Thaw:

Changing the Layer of an Object

1. **Click** Once on the object to change.
2. **Select** the desired layer from the Layer Control Box, AutoCAD will move the object to the new layer.

What do you mean by PURGE?

Purge is basically a command for removing unused named items from a drawing...

It can remove block definition, layers, dimension style, linetypes, empty text objects and text style.

Menu: Application menu ➤ Drawing Utilites ➤ Purge

Command: PU

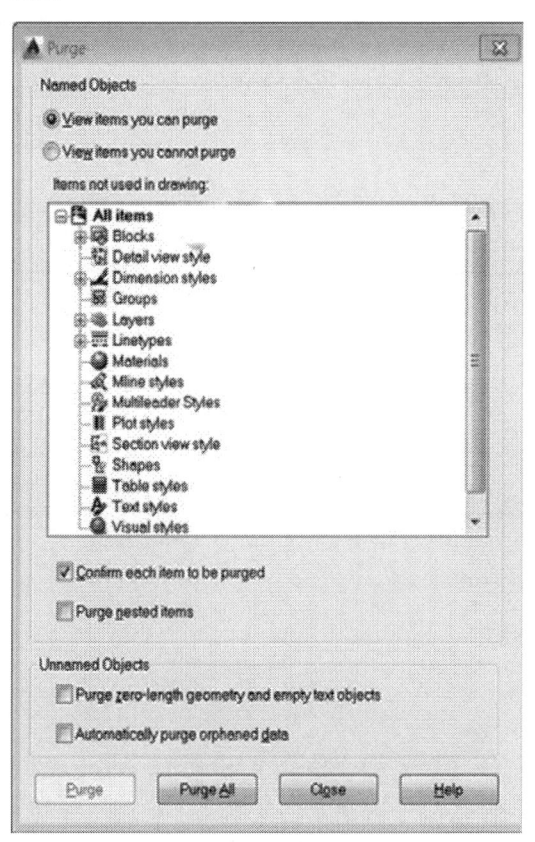

Figure 301: purge tab

CHAPTER-9

3D Modeling & View

BOX

Box is a 3D object. It can be create on X and Y plane and its height create on Z axis. Solid box create by this command.

Step 1: Ribbon- Home tab- Modeling- Box

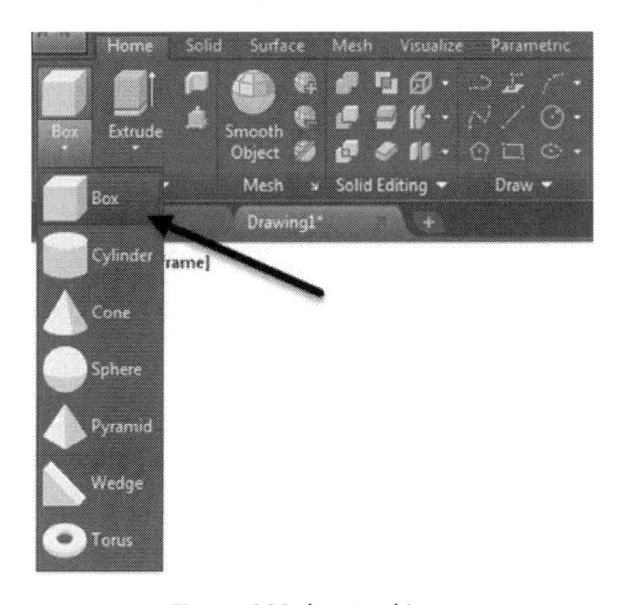

Figure 302: box tool icon

Step 2: Click first point for first corner.
Step 3: L Enter for box length.
Step 4: 60 Enter for length.
Step 5: 30 Enter for width.

Figure 303: box length and width

Step 6: 30 Enter for height.

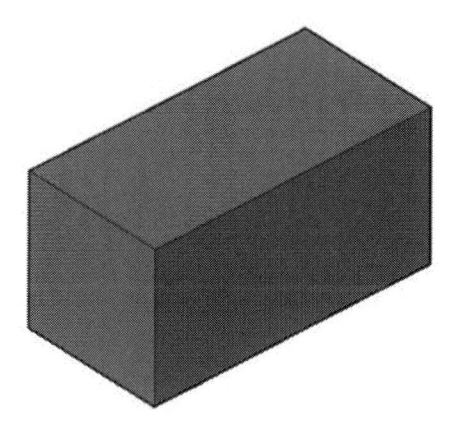

Figure 304: box

CYLINDER

Cylinder command is like a circular pipe. To create cylinder we must have radius and height. After creating cylinder on x and y plane give height on z axis.

Step 1: Ribbon ➤ Home tab ➤ Modeling ➤ Cylinder.

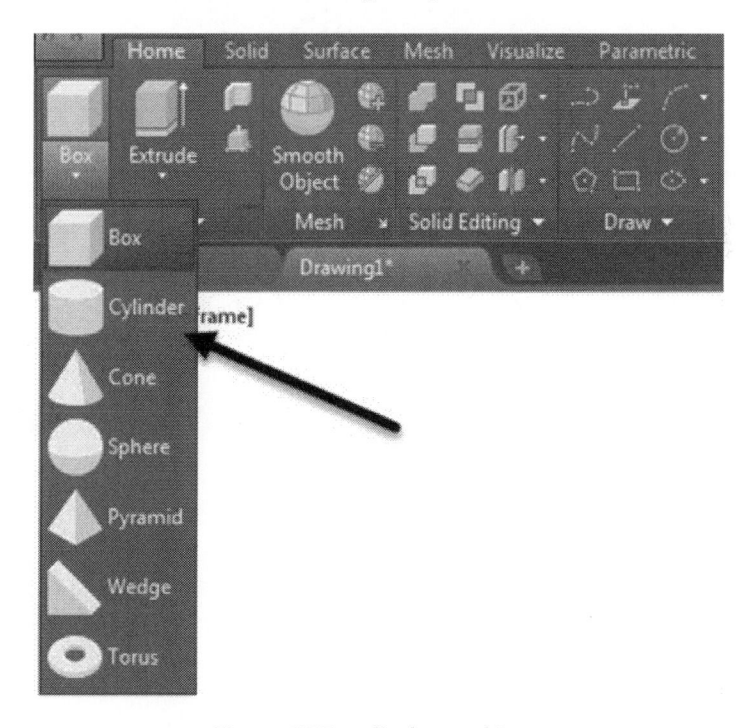

Figure 305: cylinder tool icon

Step 2: Click point for center point.

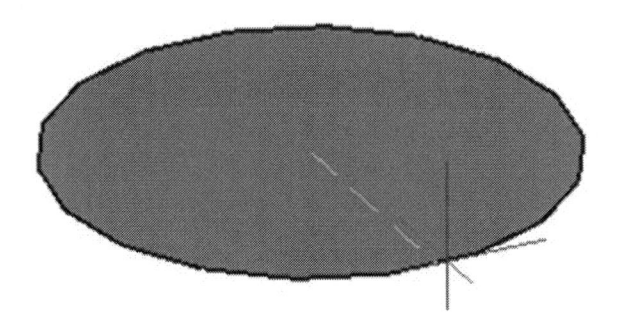

Figure 306: cylinder with radius

Step 3: 20 Enter for base radius.
Step 4: 30 Enter for height.

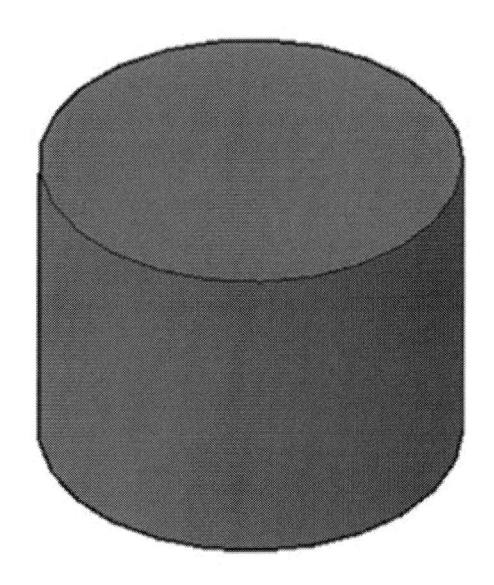

Figure 307: cylinder

HELIX

Helix command creates a spring. Firstly give base radius, top radius and height as well as turns to the use of helix.

Step 1: Ribbon ➤ Home tab ➤ Draw ➤ Helix.

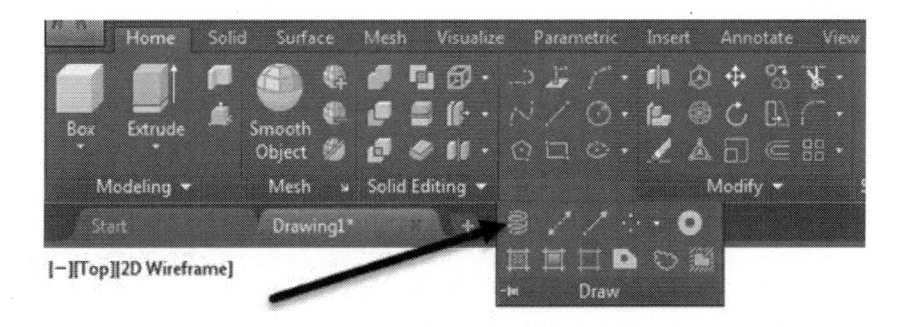

Figure 308: helix tool icon

Step 2: Click point for center base point.
Step 3: 20 Enter for base radius.
Step 4: 30 Enter for top radius.
Step 5: T Enter for helix turns.
Step 6: 10 Enter for turns.
Step 7: 50 Enter for height.

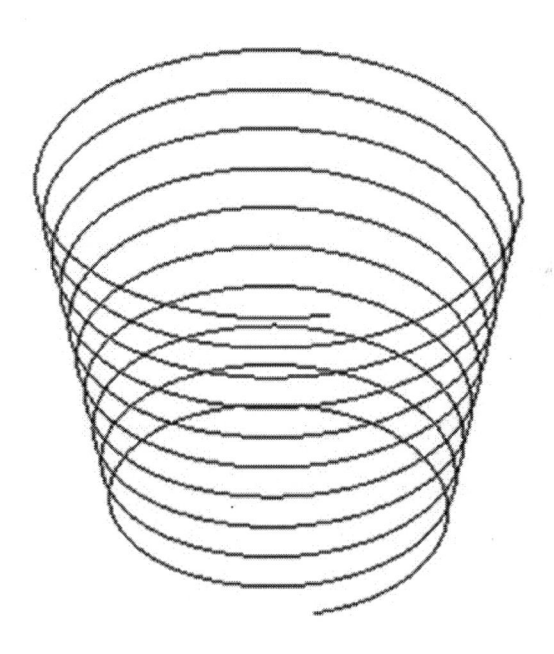

Figure 309: helix

CONE

Cone command is used to create circular cone. To create cone firstly give radius after that give height of cone.

Step 1: Ribbon ➢ Home tab ➢ Modeling ➢ Cone.

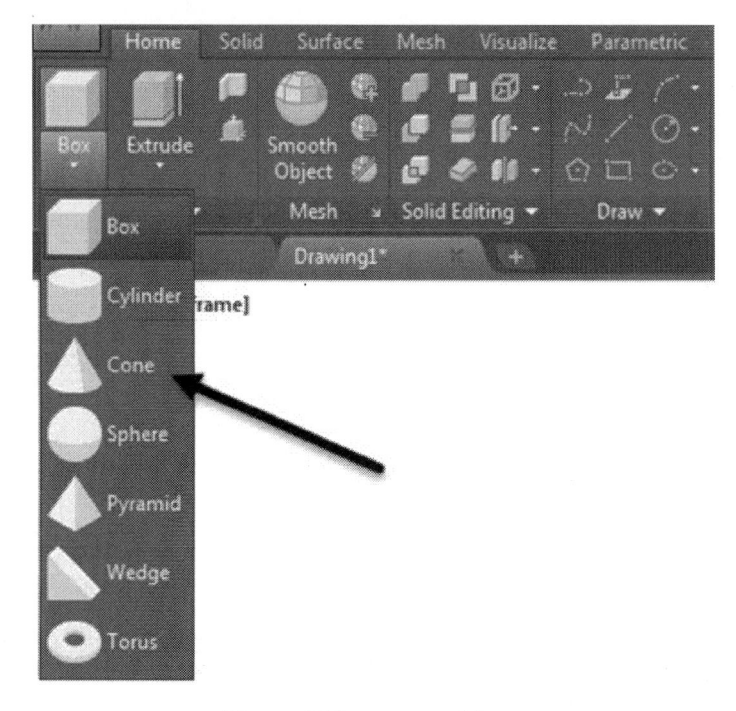

Figure 310: cone tool icon

Step 2: Click point for center point.
Step 3: 20 Enter for cone radius.

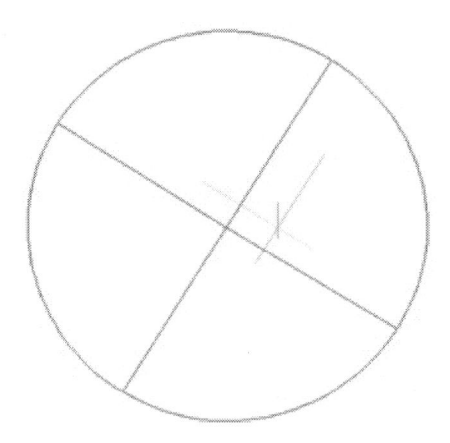

Figure 311: cone radius

Step 4: 40 Enter for cone height.

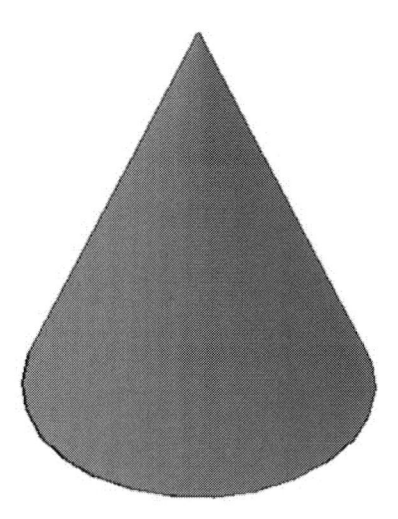

Figure 312: cone

TORUS

Torus command is used to create tube and give radius of circular tube and then give radius its thickness.

Step 1: Ribbon ➤ Home tab ➤ Modeling ➤ Torus.

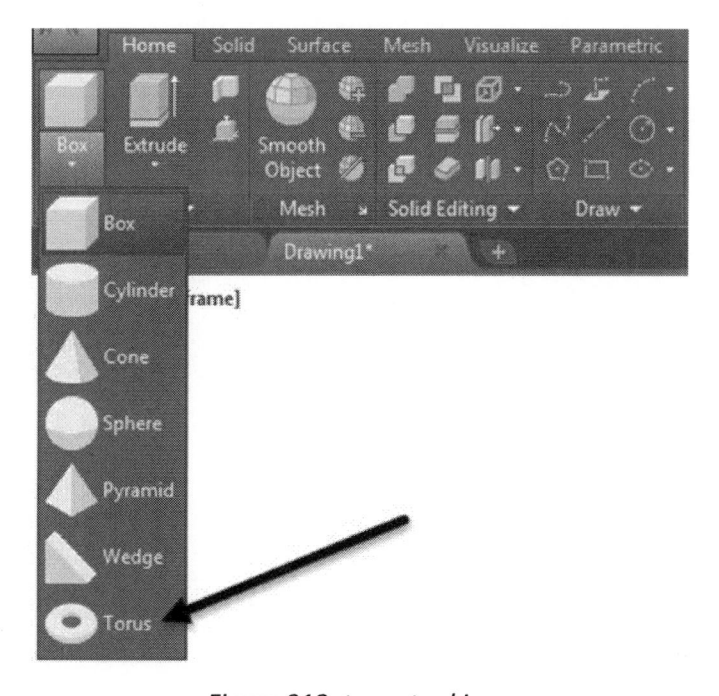

Figure 313: torus tool icon

Step 2: Click point for center point.
Step 3: 20 Enter for torus radius.

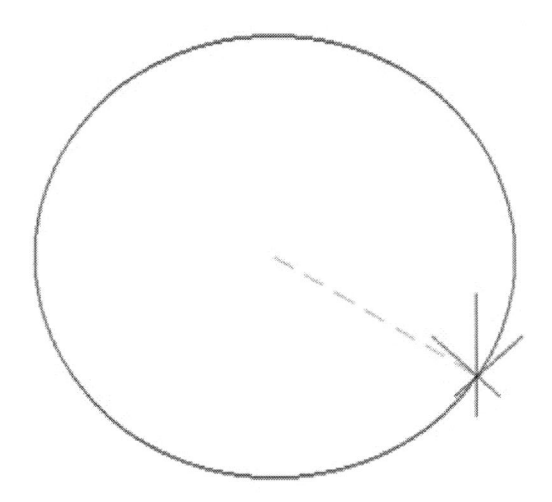

Figure 314: torus radius

Step 4: 5 Enter for tube radius.

Figure 315: torus

PYRAMID

Pyramid command is just like cone, but cone is circular while pyramid have edge, it has at least 3 edge and can up to maximum 32.

Step 1: RibbonHome tab ➤ Modeling ➤ Pyramid.

AutoCAD 2019 Training Guide **145**

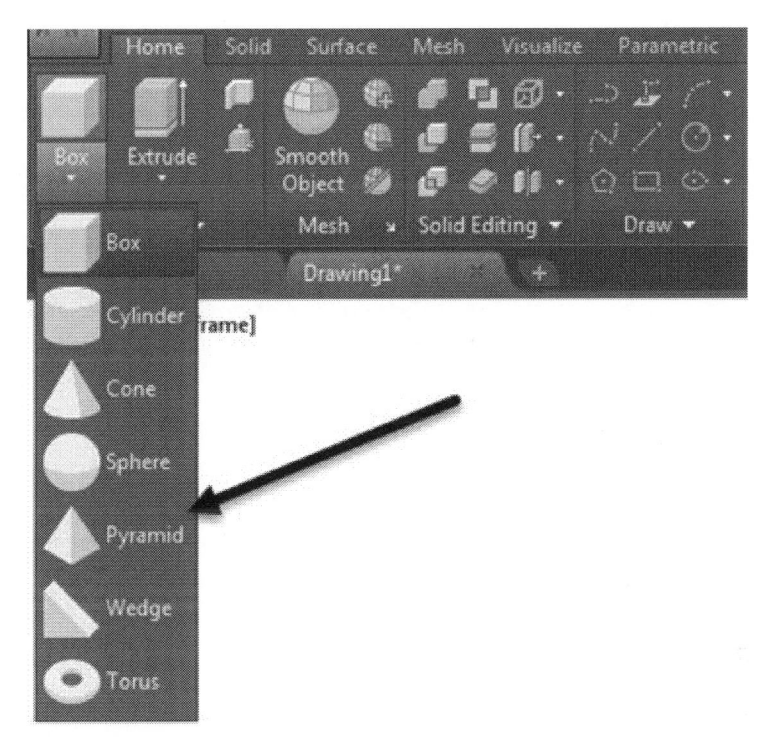

Figure 316: pyramid tool icon

Step 2: Click point for center point.
Step 3: 10 Enter for base radius.

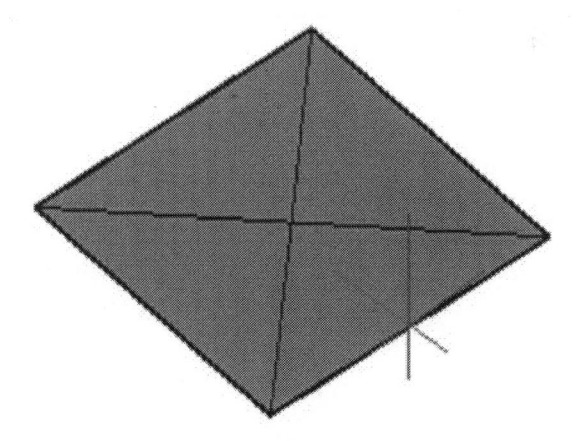

Figure 317: pyramid base radius

Step 4: 20 Enter for height.

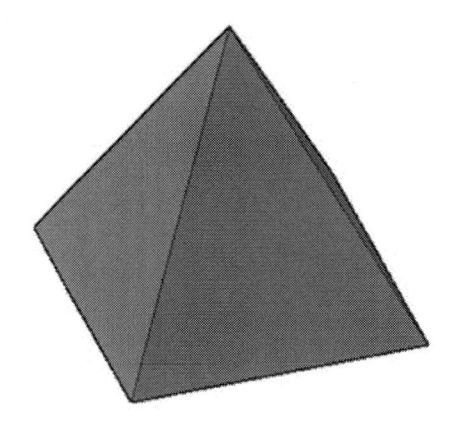

Figure 318: pyramid

WEDGE

Sphere command act like a ball, and create just like circle. But circle is 2d object while sphere is a circular shape solid 3d object, and created by giving center and radius.

Step 1: Ribbon ➢ Home tab ➢ Modeling ➢ Wedge.

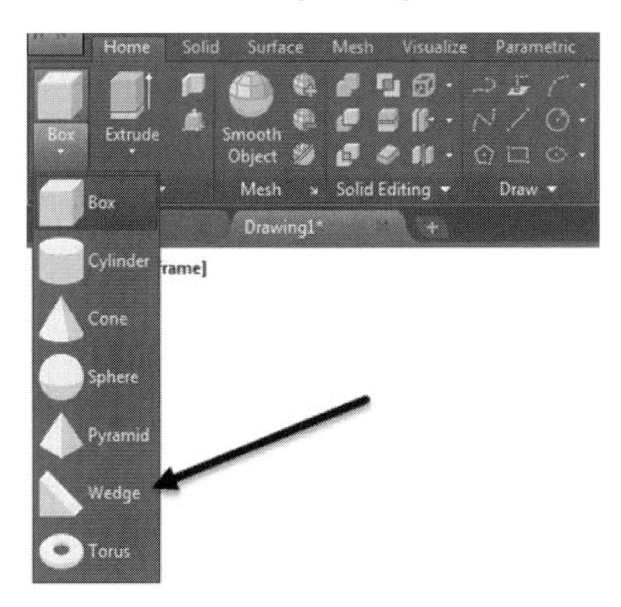

Figure 319: wedge tool icon

Step 2: Click first point for wedge corner.
Step 3: L Enter for length option.
Step 4: 40 Enter for length.
Step 5: 20 Enter for width.

AutoCAD 2019 Training Guide **147**

Figure 320: wedge length and width

Step 6: 15 Enter for height.

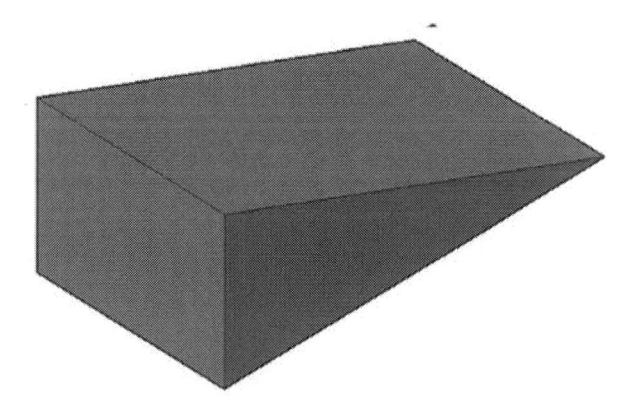

Figure 321: wedge

POLYSOLID

Polysolid command use just like Polyline, but polysolid is a 3d object so we also consider or give thickness and height.

It used to create wall or simple plane (surface).

Step 1: Ribbon ➤ Home tab ➤ Modeling ➤ Polysolid.

Figure 322: polysolid tool icon

Step 2: H Enter for height option.
Step 3: 10' Enter for height.
Step 4: W Enter for width option.
Step 5: 9" Enter for width.
Step 6: Click first point.
Step 7: Specify direction then 60' Enter.

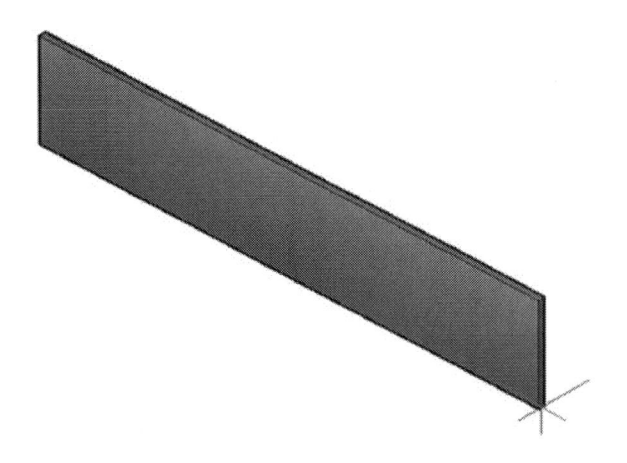

Figure 323: single polysolid

Step 8: Specify direction then 30' Enter.
Step 9: Specify direction then 60' Enter.
Step 10: C Enter for close.

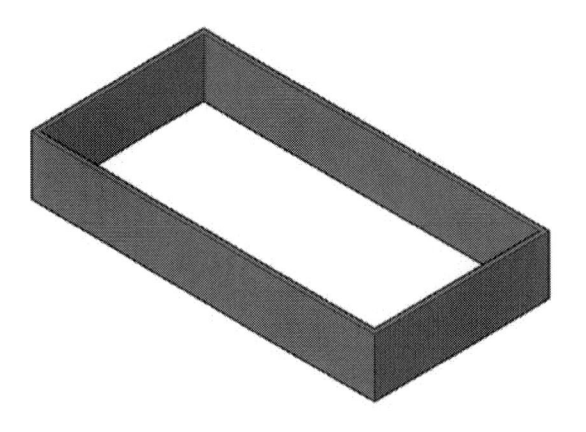

Figure 324: polysolid

SPHERE

Sphere command act like a ball, and create just like circle. But circle is 2d object

AutoCAD 2019 Training Guide **149**

while sphere is a circular shape solid 3d object, and created by giving center and radius.

Step 1: Ribbon ➤ Home tab ➤ Modeling ➤ Sphere.

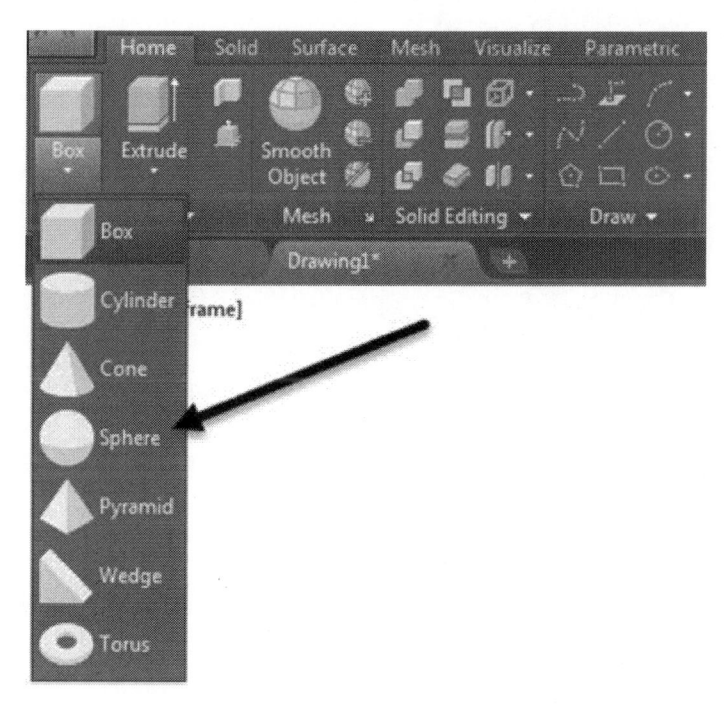

Figure 325: sphere tool icon

Step 2: Click point for center point.
Step 3: 20 Enter for radius.

Figure 326: sphere

EXTRUDE

Extrude command is used to increase the height of object like line, circle, rectangle, arc, spline etc.

That is by increasing height we convert those 2D object into 3D.

For example. If you take a circle and extend the height you can convert it in to cylinder (3D object) or convert a rectangle into box (I.e. 3D object).

Step 1: Ribbon ➤ Home tab ➤ Modeling ➤ Extrude.

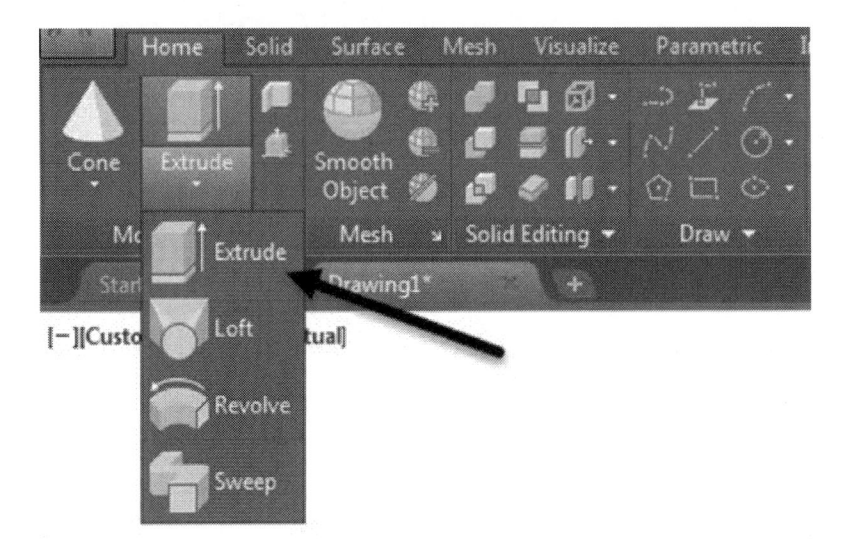

Figure 327: extrude tool icon

Step 2: Select 2D object then Enter.

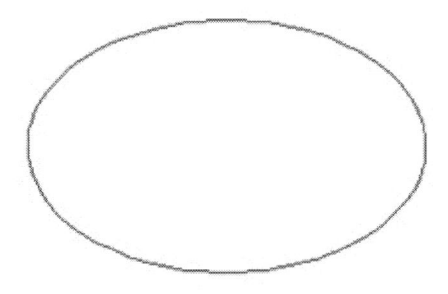

Figure 328: circle

Step 3: 30 Enter for extrude height.

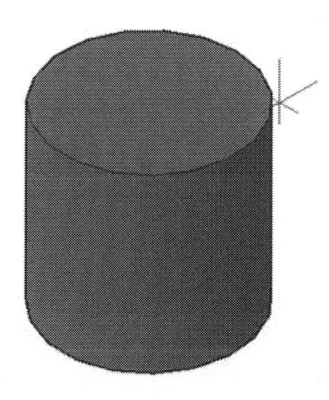

Figure 329: use of extrude

PRESSPULL

Presspull act like extrude command with a significancial difference, it allow to increase or decrease any face of the 3d object while extrude allow only increase in height of 2d.

Step 1: Ribbon ➤ Home tab ➤ Modeling ➤ Presspull.

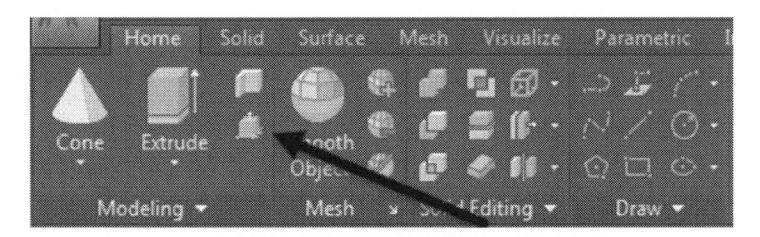

Figure 330: presspull tool icon

Step 2: Select face for presspull.

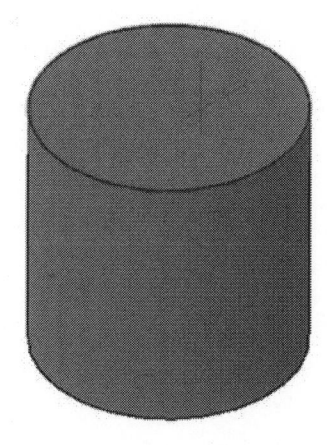

Figure 331: cylinder

Step 3: 10 Enter for extrusion height.

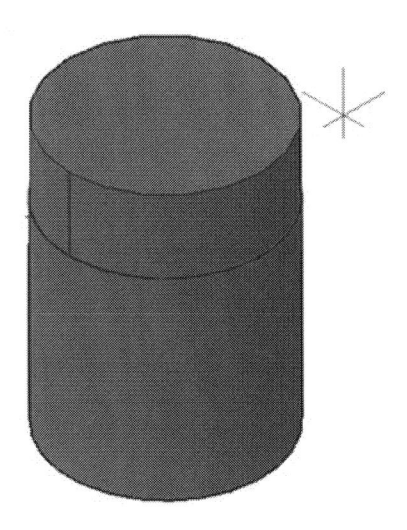

Figure 332: increases height

LOFT

Loft command is used to convert two or more than two 2d object into single 3d object. Loft command work on any 2d object which is built upon

Any 3rd object by selecting simultaneously both the object and then convert in single 3d object.

To use this command both object have different Z-axis (i.e. height must be different).

Step 1: Ribbon ➤ Home tab ➤ Modeling ➤ Loft.

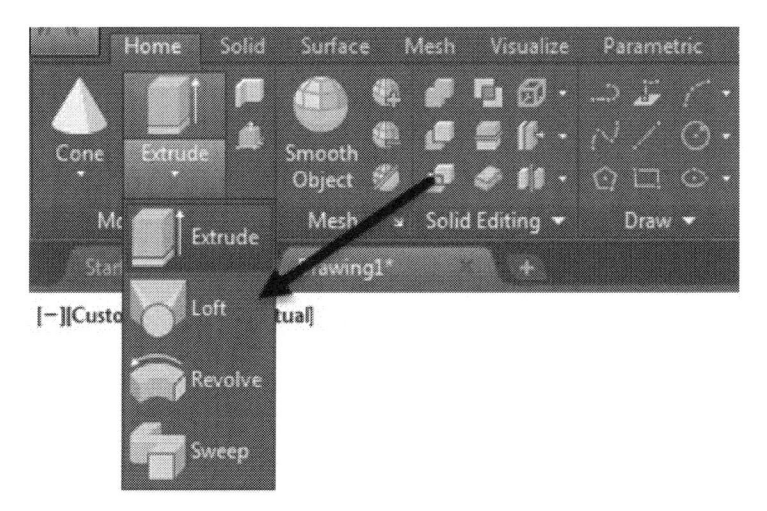

Figure 333: loft tool icon

AutoCAD 2019 Training Guide **153**

Step 2: Select first object.

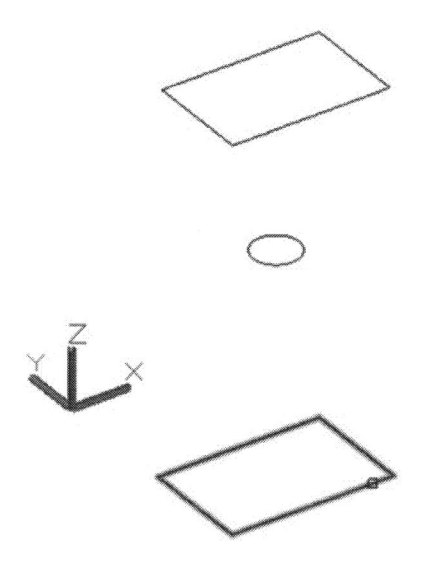

Figure 334: select first object

Step 3: Select second object.

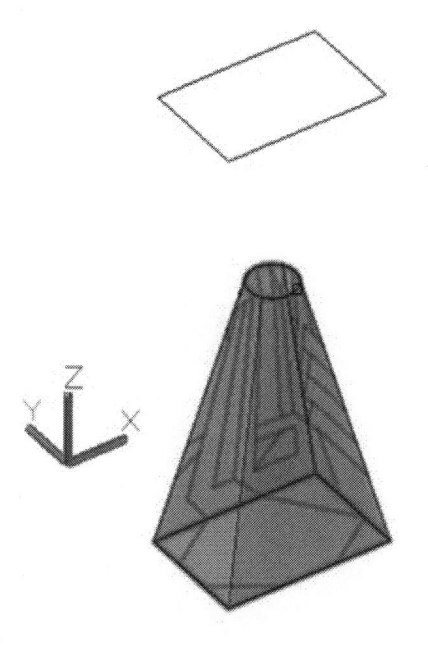

Figure 335: Select second object.

Step 4: Select third object.

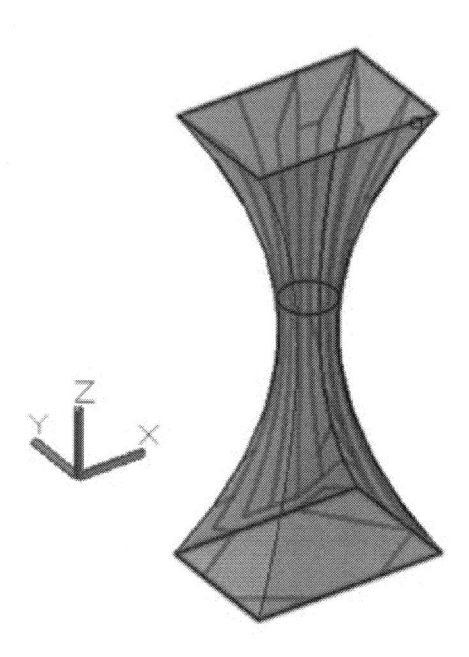

Figure 336: Select third object.

Step 5: Double enter.

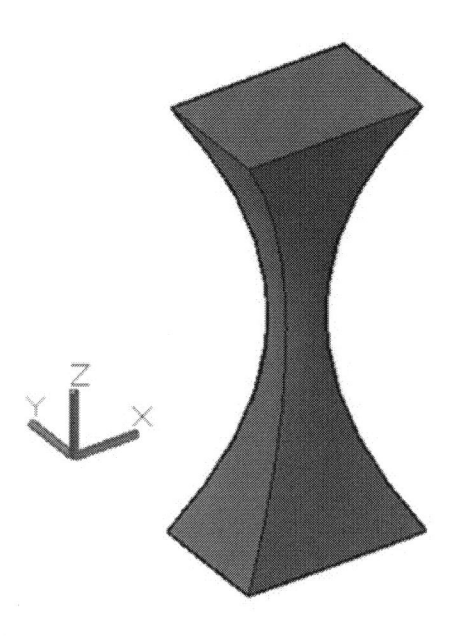

Figure 337: loft object

AutoCAD 2019 Training Guide   155

REVOLVE

Revolve command is use to convert a 2d object into 3d by revolving that object on one of any axis with respect to 2 distinguish point of that axes.

That is choose two different point on that targeted axis and revolve the object circle with respect to that point.

Step 1: Ribbon ➢ Home tab ➢ Modeling ➢ Revolve.

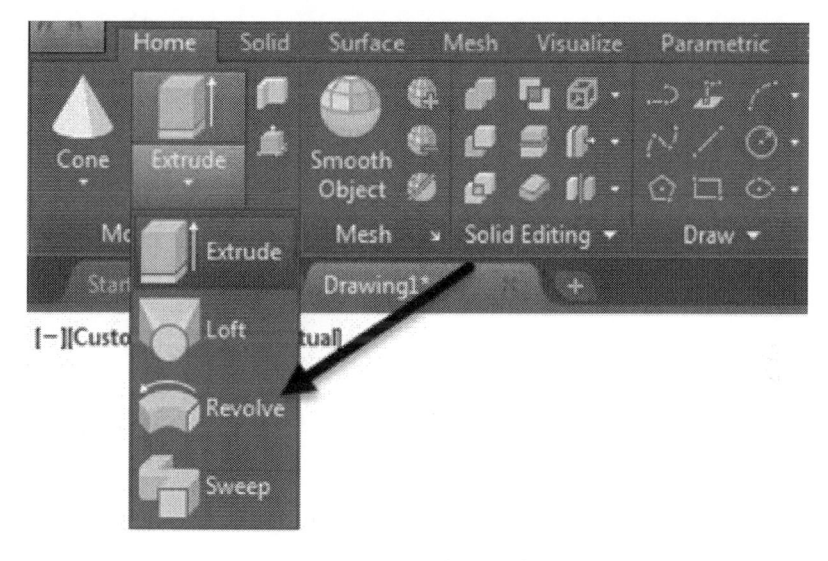

Figure 338: revolve tool icon

Step 2: Select 2D object then Enter.

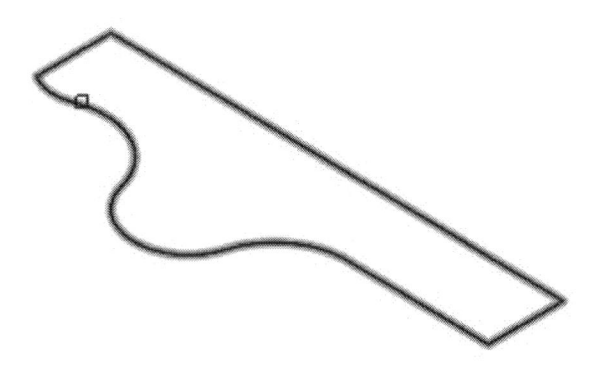

Figure 339: select object

Step 3: Click first point for Axis.

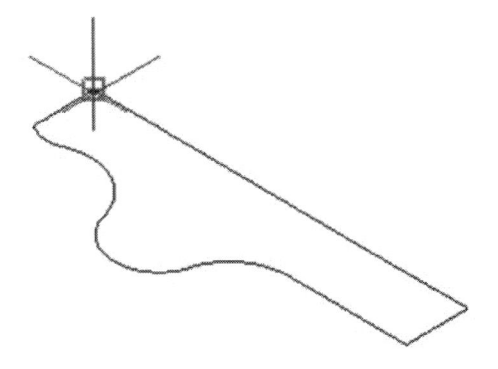

Figure 340: specify axis first point

Step 4: Click second point for Axis.

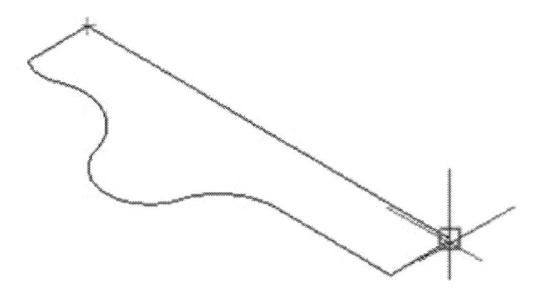

Figure 341: specify axis second point

Step 5: 360 Enter for Circular angle.

Figure 342: revolve object

SWEEP

Sweep command is used to convert into 3d object by sweeping anyone 2d object to another 2d object.

Step 1: Ribbon ➢ Home tab ➢ Modeling ➢ Sweep.

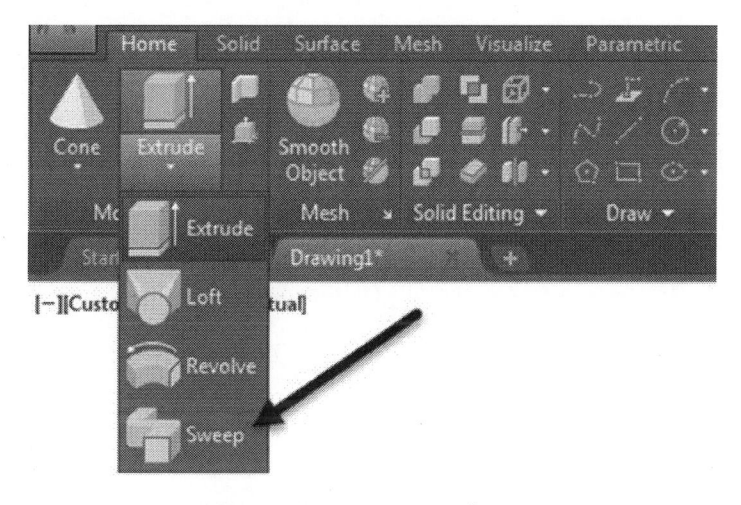

Figure 343: sweep tool icon

Step 2: Select object to sweep then Enter.

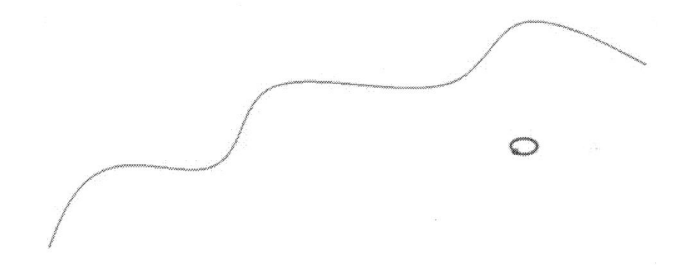

Figure 344: select circle

Step 3: Select sweep path.

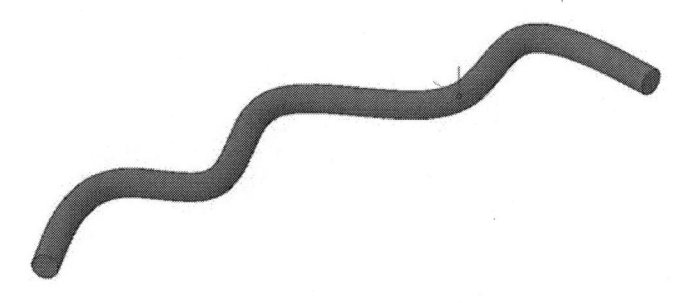

Figure 345: sweep

CHAPTER-10

3D Modify Tools

3D MOVE

3d move command is use to move an object along any of the 3 axises. To do that select the object first then select 3d move object and you will found all 3 axes appear, now move the object along the desired axes by clicking on that axes and provide move distance manually.

Step 1: Ribbon ➢ Home tab ➢ Modify ➢ 3D move.

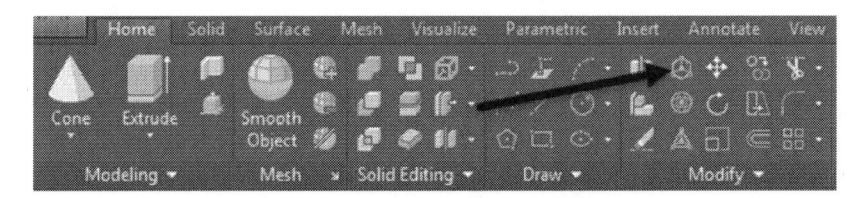

Figure 346: 3D move tool icon

Step 2: Select object then Enter.
Step 3: Click Z Axis for Z direction move.

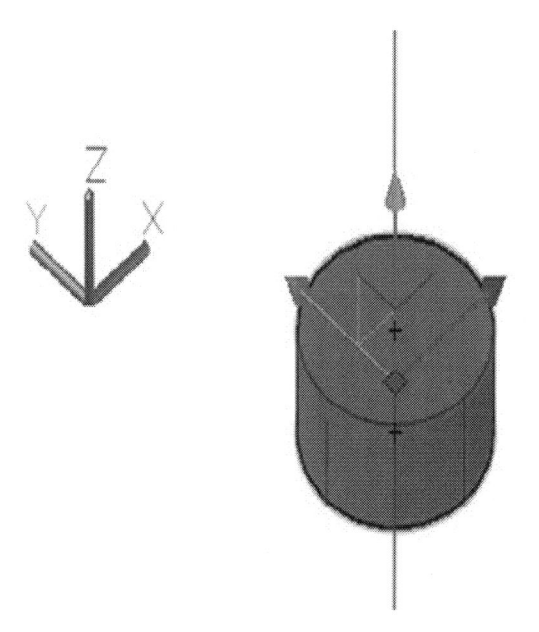

Figure 347: 3D move object

Step 4: 20 Enter for distance.

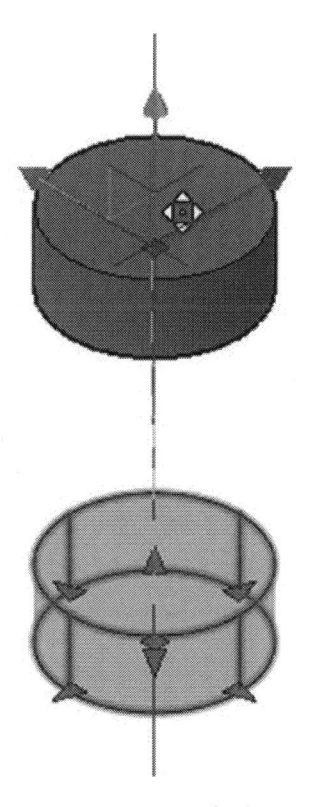

Figure 348: specify distance

3D ROTATE

3d rotate command is use to rotate an object along any of the 3 axises. To do that, select the object first then click on 3d rotate and you see object and found all 3 axes appear, now rotate the object along desired axes by click on that axes and enter the angle manually as

More you like to rotate from an angle.

Step 1: Ribbon ➤ Home tab ➤ Modify3D rotate.

Figure 349: 3D rotate tool icon

Step 2: Select object then Enter.

Step 3: Click Axis for rotate.
Step 4: 900 Enter for rotate angle.

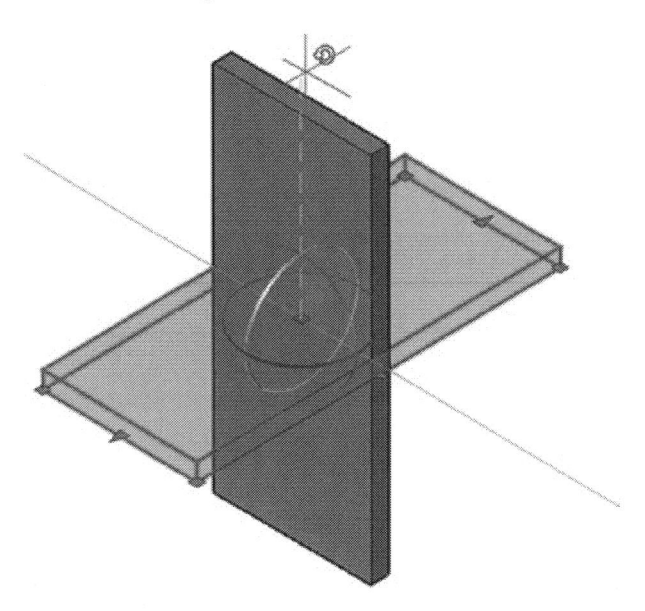

Figure 350: object rotate

3D SCALE

3d scale command is used to scale an object along any of three (x or y or z) axis, you can change scale according to length, width or height.

Step 1: Ribbon ➤ Home tab ➤ Modify ➤ 3D scale.

Figure 351: 3D scale tool icon

Step 2: Select object then Enter.
Step 3: Click base point.
Step 4: Pick axis.
Step 5: R Enter for reference option.
Step 6: 1 Enter for reference length.
Step 7: 2 Enter for new length.

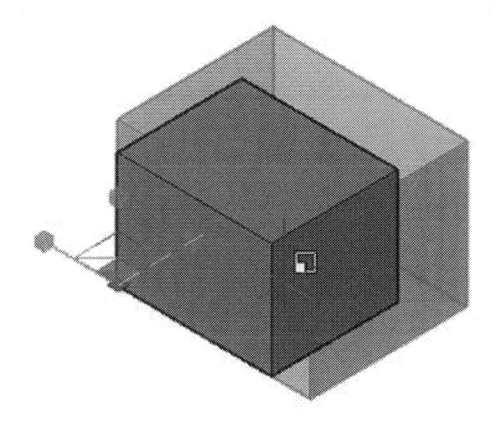

Figure 352: object scale

3D MIRROR

3D mirror command is used to create reflection or mirror object. But 3d mirror is different than Mirror, we can also mirror an object along z axis.

Step 1: Ribbon ➢ Home tab ➢ Modify ➢ 3D mirror.

Figure 353: 3D mirror tool icon

Step 2: Select object then Enter.

Figure 354: select sphere

Step 3: Click first base point.
Step 4: Click second point.
Step 5: Click third point.

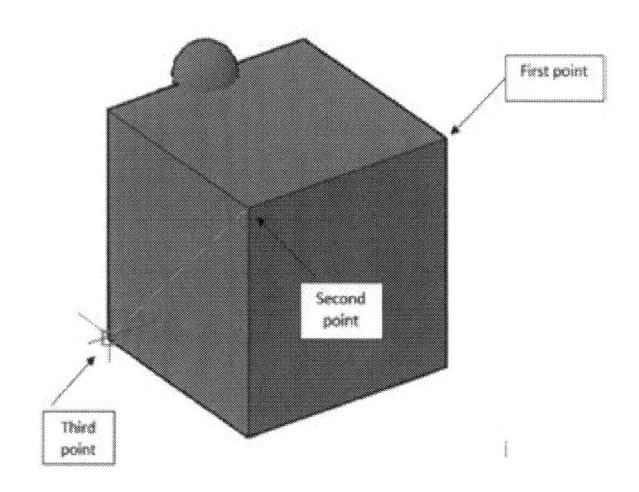

Figure 355: specify point

Step 6: N Enter for No, delete source object.

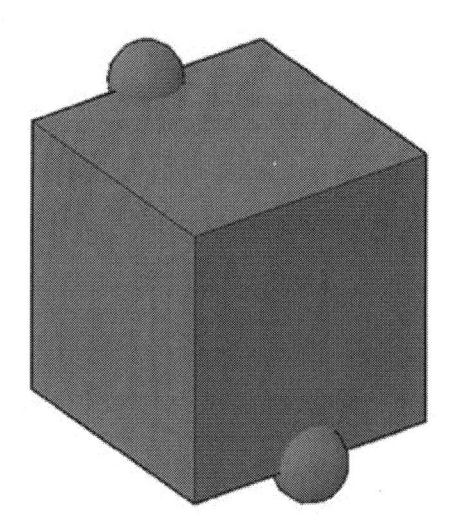

Figure 356: after 3d mirror

3D ARRAY

3D array command is used to create multiple copy of an object simultaneously along all of 3 axis.

Step 1: 3d array Enter.

AutoCAD 2019 Training Guide **163**

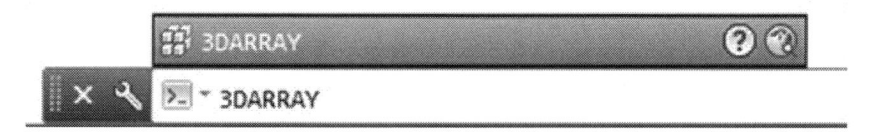

Figure 357: 3D array command

Step 2: Select object then Enter.

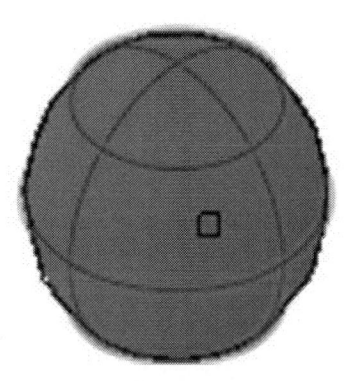

Figure 358: select sphere

Step 3: R Enter for rectangular option.
Step 4: 5 Enter for Rows number.
Step 5: 4 Enter for Columns number.
Step 6: 3 Enter for Levels number.
Step 7: 30 Enter for distance between rows.
Step 8: 30 Enter for distance between columns.
Step 9: 30 Enter for distance between levels.

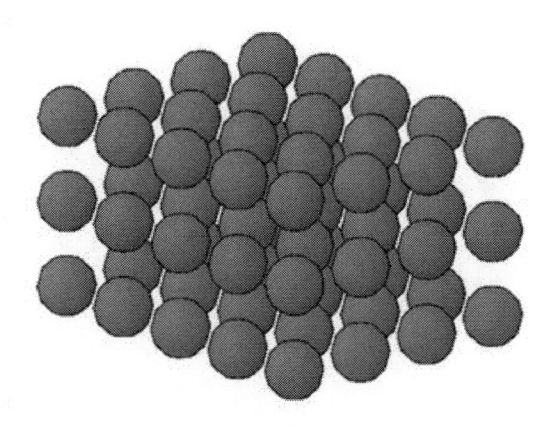

Figure 359: after array

SUBTRACT

Subtract command is used to cut the intersected part of the overlapping 3d object, For example, if you have to make a circular hole in a box then you have to intersect an object of similar radius then subtract it.

Step 1: Ribbon ➤ Home tab ➤ Solid editing ➤ Subtract.

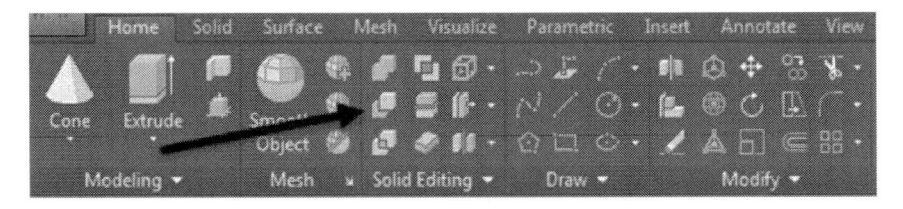

Figure 360: subtract tool icon

Step 2: Select first object then Enter.

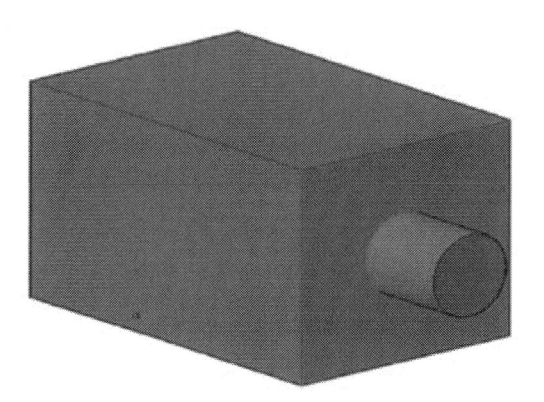

Figure 361: select box

Step 3: Select second object.

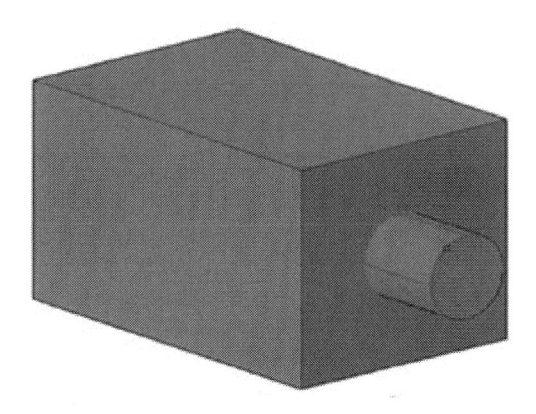

Figure 362: select cylinder

AutoCAD 2019 Training Guide

Step 4: Then Enter.

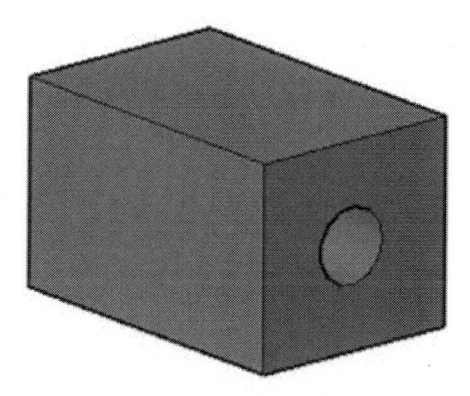

Figure 363: after subtract

UNION

Union command is use to joint or merge two or more than two 3d object. By applying this command all participated object are seems as a block.

Step 1: Ribbon ➢ Home tab ➢ Solid editing ➢ Union.

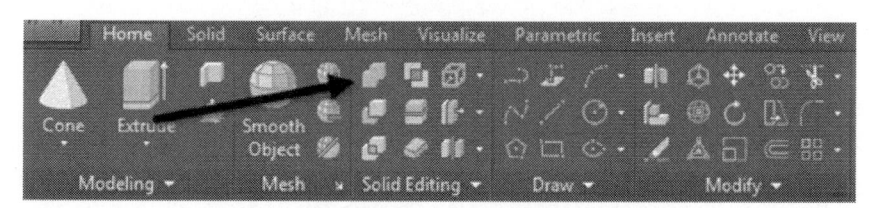

Figure 364: union tool icon

Step 2: Select first object.
Step 3: Select second object.

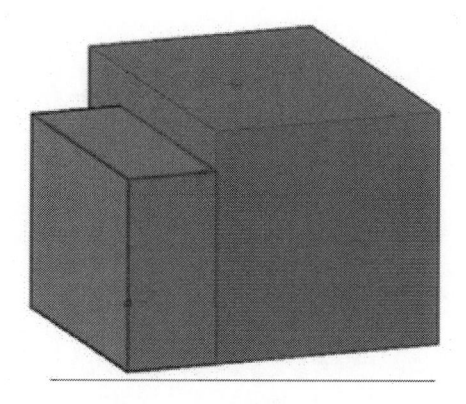

Figure 365: select object

Step 4: Then Enter.

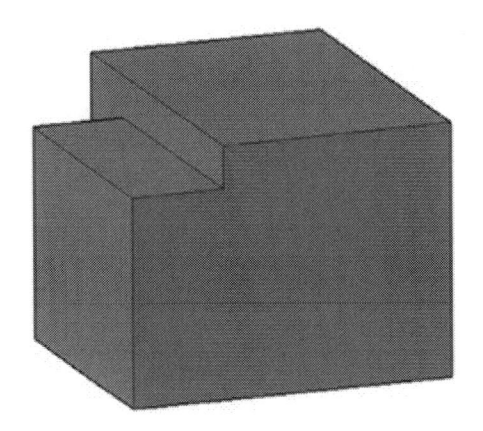

Figure 366: after union

INTERSECT

Intersect command is use to cut the rest part (i.e. except intersected part) of two 3d object who is intersecting each other.

Step 1: Ribbon ➤ Home tab ➤ Solid editing ➤ Intersect.

Figure 367: intersect tool icon

Step 2: Select first object.
Step 3: Select second object.

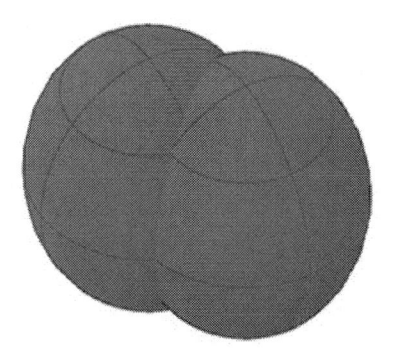

Figure 368: select sphere

Step 4: Then Enter.

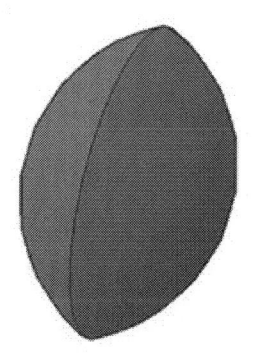

Figure 369: after intersect

SLICE

Slice command is use to cut an 3d Object, and remove the isolated part.

Step 1: Ribbon ➢ Home tab ➢ Solid editing ➢ Slice.

Figure 370: slice tool icon

Step 2: Select object then Press Enter.
Step 3: Pick first point.
Step 4: Pick second point.

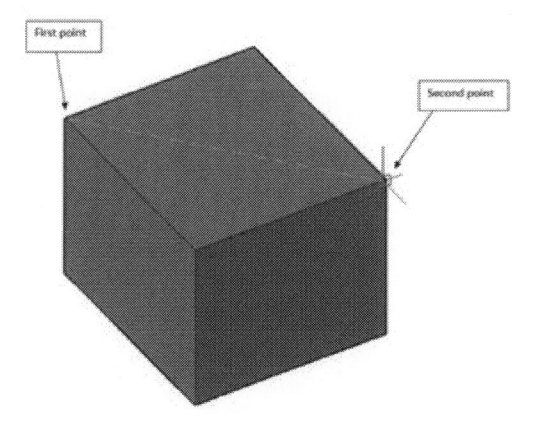

Figure 371: specify slice points

Step 5: Specify a point on desired side.

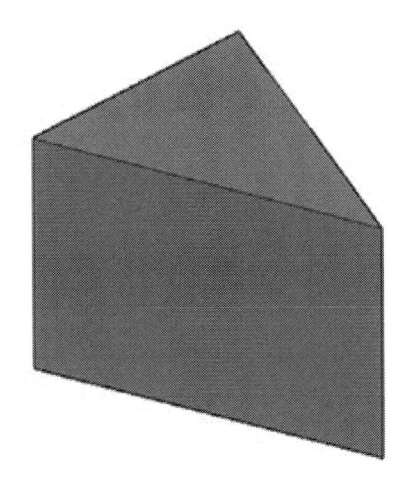

Figure 372: after slice

FILLET EDGE

Step 1: Ribbon- Solid- Solid editing- Fillet Edge.

Figure 373: Fillet edge tool icon

Step 2: Select edge then Press Enter.
Step 3: R Enter for radius option.
Step 4: Enter for fillet radius then Press Enter.

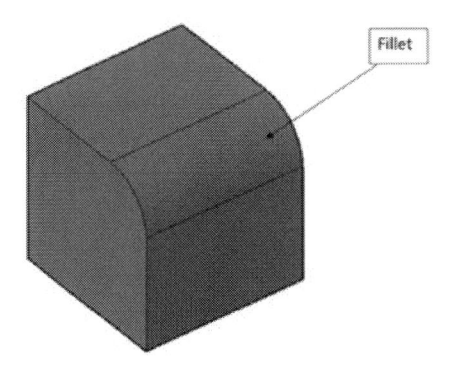

Figure 374: fillet use

CHAMFER EDGE

Step 1: Ribbon: Solid ➢ Solid editing ➢ Chamfer Edge.

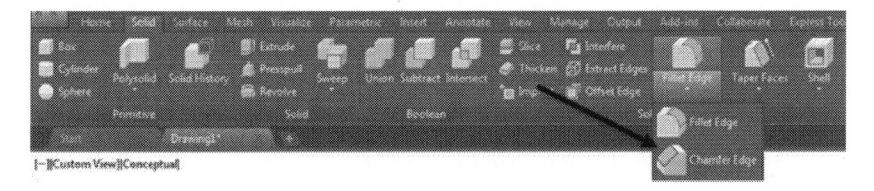

Figure 375: chamfer edge tool icon

Step 2: Select edge then Press Enter.

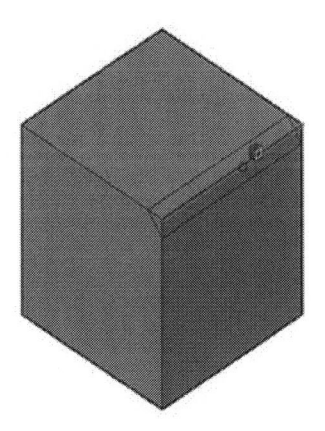

Figure 376: select edge

Step 3: D Enter for distance option.
Step 4: 2 Enter for base distance.
Step 5: 2 Enter for other distance then double Enter.

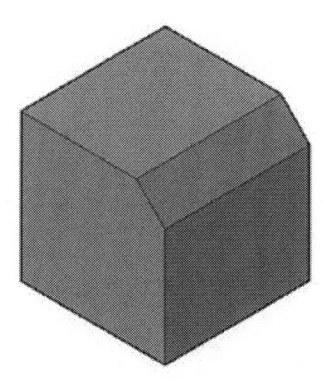

Figure 377: after chamfer

CHAPTER-11
3D Surface & Mesh

NETWORK

A network surface can be created between a network of curves or between the edges of other 3D surfaces or solids.

Step 1: Ribbon ➤ Surface ➤ Create ➤ Network.

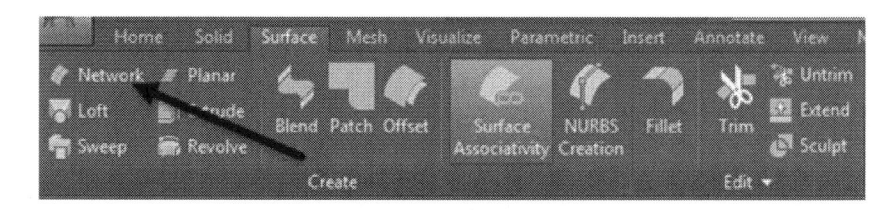

Figure 378: network tool icon

Step 2: Select all first direction edges then Press Enter.

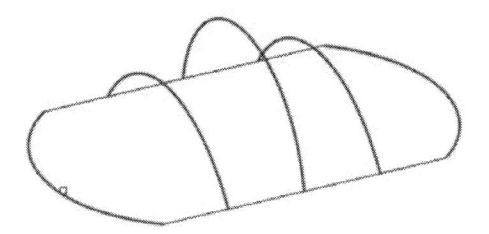

Figure 379: select all arc

Step 3: Select all second direction edges then Press Enter.

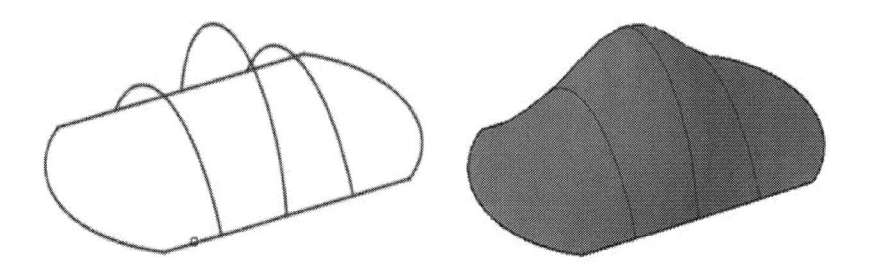

Figure 380: select line

PLANAR

Create planar surfaces in the space between edge sub objects splines and other 2D and 3D curve.

With PLANESURF, planar surfaces can be created from multiple closed objects and the edges of surface or solid objects. During creation, you can specify the tangency and bulge magnitude.

Step 1: Ribbon ➤ Surface ➤ Create ➤ Planar.

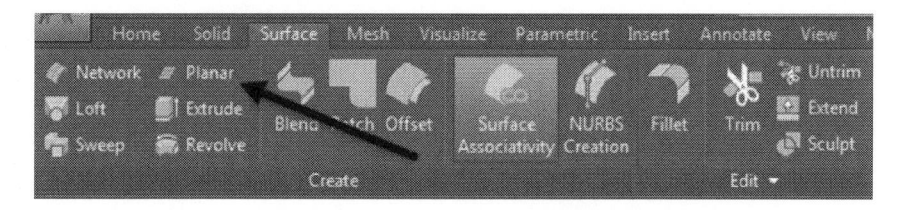

Figure 381: planar tool icon

Step 2: O Enter for object option.

Step 3: Select object then Press Enter.

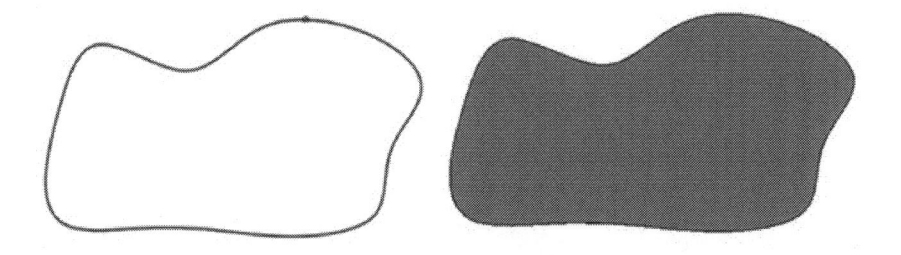

Figure 382: use of planar

SURFACE BLEND

Creates a continuous blend surface between two existing surfaces.

Step 1: Ribbon ➤ Surface ➤ Create ➤ Blend.

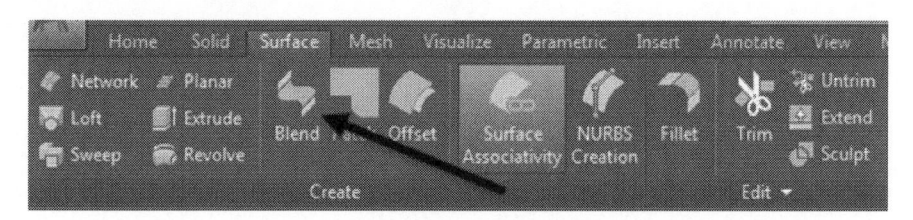

Figure 383: blend tool icon

Step 2: Select first edge then Press Enter.

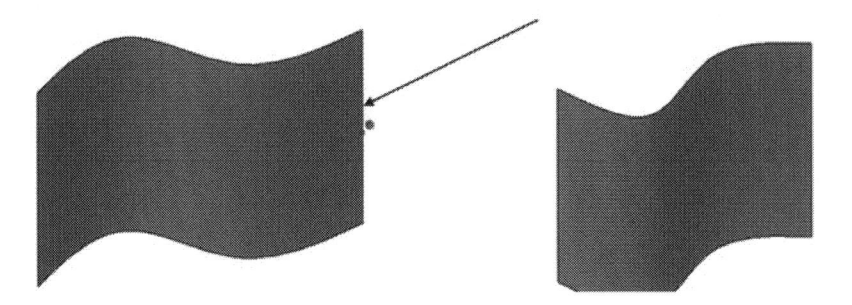

Figure 384: select edge of first surface

Step 3: Select second edge then Press Enter.

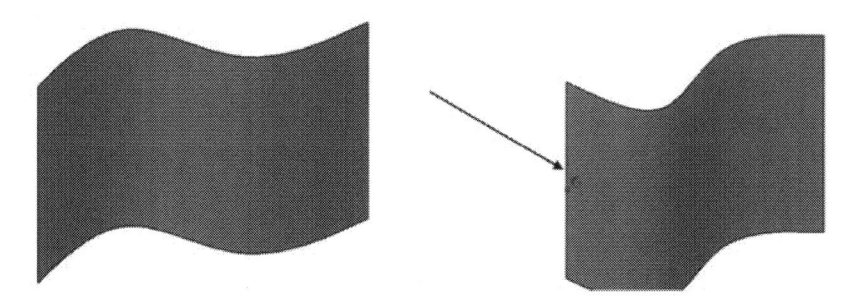

Figure 385: select edge of second surface

Step 4: Enter.

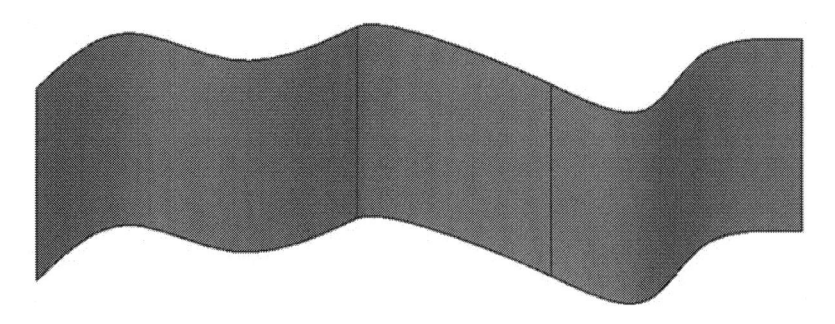

Figure 386: after blend

PATCH

Creates a new surface by fitting a cap over a surface edge that forms a closed loop.

Step 1: Ribbon ➤ Surface ➤ Create ➤ Patch.

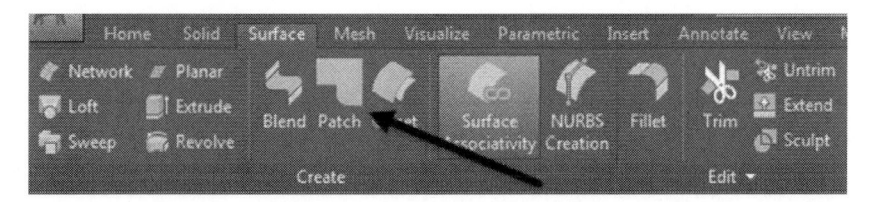

Figure 387: patch tool icon

Step 2: Select surface edge.

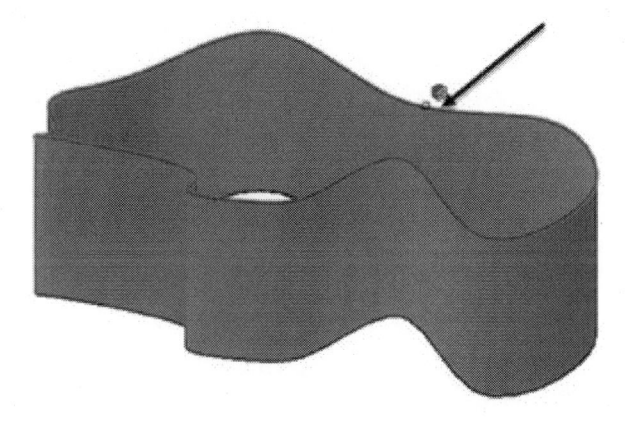

Figure 388: select edge of surface

Step 3: Double Enter.

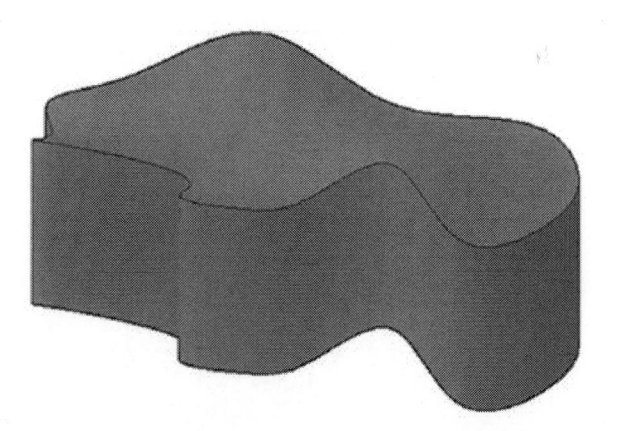

Figure 389: after patch

SURFACE OFFSET

Create a parallel surface or solid by setting an offset distance from a surface.
Step 1: Ribbon ➤ Surface ➤ Create ➤ Offset.

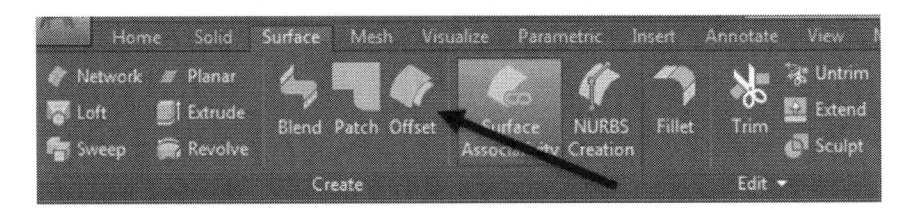

Figure 390: offset tool icon

Step 2: Select Object then enter.

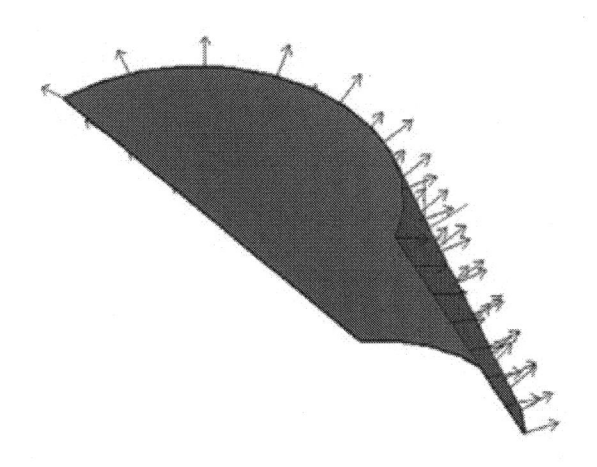

Figure 391: select surface

Step 3: 0.1 Enter for offset distance.

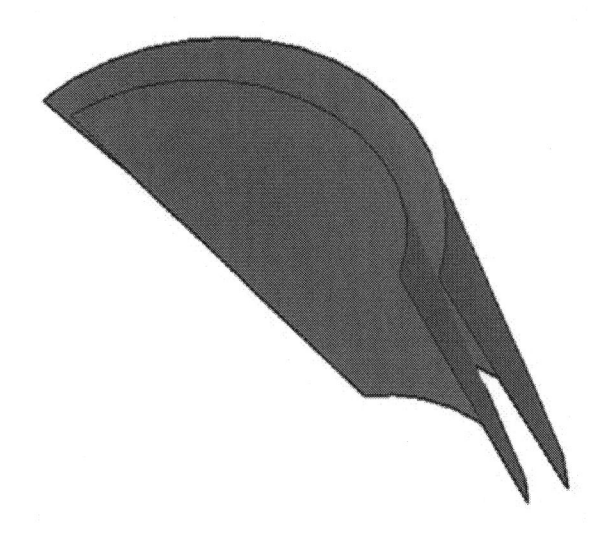

Figure 392: after offset

SURFACE EXTEND

Step 1: Ribbon ➢ Surface ➢ Edit ➢ Extend.

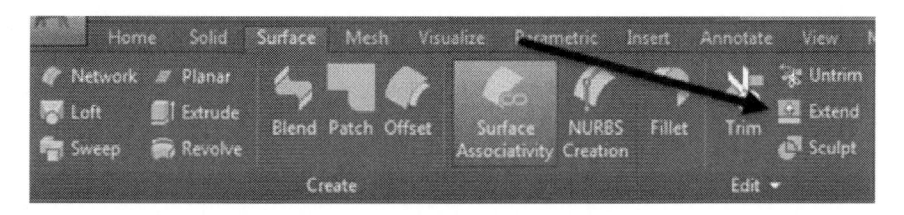

Figure 393: surface extend tool icon

Step 2: Select surface edge then enter.

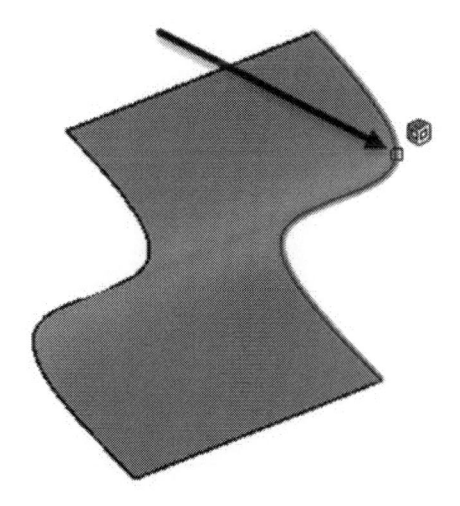

Figure 394: select edge

Step 3: 10 Enter for extend distance.

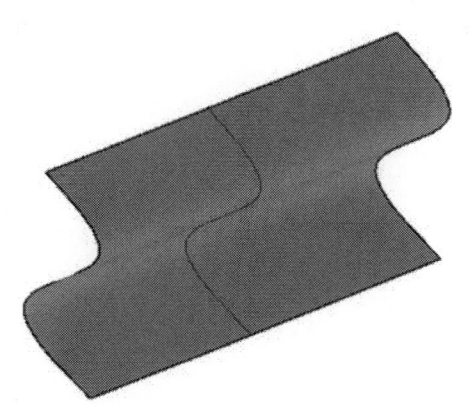

Figure 395: after extend

SURFACE TRIM

Step 1: Ribbon ➤ Surface ➤ Edit ➤ Trim.

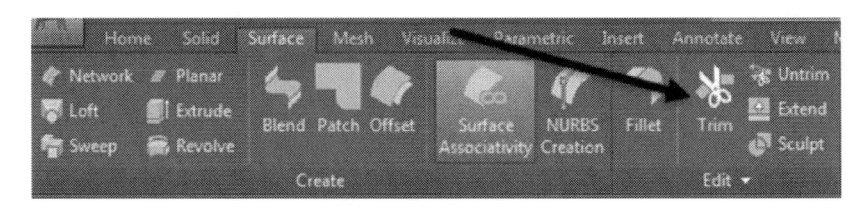

Figure 396: trim tool icon

Step 2: Select surface then enter.

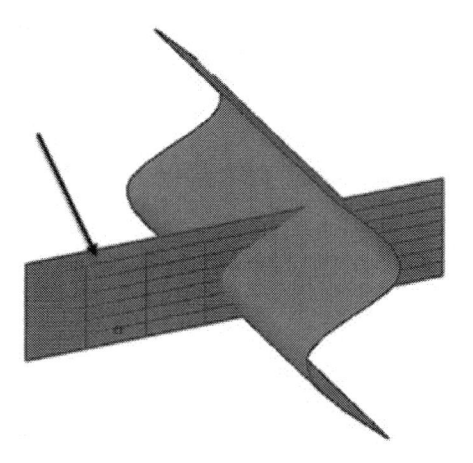

Figure 397: select plane surface

Step 3: Select cutting curves then enter.

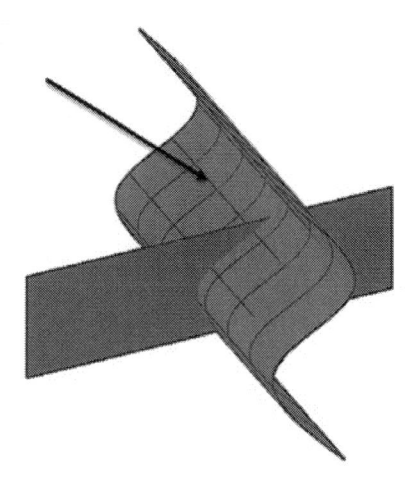

Figure 398: select curve surface

Step 4: Select area to trim.

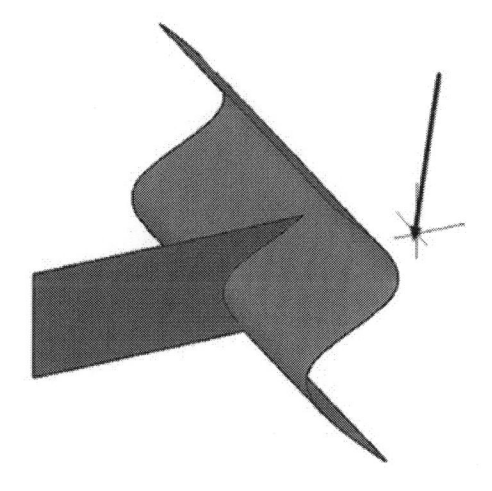

Figure 399: select trim area

SURFACE FILLET

Step 1: Ribbon ➤ Surface ➤ Edit ➤ Fillet.

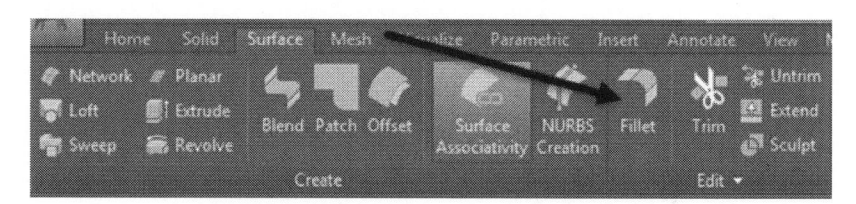

Figure 400: sarface fillet tool icon

Step 2: Select first surface.

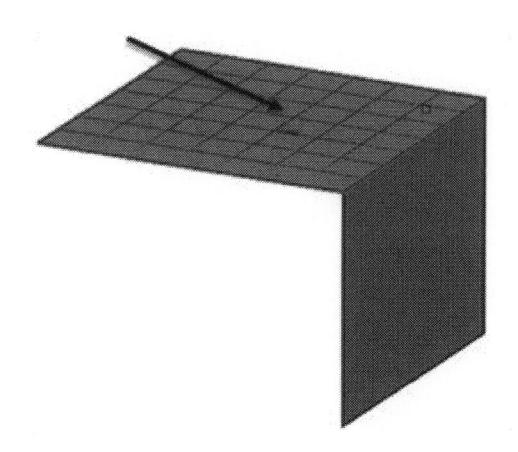

Figure 401: select first surface

Step 3: Select second surface.

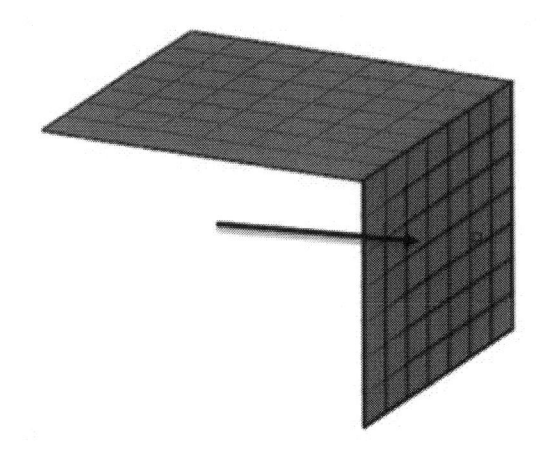

Figure 402: select second surface

Step 4: R Enter for radius option.
Step 5: 0.5 Enter for radius then again enter.

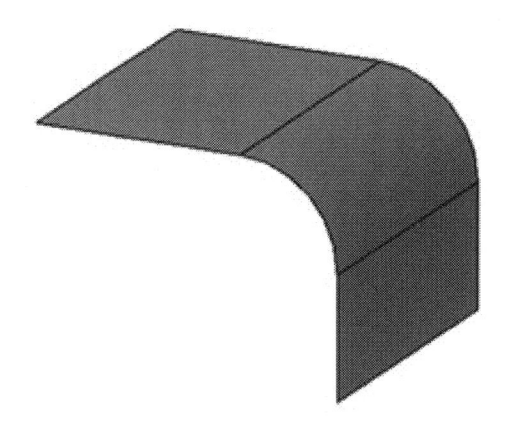

Figure 403: after fillet

CHAPTER-12

What Are The New Features Introduced in AutoCAD 2019?

DWG Compare

The same file as two, in which some changes have been made. To mark them separately or to fabricate both files, the DWG compare Tool is used.

Step 1: Ribbon ➤ Collaborate ➤ Compare ➤ DWG compare.

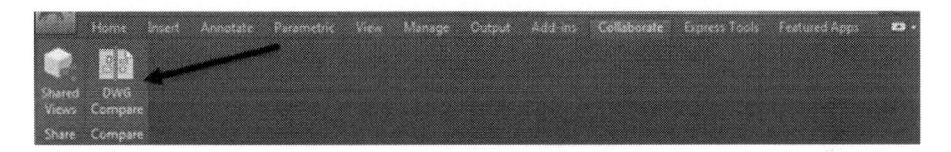

Figure 404 Dwg compare tool icon

Step 2: Click on browse button and select first file for compare.

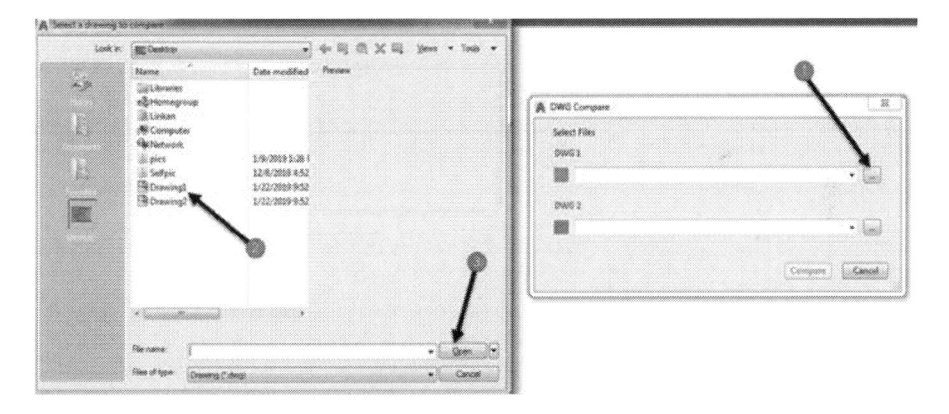

Figure 405: select first file

Step 3: again click on second browse button and select second file for compare.

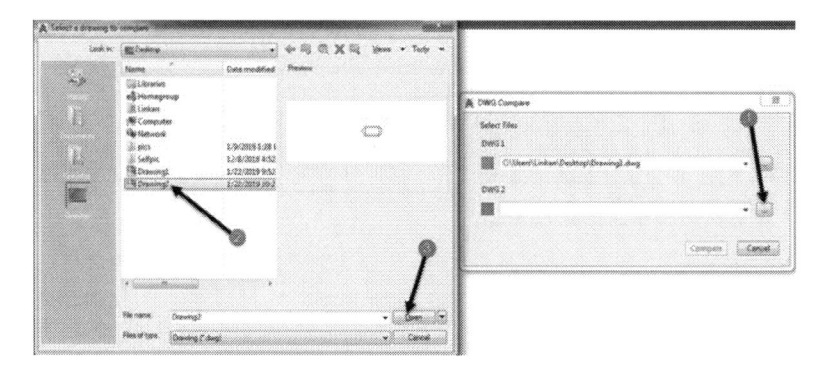

Figure 406: select second file

Step 4: Then click on compare button.

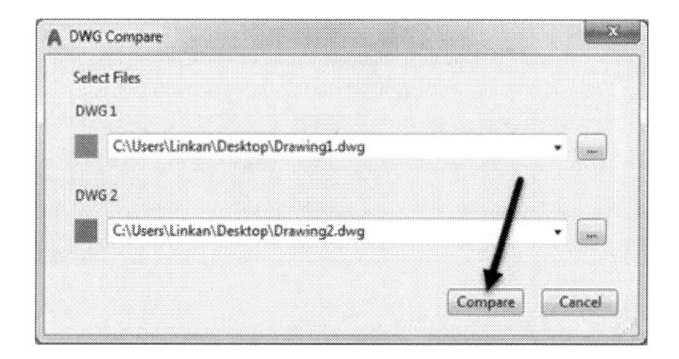

Figure 407: compare tab

Step 5: Now the different of the two files can be seen.

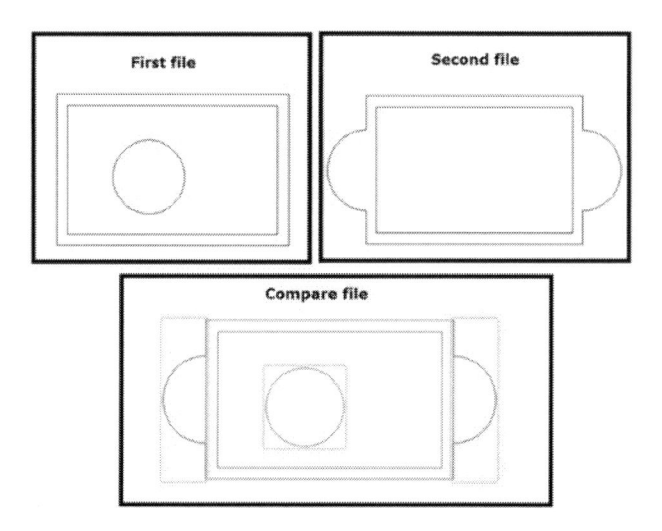

Figure 408: compare file

REVISION CLOUD

Step 1: Ribbon ➢ Home ➢ Draw ➢ Revision cloud.

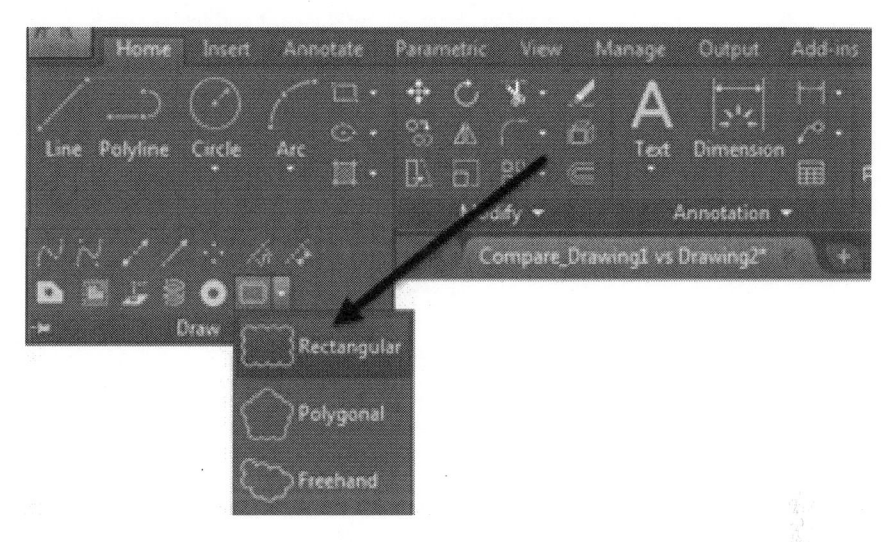

Figure 409: revision cloud tool icon

OR

Command: Revcloud

Step 2: Then R enter for rectangle shape of Revision cloud.

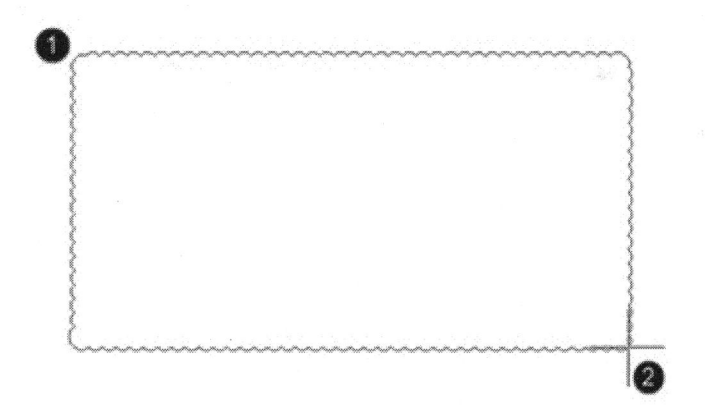

Figure 410: rectangle revision cloud

OR

P enter for Polygon shape Revision cloud.

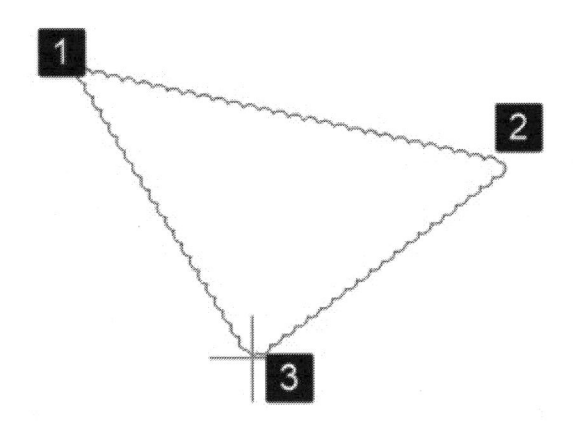

Figure 411: POLYGON SHAPE REVISION CLOUD

SMART DIMENSION

To measure the diameter of a circle as to measure the length of a line; two different tools are required for the same, But with the help of smart dimension's new feature both types of dimension's can be measure with the same tool. I.e. Smart dimension.

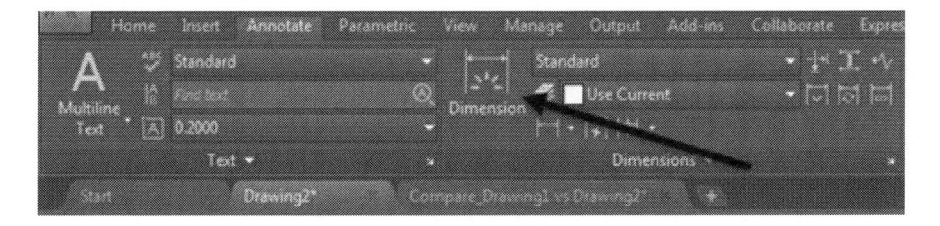

Figure 412: Smart dimension tool icon

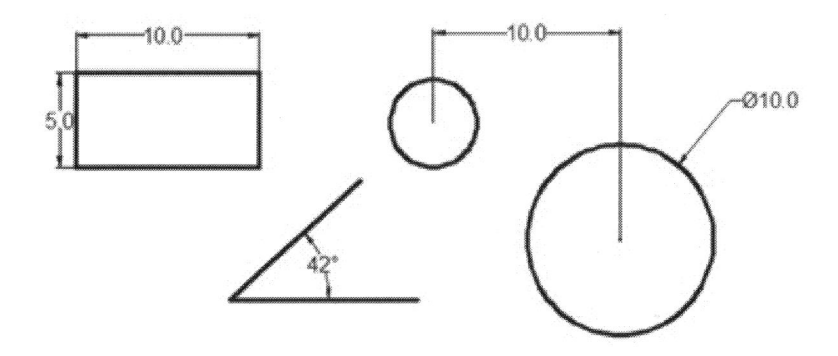

Figure 413: All dimension

GEOMETRIC CENTER (OSNAP)

Geometric any Polygon center point of it is to show. These new features are Object snapping (Osnap).

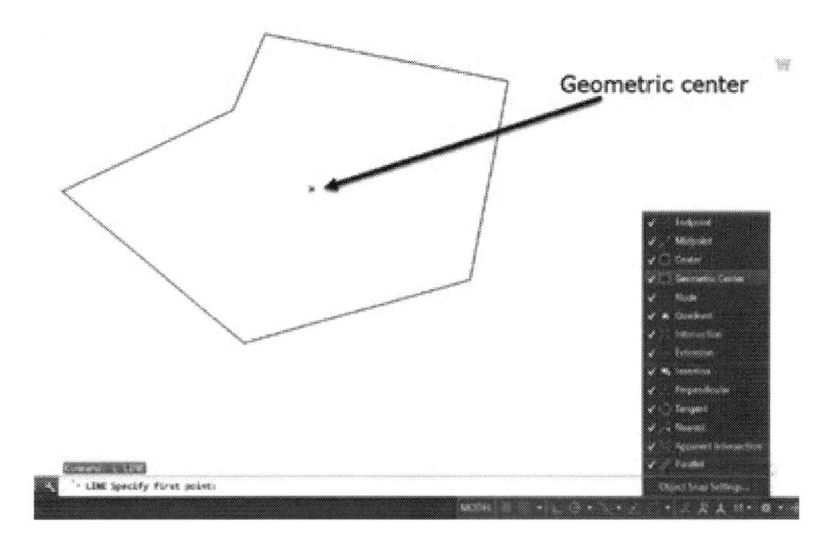

Figure 414: Geometric option

CENTER MARKS AND CENTER LINES

Step 1: Click Annotate tab.
Step 2: Click Center lines.
Step 3: Select first line.
Step 4: Select second line.

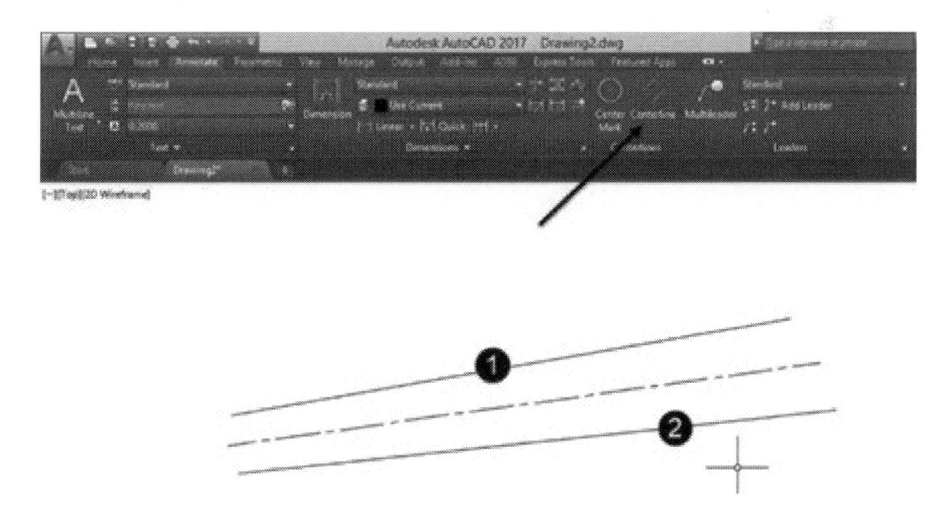

Figure 415: Center line use

OR

Click center mark then Select circle.

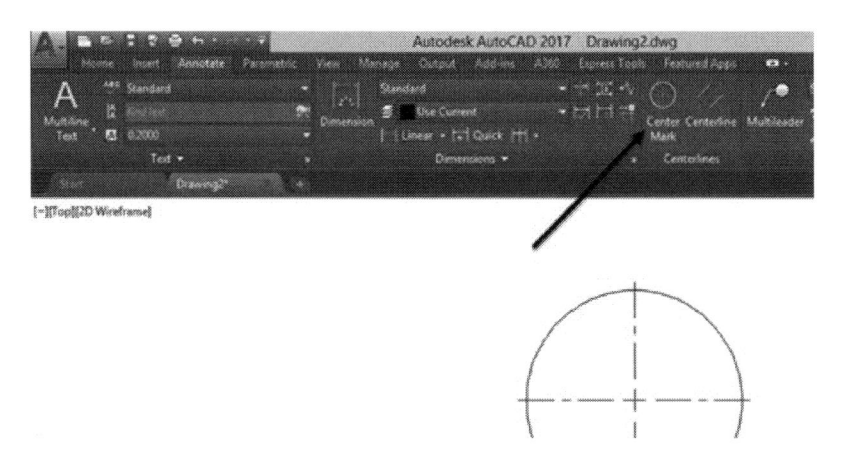

Figure 416: center mark

PDF file import

Step 1: Click Insert tab then click Pdf import.

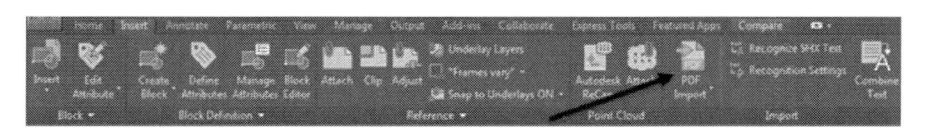

Figure 417: pdf import tool icon

Step 2: Then enter or right click.
Step 3: Select file and open.

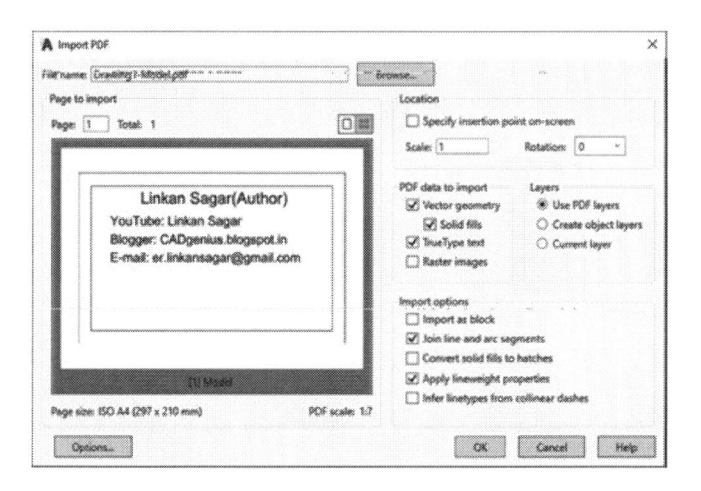

Figure 418: pdf import tab

Printed in Great Britain
by Amazon